HUEY LONG
INVADES NEW ORLEANS

HUEY LONG
INVADES NEW ORLEANS
The Siege of a City, 1934-36

GARRY BOULARD

PELICAN PUBLISHING COMPANY
Gretna 1998

*The word "Pelican" and the depiction of a pelican are trademarks
of Pelican Publishing Company, Inc., and are registered
in the U.S. Patent and Trademark Office.*

Library of Congress Cataloging-in-Publication Data

Boulard, Garry.
    Huey Long invades New Orleans : the siege of a city, 1934-36 /
Garry Boulard.
        p.   cm.
    Includes index.
    ISBN 1-56554-303-3 (pbk. : alk. paper)
    1. New Orleans (La.)—Politics and government. 2. Long,
Huey Pierce, 1893-1935. 3. Louisiana—Politics and govern-
ment—1865-1950. I. Title.
F379.N557B68 1998
976.3'35062—dc21   98-29376
                                                         CIP

Manufactured in the United States of America
Published by Pelican Publishing Company, Inc.
1000 Burmaster Street, Gretna, Louisiana 70053

For my mother,
Margaret Leonardo Boulard

Contents

Acknowledgments 9

Chapter 1 The Grand Marshall 15

Chapter 2 "A Biscuit for a Barrel of Flour"...................33

Chapter 3 "It Almost Turns My Stomach" 53

Chapter 4 "Poor C. S. Barnes".................................79

Chapter 5 Dreams of Dust...................................95

Chapter 6 "He Can't Do That" 113

Chapter 7 "We Would Do What We Were Told".........135

Chapter 8 The Most Spectacular Battle 153

Chapter 9 The Empire of Utopia............................175

Chapter 10 A Spirit Never Rests............................189

Notes 213

Index 271

Acknowledgments

Two forces fueled the writing of this book: the memories, opinions, and anecdotes of the more than two dozen people I interviewed who lived through the era of Huey Long and still vividly recall its temper and tone; and the friends, librarians, curators, and archivists who continually pointed me in the right direction. Of the latter, I am particularly grateful to Jack Epstein, Eric Heinberg, John Lawrence, John Tottenham, and Aaron Walker for reading portions of my manuscript and advising me on its strengths and weaknesses; Glen Jeansonne of the University of Wisconsin at Milwaukee and Edward Haas of Wayne State University, both esteemed scholars of Louisiana history, who helped obtain for me a copy of the Federal Bureau of Investigation's files on Long and the militia occupation of the voter registrar's office in New Orleans in 1934; and the archival staffs of Tulane University's Special Collections of the Howard-Tilton Memorial Library, particularly the collection's director, Bill Menerey, as well as James Powell, Kevin Fontenot, Sylvia Metzinger, and Joan Caldwell (curator of the Louisiana collection), who all favored me with endless courtesies as they satisfied my most obscure research request.

I also owe a debt of thanks to Wayne Everard of the New Orleans Public Library's Louisiana Division, who very kindly helped me through Mayor Walmsley's official papers while also pointing out pertinent information in the library's collection on Walmsley's successor, Robert Maestri; Anne

Smith of the Hill Memorial Library's Special Collections at Louisiana State University, for her help in obtaining transcripts of interviews T. Harry Williams conducted for his landmark biography of Long; Susan Tucker, librarian with Newcomb College on the Tulane campus, who helped me trace the life and career of Louise Jessen; and T. Semmes Favrot, Kathleen Gibbons, Samuel Price, and Carolyn King Perkins for so kindly sharing not only their time and their recollections of the late mayor but also a comprehensive Walmsley family history scrapbook.

For additional information, the help of the following individuals was essential to my work: George Dansker, reference librarian at Loyola University of New Orleans; Raymond Teichman, supervisory archivist of the Franklin D. Roosevelt Presidential Library in Hyde Park, New York; Roy Picou and J. C. Williams, who allowed me to comb through old copies of the New Orleans Athletic Club's monthly newsletter in the 1930s; Carey Alden of the Fairmont Hotel, who provided me with a wealth of information on the history of the old Roosevelt Hotel; Dale Atkins, clerk of the Civil District Court in New Orleans; Sherrie S. Pugh, head librarian at the National Guard's military library at Jackson Barracks in New Orleans, who helped me trace not only the history of the state militia, but the individual careers and lives of many of the men who made up the state guard during the 1930s; Jan Brantley, head of the photography section of the Historic New Orleans Collection; the library staffs of the New Orleans *Times-Picayune,* the Baton Rouge *Advocate,* and the *Honolulu Star-Bulletin;* and Lawrence Powell, professor of history at Tulane University, for his insights on both Col. Guy Molony as well as the Old Regulars of New Orleans.

Among those I interviewed, a special tribute must be paid to the legendary James Gillis, longtime reporter for the *Times-Picayune,* who not only repeatedly provided me with his valuable insights but also the hospitality of his home.

I am also in debt to James Fitzmorris, Lindy Boggs,

Robert Molony, Russell Long, Joe Cangiamilla, Isabel Molony, Mary Morrison, Angelo Butera, Joe Scaffidi, Charles Palmisano, Edward Gouaze, Edward P. Benezach, Jr., Joseph Biggio, William Blackwell, Howard K. Smith, Avery Alexander, Irwin Joseph, John Mahrer, James Coleman, Lawrence Eustis, and Louis Reidl, one of the last of the great employees of the New Orleans Sewerage and Water Board during the height of the Old Regulars, who gave me many amusing and clever insights on how city government in New Orleans worked at mid-century.

The staff at Pelican Publishing Company has been wonderfully supportive and helpful in seeing this book through to completion. I thank in particular Milburn, Nancy, and James Calhoun, Nina Kooij, Christine Descant, and Lynda Moreau.

Anne Compliment, without hesitation, demonstrated her selfless nature by virtually saving this entire manuscript at a crucial moment with her exemplary computer skills; Joyce M. Zaffuto graciously provided me with a photo of Mayor Walmsley and Police Chief George Reyer; while six very special friends sustained me with their unfailing wisdom and good cheer during the writing of this book: Denice Bizot, Karen Chustz, June Galloway, Nita Hemeter, Charmaine Padua, and a grand lady named Queenie.

HUEY LONG
INVADES NEW ORLEANS

1

The Grand Marshall

HUEY PIERCE LONG DID EVERYTHING with color and noise. Arriving by train in New Orleans, he presented an unforgettable picture. A boy reporter with his own aspirations for great political office who would someday serve in Congress, Hale Boggs remembered how it was as Huey came in on the old Crescent Limited as it pushed into the grand marble downtown terminal, the Southern Railway Station, "about 7:30 in the morning, and he would have this great retinue with him," Boggs recalled decades later, still awed, "with bodyguards and all that kind of stuff."[1]

"He'd come off that train, man, we'd be by the depot," the jazz virtuoso Manuel Manetta said, summoned by Long to greet him with great musical fanfare at the station. Huey always liked music and in designating Manetta as his official greeter he could hardly have done better. Manetta was one of the city's legends—he could play both the trumpet and trombone, sometimes simultaneously, and did so with the likes of Louis Armstrong. But in New Orleans parlance, Manetta always played "second line" to Huey, who, with sweeping, simian gestures, led Manetta's combo out of the cavernous depot to the steamy streets outside. Huey, Manetta put it many years later, was one of a kind, once and forever, "the grand marshall."[2]

Huey was also by the summer of 1934 one of the most prominent and ominous men in the country. A one-term governor who transformed Louisiana by brute force and a

15

*Huey visits New York and shows the Yankees how to make a Ramos gin
fizz like the ones he drank at the Roosevelt Hotel in New Orleans.* (Photo
used by permission of Photofest)

fevered imagination, he was now the state's senior senator and the spouting head of an angry people's movement that was frightening many but sweeping the nation. It was a movement, he was chillingly certain, that would also sweep him into the White House in the next presidential election.

He wore wild clothes—pink suits, purple shirts, yellow ties, and spit-polished spats—and looked like nothing less than a happy convention Rotarian returned to the flock. "A chubby man, he had ginger hair, and tight skin that was the color of a sunburn coming on," as acerbic A. J. Leibling, who covered Huey for the *New York World,* put it. Tightly surrounded by a knot of beefy guards with grim dark faces— one even clutched a sawed-off shotgun concealed in a brown paper bag—Huey would then briefly take in a slice of the city.[3]

From the Southern Railway Station, Huey and his contingent paraded down the wide vista of Canal Street, which was alive and loud with rattling streetcars, vegetable vendors, horse-drawn supply wagons, and newsboys singing out the headlines from the city's four daily papers. There were fur dealers and clothing stores and liquor shops on either side of a street whose splendid neutral ground was paved in white-and-red terrazzo marble. To Huey's left stood the monumental Saenger Theater, self-billed as a Florentine palace. To his right rose the intricately designed edifice of the Pickwick Club, a private oasis for the white aristocratic men of the city where Huey, despite all of his powers, could never gain entry. He would fly by Marullo's Physical Culture Gym for Ladies and the American Drug Store with its huge banner advertising five-cents double-dip ice-cream cones. But even here, the presence of his greatest enemy, Pres. Franklin D. Roosevelt, a man he had come to hate with an almost ferocious intensity, was felt: from the windows of the White Brothers Jewelers, Mayer Israel's clothing store, and Maison Blanche's huge, popular department store waved the Blue Eagle, symbol of one of the president's popular New Deal programs designed to whittle down the effects of the

Great Depression. Huey, now an ardent critic of such FDR efforts, could be excused if he snorted in response.[4]

A swift right shift suddenly brought Huey's party to University Place, a street of imposing significance. Here stood the gleaming terra cotta of the Orpheum Theatre, a shrine-like playhouse built for vaudeville but now showing daily movies. One day many years later, Huey's son Russell would remember how excited he was: his father, always busy running Louisiana, was taking him to the Orpheum. Together father and son sat in the darkened theater as the film fare began, but when the lights returned Huey was gone, and Russell, always forgiving, just knew his father had more important things to do. Huey had gone across the street to the bustling Roosevelt Hotel, his headquarters in New Orleans, where he reigned rent-free in a spacious corner suite on the hotel's tenth floor.[5]

"The Roosevelt Hotel was the only place to go in those days," remembered James Gillis, a New Orleans reporter who wrote about Huey for the *Times-Picayune*. "With Long staying there, it was even more important."[6]

"We were *all* there," patiently explained Cecil Morgan, an erudite state legislator who loathed Long for his crudeness and corruption. "The anti-Longs were there to see what the pro-Longs were up to and vice-versa. Everyone could be looked upon as a spy. If you wanted to have any notion of what was going on, that was the hotel you hung around."[7]

Advertised in those kinds of shiny, sleekly designed brochures that hotels and chambers of commerce put out when they want to promote something, the Roosevelt Hotel was the "Pride of the South" and by 1934 a New Orleans cultural institution second to none. Opened in 1893 by Louis Grunewald, an ambitious financier with dreams of glory, it was originally called the Grunewald Hotel, with some two hundred delicately decorated rooms spread over six floors. The name change came thirty years later to honor the always-bellicose Theodore Roosevelt, who was, from all reports, silent the night he slept at the hotel. A 400-room,

The Roosevelt Hotel. Huey's home away from home, it was the scene of endless political intrigue in the 1930s. (Photo courtesy The Historic New Orleans Collection, Acc. No. 1979.325.4591)

14-story annex was added to the main building and unveiled to the public in a lavish, gay celebration at the flash of midnight 1908, offset by another 16-story annex on the Baronne Street end of the building some seventeen years later. Through it all, Louis and then his son, Theodore Grunewald, devoted themselves to the stuff of myth and fantasy. Their hostelry luxuriated in opulence, a palace gleaming out of the otherwise dormant sahara of the Deep South with detailed cornices decorating thirty-foot-high ceilings, French, African, and Italian marbled-covered walls, and massive columns of gilt and gold.[8]

By 1932, the Roosevelt, already established as a place of local legend, went national: radio station WWL brought their broadcast studios to the hotel and soon evening shows from the Blue Room nightclub beamed out to millions of listeners across a lonely, dark land scarred by the Great Depression. The melodic deep voice of the program announcer, the sweet, lifting strains of a dance orchestra, the scat nonsense of singer Phil Harris, or the barrelhouse blues of vaudeville trouper Sophie Tucker all suggested the mystery, glamour, and elegance of the big, busy city very far away. And the very tangible beauty of the Blue Room itself—as reported in the national press—only added to its allure. Blanketed in a painted ceiling of blue that was punctuated with a splash of glittering stars, all of which was subdued with soft blue neon, the nightclub, said one columnist who dined and wined there, was "both startling and entrancing."[9]

"Huey would come into the club every time he stayed at the hotel," Joe Scaffidi, a bartender at the Roosevelt, later recalled. "Usually he'd have a couple of drinks and talk. Man, he'd talk to anybody who was there." But sometimes Huey also came simply to listen, to only momentarily douse that frightening fire that burned within. "When he was dancing in the Blue Room, he was in heaven," Castro Carazo, the nightclub's longtime orchestra leader, later said. Huey liked it when Carazo had the boys play "Smoke

Gets in Your Eyes," and "That Lonesome Road." But nothing could top "Harvest Moon," a simple, sweet dance tune of the day. "He would look dreamy and blissful," Carazo said of the temporarily sedated Huey, "and look at me as if to say thank you," as he floated "with his eyes half-closed."[10]

Guests at the Roosevelt Hotel lived in a small world of wonder. Bridge tournaments in the hotel's palmed foyer were a popular afternoon activity. There was a man and woman's hat shop, a beauty parlor, three separate restaurants, dozens of smiling and accommodating bellmen and doormen, 24-hour food service, valets, secretaries on staff to take dictation from the many famous people who were guests there, and a basement barbershop with a team of barbers and manicurists on staff. "It was a very classy operation," remembered Russell Long, who accompanied his father there. It was "the kind of thing you'd expect to see in the big city."[11]

A Turkish bath added to the sense of exotica: manned by a soft-spoken black Mississippian named Niclaise Mitchell, who just seemed to know his longtime customers the way a bartender or bookie does. Huey, Mitchell quietly ventured decades after the fact, was "a good man, but nobody understood him."[12]

The Roosevelt Hotel was also home to a New Orleans sensation: the famous Ramos gin fizz. Composed of gin, milk, powdered sugar, and both lemon and lime juice, the "fizz" came, once shaken, with the addition of several drops of orange-flower water over ice. It was a perfect afternoon cooler.[13]

Huey so liked the Roosevelt's gin fizz that he once made headlines in New York by flying up one of the hotel's bartenders, Sam Guarino, to a hotel he was visiting there so that the Yankees could see for themselves what a real gin fizz was all about. With a throng of afternoon drinkers and journalists—perhaps one and the same—laughing appreciatively, Huey and Guarino elaborately mixed their concoction. Then Huey, holding a wet glass up high, solemnly

An ad for the Roosevelt Hotel's famous Ramos Gin Fizz in the 1930s. (Courtesy the Fairmont Hotel of New Orleans)

announced he would taste the first drink to verify its authenticity. "Better be sure about it," Huey said as his curly hair licked his forehead. Finally, five drinks later, Huey was sure and declared in triumph that the gin fizz from the Roosevelt Hotel of New Orleans was his personal gift to New York.[14]

Huey and the Roosevelt Hotel: the stories the guests could tell. There was something about the place that prompted even the normally expansive Huey to uncoil, a home away from the real home he shared with his wife and children in Uptown New Orleans. Who could forget the time he gaily greeted—all done up in silk pajamas, a red-and-blue robe, and bright blue slippers—the puffed-up German consul who promptly departed from Huey's suite while declaring Huey's rainbow attire an affront to his foreign station. Or when a former governor, finally driven to distraction by Huey's taunts, chased Long down the Roosevelt's lobby and cornered him in an elevator with ham-fisted blows.[15]

One day reporter Gillis was on assignment, hoping to interview Huey, when he saw his man loudly passing out dollar bills to members of the Louisiana State University marching band in the lobby of the hotel. Here was Gillis's chance for an interview, but before he even got to say hello to Huey, the young reporter suddenly felt two men grab him and point him in the direction of the exit door. He was ominously warned to leave, "if you know what's good for you." Gillis admitted he was startled. "They looked like gangsters, which most of them were," he said. But, laughing at the memory, Gillis said he took their advice and quickly departed.[16]

In retrospect, it made perfect sense that the Roosevelt Hotel would be Huey's home. It was a place where the young went, and Huey was one of the youngest governors and then-senators in the nation. It was where reporters lived and movie stars visited. A man like Robert Maestri, a first-generation Italian who had made a fortune in real estate even though he still lacked social graces, was welcome there. None of that was true for the much older, socially pretentious St. Charles Hotel, the home of the city's Uptown elite.[17]

There were, in short, plenty of reasons why Huey Long should stay at the Roosevelt, but a man named Seymour Weiss was the most important. And by 1934 Weiss not only owned the Roosevelt Hotel, although he was only in his late thirties, he was also a self-made millionaire. Now, next to Huey himself, he was the most important person in Long's vast, complex, and rich network.[18]

The Roosevelt Hotel was virtually an incubator of democracy: Huey, the redneck son of a hardscrabble farm family; Maestri, the uneducated but astute New Orleans Italian; and now Weiss, a Jew from Bunkie, Louisiana, who owned the place.

The Deep South in the early part of this century was hardly a welcome place for most minority groups. But New Orleans was unique and Weiss resilient. He came to the city when he was only twenty and his blonde hair was already thinning. But his blue eyes revealed a hard-edged, intuitive intelligence, and he had a burning desire to get ahead. The climb had begun.[19]

First he got a job as a clerk in a downtown shoe store. But in the mid-1920s, as New Orleans and the Roosevelt Hotel prospered in the glad riches of that era, Weiss, found himself at the hotel after he landed a plum job: manager of the basement barbershop. This was where the younger men went, men about to make their fortunes—politicians, salesmen, investors, gamblers. How many deals were sealed beneath the soft clipping of falling hair?

In rapid succession, Weiss proved his worth to the hotel through his managerial efficiency. There was just something about him that people liked, and Weiss was always happy to hear other people's problems. Within five years, Weiss moved up to the assistant manager's job, then he was the manager, and finally, by 1931, he was the hotel's director and principal owner. It had all happened so quickly. He was only thirty-five and already had his first million, a figure that would grow fourfold after Weiss and Huey met up.[20]

In later years, Long's many biographers would have a hard time getting a fix on Weiss. He was dismissed as an insider, a craven pretender to the throne, and portrayed in vaguely anti-Semitic terms as something of a smoothie, a crafty operator who just must have gotten his riches dishonestly. How else could such a young man do so well? Others viewed him as a dark, controlling force within the kingdom of Huey Long. But the descriptions were one-dimensional treatments of a multidimensional man. In real life Weiss was many things: he loved chicken, baked, fried, or broiled, as long as it was chicken, and Hawaiian music, which was briefly popular in the 1930s. He was a kind boss to his many employees, unfailingly pleasant, always requesting, never ordering, and passionately patriotic. Weiss was also, in the early 1930s, worried. People in Bunkie, Louisiana, were starving. So were they in New Orleans. There was talk that somehow America had finally gone wrong for good, that it was all about to collapse. Weiss knew what was wrong. The old men, the men who made their money in cotton and public utilities, the aristocrats who stayed at the St. Charles Hotel, Pres. Herbert Hoover's kind of men, were too old. They were tired and selfish and kept their money for themselves. America could only be saved if it were turned over to men like Seymour Weiss—young, vigorous, dynamic comers who would try this and that, but mostly would just try something to save the country from itself. Significantly, Weiss had two heroes: Franklin D. Roosevelt and Huey P. Long.[21]

"Mr. Weiss was a very good man, very loyal to his employees," Angelo Butera, a longtime bell captain at the hotel, later said. "And he didn't believe in firing anybody either. You had to do something really bad to get fired by Seymour Weiss." Bartender Scaffidi had his own take: "Seymour Weiss? He was a prince. That's all I got to say."[22]

Three years Huey's junior, Weiss rapidly became one of

his closest friends. "He was the most astute politician I ever knew," said Weiss, who also called him brilliant. Weiss added: "We were inseparable friends."[23]

The friendship was first sparked in 1928 when Huey, still a country boy in the city, picked the Roosevelt as his New Orleans headquarters. Already Weiss had seen his fair share of national and local politicians. Many of them seemed alike: dull and pedantic, they relied on tired bromides and hoped to succeed by doing as little as possible. Until Huey, many of the city and state leaders were indistinguishable from the ancients who ruled the city from the St. Charles Hotel: gray, tired men. But Huey was entirely different, he brimmed with ideas, passion, and energy, and he was politically clever; Weiss could see that right away. He gave the young candidate money for his campaign, offered him suite space, and attempted to subdue Huey's outlandish clothing and sometimes mawkish manners. Huey, in return, saw that Weiss was smart and rich too, not always an inevitable combination in New Orleans, and made him his official campaign treasurer. But it went further than that. Huey won that 1928 election and soon was building a political patronage system that would scandalize the elite by rewarding good jobs—state jobs—to men and women loyal to him but asking in return not only their political fealty come time for the next election (a fealty most displayed with natural affection) but also their money. Thousands of workers gave a percentage of their salaries out of every check to Huey. He was building a massive account for his own personal and political use; everyone called it the "deduct box," and Weiss was given charge of it all. The box, of course, was not without controversy. In fact, it was soon one of the most enduring parts of the Huey Long legend. Everyone, reporters in particular, and one day even the Internal Revenue Service, wanted to know how much was in it. What was Huey going to do with all of that money? At Charity Hospital, the public institution Huey did so much to make modern, employees glanced at the diminished size of their paychecks and just

Save for Huey himself, no one knew as much about the intricacies, secrets, and finances of the Long organization as Seymour Weiss. Urbane, Jewish, and temperate, Weiss was one of the few restraining forces in Huey's life. (Courtesy the Leon C. Trice Collection, Manuscripts Division, Howard-Tilton Memorial Library, Tulane University)

shrugged it off: it was because of the "de ducks," they said, as they flapped their arms as wings. No one knew for sure just how much money Huey had, except for Weiss. But this much was certain: with that kind of money (it was thought to be in the millions by 1934), Huey and Weiss had one of the largest cash reserves at their disposal of any politician or political organization in the country. And it was all hidden away behind the double-door cast-iron safe of the Roosevelt Hotel.[24]

Once, under questioning, Weiss gave a hint of how the deduct box could work. He would solicit money from Huey's rich supporters, men like Maestri and Oscar K. Allen, the governor Long designated to succeed him after 1932. Sometimes either man gave Weiss cash donations, depending upon the campaign and election Huey needed money for. Was $5,000 enough? How about $10,000? Other contributors might pony up $1,000—nice chunks of money in the depths of the Depression when you could get an apartment for less than $50 a month and those five-cent double-dip ice-cream cones at the American Drug Store. For any given race, Weiss explained, he might raise as much as $50,000. But he would spend every cent of it and nothing was accounted for—there were no records or notes made of any transactions. Or at least none that Huey and Weiss wanted anyone else to see. "I didn't have any bank accounts," Weiss said without blinking. "I paid cash for everything."[25]

Candidates running on Huey's ticket were lucky anyway. They shared their ticket with the state's most popular, if detested in certain New Orleans quarters, vote-getter. But Weiss and Huey gave them more: free room and board at the Roosevelt Hotel, especially if the campaign just happened to fall during August and September, monstrously hot months in New Orleans, and, said Weiss, the "dull season" for occupancies. Huey was a big believer in flyers, long, densely written, sometimes hilarious, oftentimes vicious tracts that would explain the Long ticket's position on the issues of the day. But it cost money to print and distribute them by the thousands. Weiss would dole out another $9,000. How about a radio speech, particularly with Huey, and a dance band to open and close the show? $1,000 cash. But by far the biggest expense came on election day: Huey knew that people might want to vote for you, they might say they were going to, but you had to do everything possible to make it happen. Drivers then got cash, hundreds of dollars, for a grueling day's work rounding up as many voters in every far-flung corner of the state as possible. The farmers loved Huey. He was one of them, they thought. And they voted for him in avalanches. Without their support, he would have never been elected governor in the first place. But it was absolutely essential for him to get those farmers out in the field who were too busy or didn't even have enough money to buy gas to drive to the nearest precinct station to vote. In 1932, for an election Huey was not even running in, Weiss peeled off $14,000 for drivers.[26]

Putting Weiss in charge of Huey's financial empire just made good sense. Weiss obviously knew how to manage Huey's money, and Huey trusted him, at least more than he did anyone else. But the Weiss appointment also freed Huey to devote himself exclusively to politics, which Weiss saw as Huey's God-given calling. Even two decades later, Weiss could still recall the day Huey, on a moment's notice, spontaneously drafted his historic proposal for free school textbooks, one of the most important tenets of his entire administration, all on the cardboard backing that came with one of his starched shirts. Huey was quick and smart and, some were already saying it, a genius. He was destined, Weiss said, for great things.[27]

Except he had a problem. Huey was headstrong and sometimes mean, and Seymour Weiss, this gentle man who never raised his voice even to those on his payroll, was sometimes the only person in the world who could talk Huey out of his worst inclinations. It was Weiss who told Huey he should apologize to the German consul for his undignified dress, even talking Huey into a swallowtail coat and striped trousers for a later visit of contrition to the consul's cruiser, docked at the Port of New Orleans. It was also Weiss who got Huey to promise he would not attack President Roosevelt during the early months of FDR's administration. He argued that under the Hoover Republicans "we have suffered like hell. . . . Now we have a Democratic president and for God's sake promise me you will not fall out with this man." Huey even kept his promise, for at least six months. And Weiss was also a prominent voice warning Huey not to get involved in the factional politics of New Orleans. In January of 1934 there would be a mayor's race, and Weiss saw no advantage for Huey getting into it. Huey ignored his friend's advice and soon came to regret it. In fact, the election results became an obsession for Huey.[28]

But now, in the final days of July 1934, Huey Long wasn't looking for advice. He had returned to New Orleans from Washington in a dark mood and soon summoned the vanguard of his empire into his suite at the Roosevelt. Earl Long, Huey's unpredictable brother, was there, as was Governor Allen, gray and cordial; Robert Maestri, now a major backer who admired Huey for the ruthless way he produced results, came in, as did the coolly confident Raymond Fleming, the state's adjutant general, who had overseen a massive buildup of military power under Huey's watch.[29]

The men had barely settled in before Huey thrust a sheet of paper into Allen's hands and ordered him to sign it. Allen was, after all, the governor of Louisiana now, at least officially, although everyone knew that Huey was still the power behind the throne. "Partial Martial Law," the document proclaimed, as Allen, without hesitation, signed it. Huey then passed the paper to Fleming, always impeccable in his military dress, for his comment. But before the general could respond, Huey explained his move. He was on the precipice of real national power; polls showed him a threat to FDR's re-election. Huey's office was getting sixty thousand letters a week, while his Share Our Wealth clubs, a national network of groups dedicated to his calls for a radical redistribution of wealth, would soon have a registered membership of more than eight million. Next to FDR, no other political figure in the country received as much attention in the nation's press as Huey did—even if some of the stories were unflattering, pointing out that he ramrodded bills through the state legislature, intimidated opponents, and, in general, circumvented normal democratic procedure. By any measure Huey was a national phenomenon ready for the next step: the White House. But New Orleans and its stubborn leadership in the person of the city's mayor, the patrician T. Semmes Walmsley, and the machine that dominated the city's politics, the Old Regulars, stood in the way.[30]

Repeatedly the Old Regulars and Walmsley thwarted Huey. They instructed the block of legislators representing New Orleans to oppose him, they ran city candidates who pledged to battle Huey, and they now were even in contact with the White House and conspiring to deny Huey any New Deal federal money coming to Louisiana. They wanted to make certain, instead, that Washington's money went to Huey's foes. As long as they persisted, Huey's hold on the state would be challenged. And without the solid backing of his own state, a bid for national office would be that much harder. Something had to be done, and Huey had an idea: on the city's borders that very night, resting at the Jackson Barracks, were nearly two hundred armed militiamen who would instantly respond to Huey's command. They could easily be re-enforced, Huey knew, because General Fleming told him so, by up to 3,000 additional men from across the state if need be. They had tanks, trucks, machine guns, and hand grenades, and soon, by order of Huey, they would have the city of New Orleans too.[31]

Tomorrow night, Huey told his surprised guests, the soldiers would come into the city, without first telling a single city official, especially Walmsley. Their specific assignment was bust into and take over the building that housed the voter registrar's office, which was right next to Walmsley's official address at Gallier Hall.

From his hotel suite, Huey could survey the sweep of the Mississippi River and the barges and ferries it carried all through the night and day. He could see the decaying rooftops of the French Quarter, and, in the opposite direction, the gleaming white edifice of Gallier Hall. It was an expansive, thrilling view of a dynamic city, a city that, in a short 24 hours, Huey would invade.

2

"A Biscuit for a Barrel of Flour"

THOMAS SEMMES WALMSLEY, the well-intentioned, frequently combative mayor of New Orleans during the 1930s, betrayed his feelings about Huey Long in the summer of 1934 during a talk with *New York Times* reporter Raymond Daniell: "Nobody invites him anywhere. He knows he doesn't belong and he can't take it," said Walmsley in a particularly exasperated moment.[1]

To Walmsley, who was raised in a world of rank and power in an Uptown New Orleans mansion with thirty rooms surrounded by an imposing cast-iron fence and a grove of palms and oaks, Huey was a misfit, a pretender to the throne, a coarse and common man who had bullied his way to power and was now in a position where he was not only Walmsley's political equal, but, maddeningly, his superior. "Decent people," Walmsley almost sneered, would never invite such a ruffian to dinner, a man who was required to "take bodyguards along to protect him from the wrath of the people."[2]

A member in good standing of the exclusive Boston Club and a graduate of Tulane University, when it was still the city's premier enclave of effete white culture, Walmsley lived in a world of rank and noblesse oblige. His circle of family and friends was inhabited with men not unlike Binx Bolling's Uncle Jules in Walker Percy's *The Moviegoer*, a man who was once Rex of Mardi Gras and wanted to keep the city the way he thought it should be: "a friendly easy-going place of old-world charm and new-world business methods where kind white folks and carefree darkies have the good sense to behave pleasantly towards each other."[3]

Born in 1889, just four years before Huey's birth in remote Winn Parish, Walmsley was the son of Sylvester Pierce Walmsley, who was well known and regarded in the local lucrative cotton exchange and who was also Rex in 1890. His grandfather was Robert N. Walmsley, who once served as the president of the prestigious Louisiana National Bank. A cousin, Adm. Raphael Semmes, was the naval commander of the CSS *Alabama* for the Confederacy during the Civil War; while an uncle, Thomas J. Semmes, rose to become Louisiana's attorney general.[4]

Educated at a local military school before entering Tulane, where he excelled in athletics and won a coveted varsity "T" in no less than five sports, Walmsley lived an unencumbered life where the social order of things was treasured and religiously observed. "We were the old families," one woman member of the upper caste later recalled. "We had what we wanted . . . all we wanted was to keep it." A later historian who studied the Uptown elites noted that the men in Walmsley's world served on the board of administrators of Tulane or the Hibernia or Whitney banks, they lunched and made deals at the Boston, Pickwick, and Stratford clubs, and nearly always held sway at Gallier Hall, the official city hall.[5]

Sumptuous dinner parties at the Walmsley estate on Prytania Street were a nightly affair and were attended by dozens of Walmsley's immediate and extended family members. "That's why the dining room table was so big," Walmsley's niece, Kathleen Gibbons, remembered. "In fact, the children were not allowed to sit at that table, there wasn't enough room. Behind the dining room was an enormous hall going to the kitchen, the pantry, and then another room just for washing dishes. If one adult wasn't at the table, one of the children would be allowed to join them and we took turns doing so. It went on every night, with the men wearing white coats and everything."[6]

Nowhere in the public record of T. Semmes Walmsley is there a hint of scandal or anything amiss. Everything was as it should be, everything Walmsley did was as he should do, and his family properly took pride in the young man's obvious ability to carry on the honor of their name.

He was married on April 15, 1914, to Julia Havard, also to the manor born as the daughter of Augustus D. Havard, a country gentleman and plantation operator from Cheneyville, Louisiana. Walmsley and his new wife soon moved to a two-story estate fronted by four Roman columns and shaded by a line of imposing oaks on Palmer Avenue in Uptown New Orleans, only blocks away from the campuses of Tulane and Loyola universities.[7]

At the same time, the young Walmsley, his red hair already disappearing to reveal a prominent, smooth dome, joined one of the city's oldest and most respected law firms—Saunders, Dufour, and Dufour—before serving in the U.S. Army's air corps overseas.[8]

Walmsley's political career did not blossom until the early 1920s when he was appointed as an assistant attorney general for the state in charge of criminal law. But between 1924 and 1929, his rise to political prominence was swift. The legendary Mayor Martin Behrman made Walmsley his city attorney in 1924. But the frailties of his superiors gave Walmsley his most fortuitous advances: in 1926 the great Behrman, dominant in New Orleans politics for more than a generation, suddenly died. Arthur J. O'Keefe, the city's public finance commissioner, replaced Behrman as Walmsley, in turn, succeeded O'Keefe. This was an enormously important position for a young man who was still only thirty-seven years old: there were only five members then on the city commission and they virtually shared power with the mayor, who was also a member of the commission. But the hand of providence intervened on Walmsley's behalf again in July 1929 when O'Keefe declared he was too ill to govern,

and Walmsley became the city's new chief executive without
the benefit of an election. They would call him, and he
would call himself until the next scheduled election, "acting" mayor, but in power and reality, there was only one
mayor of New Orleans by the fall of 1929, and his name was
T. Semmes Walmsley. He had just celebrated his fortieth
birthday.[9]

In the city's top post, Walmsley instinctively represented
the commercial-business elite that gave him life. Just one
month after O'Keefe turned Gallier Hall over to him, Walmsley won rave reviews in the local conservative pro-business
press when he responded with studied outrage to a mob of
angry striking streetcar drivers who flooded the commission
chambers and verbally accosted the new mayor and his fellow commission members. It was a frightening moment,
one more unfortunate, ugly scene in a summer of hot confrontation surrounding the streetcar drivers. Only several
weeks before, Walmsley even surprised some of his conservative friends when he sought to seek a peaceful solution to
the strike and even went so far as to suggest that the drivers'
union be recognized. But now, in a dramatic outburst, he
declared that he had had enough of violent talk and action.
In 1930, he promised, he would run for his own term as
mayor, predicating his effort on one of the enduring shib-
boleths of conservative thought: the need to restore law and
order to a society run amok. Two years later, after Walmsley
was overwhelmingly elected, he gave more evidence of his
thinking when he introduced before the city commission an
ordinance prohibiting the "teaching, uttering, printing, or
advocating of anarchistic, communistic, or radical doc-
trines" within the city's borders.[10]

Walmsley never betrayed the world of breeding and manners that nurtured him. Throughout his public life he sym-
pathized with the plight of less fortunates because that was
what the more fortunate were supposed to do. Cheerfully
he gave his name and presence to dozens of charity balls
and parties. As the Great Depression slowly strangled New

Orleans, too, and local banks suddenly questioned the city's solvency, Walmsley made a typically grand gesture: "We are going to pay in cash to protect the city employees," he announced, preventing the possibility that any city employee would be the unlucky recipient of a bounced paycheck. Even in the midst of his greatest moment, the May 1930 inauguration making official his landslide electoral victory of the month before, Walmsley was mindful of those who would never share in his world: the mass of beautiful and abundant floral arrangements prepared especially for this most special day, he declared, should be sent to the city's asylum and rest homes by night so the people there could enjoy them too. Walmsley's attention to details extended to even the briefest encounter—one afternoon a slender, hungry, dark-haired boy appeared at the front door of the mayor's Palmer Avenue estate in desperate circumstances. He had received a mayor's scholarship to attend Tulane, the boy said, but it was somehow now lost, and he was too poor to go on his own. Decades later, the veteran newsman Howard K. Smith recalled stating his case breathlessly. "He said he never heard of it, but he would look into it, and he dismissed me. No trace of compassion or even of interest." But the following morning, first thing, Walmsley's office called Tulane, and Smith was in. "He was," Smith later said of Walmsley, "an altogether good citizen."[11]

Good citizen or not, Walmsley was never entirely removed from the more sordid aspects of politics in New Orleans. Indeed, it could be argued that he owed just as much to the corruption of others as he did to the death and sickness of Behrman and O'Keefe, for surely without the Old Regulars' seal of approval, Walmsley most likely would never have gotten beyond the Boston Club.

The Old Regulars, in fact, had a club too, known as the Choctaw. "Not only is it a political organization," a 1930s book underwritten by the Old Regulars proclaimed, "but it is a place for social gathering . . . where its members can find diversion and recreation." Housed in a three-story

The Choctaw Club was far less elegant and decorous than the Boston and Pickwick socially elite clubs, but because it was home to the politically omnipotent Old Regulars, it was more important. (Photo courtesy The Historic New Orleans Collection, Acc. No. 1981.20.28)

brick building decorated with wrought-iron balconies, the Choctaw Club, remembered James Fitzmorris, who was a young boy when the Old Regulars reigned, "was a private club of a totally different sort from the genteel Boston Club and others in its social strata." Fitzmorris, who would rise to political prominence in the next generation, added that the club, one block down from Walmsley's Gallier Hall, was "musty" and "antique-filled . . . with no dining room or bar," although food was frequently catered from a restaurant below. But Fitzmorris was far more impressed with the men who ran the Choctaw: "The Old Regulars were the most important force in the city in those days," he said later. "They went out and they worked diligently, knocking on doors—door-to-door—in their own precincts, to be sure that they got their vote out on election day."[12]

Robert Maloney, the grandson of Democratic Congressman Paul Maloney (a man who somehow managed to remain friends with both Huey Long and the Uptown Walmsley faction), said the Old Regulars were "*the* organization. That was what got people elected, because the people did what they were told to do."[13]

The Old Regulars, continued Maloney, won elections in New Orleans because they sold their promises on a retail basis. "In other words, if you wanted your assessment lowered, you went to see the person who ran the Old Regular organization in your block, and he brought you to the right person or he made the contact for you."[14]

Said assessment lowered, the now-happy homeowner was in the debt of the Old Regulars, who were only too happy to remind him of the favor rendered when the next important election rolled around. But historian T. Harry Williams claims the Old Regular organization triumphed for other reasons as well: "It controlled the registration office and padded the rolls generously, with the names of dead people, imaginary people, and people who moved elsewhere."[15]

Another expert with a good memory was Pershing Gervais, who, as a young street tough, rendered with his friends an important service for the Regulars: he disrupted elections. "The guys at the campaign headquarters would call us in and tell us that at such and such a place there was some cheatin' going on and to take care of it." The "cheatin'" in such cases meant an opposition candidate was getting too many votes. Gervais would respond enthusiastically, under the direction of the Old Regulars, by staging a fight with his pals outside a polling place in the hope of enticing the unsuspecting commissioner to also come outside and see what all of the fuss was about. That task accomplished, a member of Gervais' group would glide back into the building carrying a small bottle of ink, which he then poured into one of the wooden ballot boxes, rendering the accumulated ballots useless. "We made sure them bad guys weren't cheatin.'"[16]

There were other ways of winning elections: Paul Maloney never forgot how the Old Regulars deprived him of a win in the 1925 mayor's race against Behrman. "He always told us that after Algiers reported their vote, he had edged out ahead of Behrman," said Robert Maloney of his grandfather's big victory across the river. "But the ballots from Algiers were lost after they fell off the ferry carrying them across the river."[17]

Given such tactical advantages, the Old Regulars were unvanquished, wrote George M. Reynolds in the only comprehensive study of New Orleans machine politics written when the Regulars were in their prime: "Power begets power, and a feeling grew up in New Orleans that the Choctaws were invincible."[18]

Invincible, and indispensable. In a city of more than one-half million, where jobs were at a premium and people short of food, the Old Regulars had work. If you were willing to work for them, they could provide work for you: the city sewerage and water board alone was worth more than four thousand jobs; there were jobs in the police and fire departments, jobs on public-financed construction projects, jobs hauling garbage, jobs working in city hall. Only through the Old Regulars could New Orleanians gain access to these jobs, and during a time when the Port of New Orleans was in decline, when private manufacturing had gone flat, and the city's grand financial institutions were even more tight-fisted than usual, the Old Regulars were the city's salvation, saving thousands of people from despair and a yellowed sheriff's eviction notice, giving thousands more a place in an organization where every person was valued, and used.

But from the standpoint of good government reformers in New Orleans—curiously the same people who enjoyed Walmsley's society—the Regulars were rotten. They were unethical, the reformers said; they paid to win elections, and they arbitrarily planted people in jobs with little regard for the quaint notion of ability and entirely too much regard for how many Old Regular votes could be spawned from the same precinct the job-seeker claimed to hail from. They were also, in the eyes of the elites, illiterate, rough, and common men, the direct descendants of the city's working class who could never sup at the Boston Club, even though their votes were required to support the political rule of those who did.

It was one of the greatest ironies of politics in New Orleans that the Old Regulars, the gallant friend of the city's working stiffs, were actually anti-labor and willing to vote in the state legislature against any measure that might improve the lot of the working person's condition. Years before Walmsley arrived on the scene, the Old Regulars and the city's business elite had made a devil's bargain, and both sides honored the commitment for decades to come: the Uptown elite, despite their many misgivings, would give to the Old Regulars the plunder of political patronage provided that the Old Regulars agreed to support the business elite in the legislature. This was done, historian Pamela Tyler later observed, "even when those policies hurt their loyal working class followers."[19]

This made the Old Regulars omnipotent, another historian,

Edward Haas, would conclude, and created a "tightly knit
system of patronage-fed ward and precinct organizations
that effectively controlled the political behavior of the low-
voting population of the city."[20]

Indeed, by 1930 it was clear that the Old Regulars and
the elites had a lock on New Orleans and all was harmony:
Walmsley made the city his own, winning election to a full
term at the head of the ticket by sweeping fourteen of the
city's seventeen wards. Other Old Regulars on Walmsley's
ticket won virtually every other race, including all of the
seats on the city commission. On election night, a gleeful
band of local musicians marched to the front lawn of
Walmsley's Palmer Avenue home to serenade the happy
mayor to the tune of "Hail, Hail, the Gang's All Here,"
Walmsley's deliciously ironic campaign theme song. The
riveting theme of Walmsley's campaign was ironic too: efficiency and economy in the same office that thrived on one
of the most porcine political machines south of the Mason-
Dixon.[21]

Walmsley's inaugural celebration, on the front steps of a
Gallier Hall bathed in bouquets, was a hopeful, festive occasion that spring. Uptown families in sartorial splendor mixed
amiably with the Old Regulars, some of whom spoke in distinct Italian, Irish, and Jewish accents as they shook hands all
around and somehow seemed too excited and loud.

Walmsley, however, was quite taken with his new friends.
First he lavished praise on the departed patron saint of the
Regulars, Martin Behrman, for all he had given the city.
Then, gladly accepting a huge wood-carved chair bearing
the insignia of the Choctaw Club from the Old Regulars'
women's chapter, Walmsley plopped in it and waved to
applause all around. The Old Regulars, it was clear, liked
Walmsley. He was a proven winner and that meant they
would have their jobs for at least another four years. Walmsley, in turn, returned their affection in the way he might the
servants on his Uptown estate because that was the socially
gracious thing to do.[22]

And it *was* good to be the mayor: the Old Regulars also chipped in to give Walmsley a new 1930 Pierce Arrow sedan, which he himself drove, frequently at breakneck speed, through the city. He became New Orleans' official greeter, meeting foreign dignitaries, presidents, and even movie stars. And on Mardi Gras, Walmsley reveled in the moment of glory any New Orleans mayor is given as Rex paraded by Gallier Hall to offer the mayor a ceremonial toast. Carnival traditions, in fact, were nothing new to him: he belonged to several of the most prestigious private carnival clubs himself.[23]

In office, Walmsley was amiable, signing off on most of the Regulars' patronage decisions while striving to maintain a certain "way of life." That way included race, and Walmsley was a traditionalist; he saw blacks as his social inferiors. In late 1931, Walmsley invoked a forgotten ordinance first enacted in 1908 that prohibited the city from hiring any worker who was not also eligible to vote. In one fell swoop, nearly two thousand black employees who were prevented from voting by Jim Crow laws lost their jobs. In a less traumatic but equally telling moment, Walmsley also demonstrated his feelings when he took issue with the *Times-Picayune* for running a story that revealed the mayor had recently had dinner at the same table with a black man, Illinois Congressman Oscar De Priest. In response, Walmsley declared: "I am just as passionate an adherent to the cause of white supremacy as it is possible for any human to be." He only broke bread with De Priest, Walmsley insisted, to avoid offending his white hosts on an out-of-town trip.[24]

By New Orleans standards, it seemed as though Walmsley could do no wrong. Widely admired by the Uptown elites, respected by the Old Regulars who basked in his political popularity, Walmsley was even forgiven when he sometimes showed that he, too, could be a petty politician. Furious over the *Times-Picayune*'s unflattering coverage of him—the most important paper in New Orleans found Walmsley's liaison with the Old Regulars unbearable—he launched an effort in the fall of 1931 to encourage all city employees to subscribe

to the more supportive *Item-Tribune*. If his fellow Uptowners
found such maneuvers unseemly, they never said so.[25]

Gregarious, cultured, lucky, sometimes vindictive, abun-
dantly robust, Walmsley could have eventually rivaled
Behrman as the most popular and powerful mayor in New
Orleans history. But a cloud was on Walmsley's horizon,
one that, before it passed, would turn into a deadly storm:
Huey P. Long by 1928 was governor, and he suddenly
injected a strange and unsettling force into the small world
of favors granted and shared by the Old Regulars and the
Uptown elites.

Initially, they locked him out. Two times Huey tried to get
in, and two times he was rejected: in 1924, his first unsuccessful run for governor, and in his victorious bid in 1928,
Huey sought the support of the Old Regulars. Although he
realized the cultural and political gulf that divided them, he
never made a serious bid for elite support. But neither
group liked or needed Huey. He was, instead, the exact
kind of politician both factions avoided: an upstart from the
north country, and worst of all, noted Congressman Maloney with a certain amount of affection, the kind of guy
who always "wanted to be boss. He wasn't going to take
orders from them." Used to dominating their candidates,
the Old Regulars wanted nothing to do with Huey.[26]

The enmity was seen in the results: in 1924, as Long was
winning 25 percent of the vote statewide and running, for a
first-time outsider, a strong third-place finish, he was flat-
tened in the city at less than 18 percent. He hardly
improved those numbers four years later when the Old
Regulars and the elites combined kept his vote down to 23
percent. That showing was so bad that the Old Regulars
celebrated early: it seemed unlikely Huey could overcome
his poor New Orleans showing with the rural vote, and they
laughed as they marked the bumpkin's second defeat in a
row. But then something remarkable happened: returns
from Acadiana and the north country gave Huey a commanding lead, pushing him first even with his nearest

Walmsley. By the early 1930s, T. Semmes Walmsley, demonstrating the warm touch that helped him win two landslide elections, was one of the most popular mayors in New Orleans' history, the confident scion of a sturdy Uptown lineage. (Courtesy of the Walmsley family)

opponent, then ahead by 20,000 votes, then 35,000, and finally, by morning, Huey had a margin of more than 45,000 votes—a margin his seasoned opponents knew would be nearly impossible to overcome. His likely runoff competition withdrew and Huey Long, improbably, unpredictably, was the new governor. Addressing a wild crowd at the Roosevelt, which included an exultant Seymour Weiss, Huey said he would someday be president.[27]

It would have been instructive at this point for the streetwise, cigar-smoking, plebeian Old Regulars to pause and size up this pugnacious man who sought to lead them. Had they done so, before them would be revealed an individual of uncommon dimensions, with an unlimited capacity for industry, an unquenchable thirst for power, and narcotic notions of conquests far beyond their more provincial neighborhood concerns. Although Huey was only thirty-four at the time of his inauguration and without a political or economic power base to call his own, he was nevertheless quite unlike any previous politician in Louisiana, and that was what was good about him.

He came out of the gray, backward farm country of north-central Louisiana, a place far more Celtic than New Orleans, where Protestants and Anglo-Saxons were in abundant dominance, and a kind of dark, relentless poverty shadowed the lives of generations. Huey was the eighth of nine children in a household where reading was encouraged and politics discussed. The Long family home was comfortable, although it was nothing more than a one-room cabin to hear Huey describe it in later years. Huey's father even owned 320 acres of land, some of which he sold to the Arkansas Southern Railroad when a small road was carved out for hauling lumber through around 1900.[28]

This was Winn Parish, a lonely place unvisited by electricity, gas heat, and running water for nearly all of Huey's youth, where people, not Huey's family, lived in decaying cabins with dirt floors. The surrounding countryside was mostly untamed and unattractive, sometimes savagely wooded, other times broken up by a few clearings containing paltry cotton patches. The people in this country gave birth to children with distended bellies and hopeless futures mired in the exact kind of poverty that had destroyed their parents. This was also a country ripe for revolution where both Socialists and Populists had won respectable votes and the planter aristocracy was openly reviled for the scourge that it was.[29]

Cultural and religious prejudice prevented poor Protestants from north Louisiana from aligning with the equally destitute Catholics in southern Acadiana, thus making it inevitable that the state's conservative elite, which also had the Old Regulars in their pockets, would glide through life unchallenged. That the elites did so with a vindictive, monstrous indifference to the people they ruled was a measure of their reign. "The oligarchy that ruled Louisiana all those years was one of the most powerful and heartless in the annals of the Republic," two veteran reporters, Neal R. Peirce and Jerry Hagstrom, later judged. "Virtually nothing was done to cope with overwhelming problems of illiteracy and crushing poverty that left most Louisianians with inadequate food, shelter, and clothing well past the year 1900."[30]

But at the same time, historian Allen Sindler later perceptively observed, well-defined class antagonisms had emerged, which, if the "appropriately charismatic leader appeared," could lead to another, perhaps more lasting, shot at protest politics.[31]

That person was Huey Long, who, beginning in his early twenties, was less firm in body than he was in conviction, melding the dire times with his own passions of youth and coming to a striking conclusion: the system stunk. He could see for himself how it worked. There were cotton farmers and fur trappers and plowmen and tree cutters all around him who worked in medieval conditions and never got ahead. There were men and women who never knew a member of their family who went to school, and they never got ahead. Parents hoped they would not get sick and prayed that their children would not get sick, because they could not afford medical care and there was no hospital nearby, anyway. And they never got ahead. Common laborers did not know how to write or read, had no friends who were lawyers or politicians, knew absolutely no one who could help them, and they never got ahead. They were an old story, a story whose roots reached back to the Bible and told an eternal tale of masters and slaves, of power and bondage. United, Huey grasped, their numbers could overwhelm; divided, their toil would forever occur in darkness.

Huey was not the first who sought to lead a movement of mass discontent. Others had done it before him with varying degrees of success: Andrew Jackson went all the way to the White House in 1828 on a platform seeking a more equitable distribution of the nation's wealth, and even though he was one of the country's great military heroes and a man of unquestioned integrity, the lot of poor farmers and laborers remained pretty much the same after he left the presidency as it was before. William Jennings Bryan didn't even get that far: the Great Commoner three times won the Democratic nomination for president before and after the turn of the century by running on a platform of agrarian upheaval, and three times he was defeated. During Huey's boyhood, another voice echoed across the South. It was an angry voice of protest belonging to an angry man of vision, a fire-breather named Tom Watson out of Georgia who hoped to lead a farmers' revolt bathed in the populism of his day. But Watson, too, was unsuccessful, largely because he failed to move off the farm and invite the disenchanted of the small towns and the great cities into his coalition. Huey would be different. He would be the first leader of a mass uprising who would actually make rhetoric reality, implementing through programs the ideas he decreed as a campaigner. This made him a great hero to millions of Louisianians who would soon be repeating his name in idle conversation and cutting from newspapers faded likenesses of his face. It also made him dangerous.[32]

Married in 1913 to Rose McConnell of Shreveport, a dark-haired, dark-eyed stenographer for a local insurance company, Huey and his wife boxed their few belongings for New Orleans, where the young couple lived in a plain, two-story house near the river's edge as Huey completed enough law classes at Tulane University to pass the state bar examination only three years later. For a while he specialized in injured workers' cases, but in 1918 Huey ran for and won a seat on the State Railroad Commission, giving him his first real opportunity to make his Populist visions real. He was only twenty-five, and the commission, which regulated railroads, telegraphs, telephones, and steamboats, would never be the same again. Slowly forging a narrow voting majority on the board, Huey soon built an impressive Populist record by denying rate hikes to utility companies and even forcing one telephone company to return to its customers the proceeds from an earlier hike. He saved his greatest effort for an unbridled attack against the Standard Oil Company, both raising the company's taxes and regulating their rates. The word spread that here, finally, was a man, a very young man at that, who was fighting for the working man's interests. In a society defined by caste, that was very big and troubling news indeed.[33]

Huey's battles on the commission, his unsuccessful run for governor in 1924, and his successful re-election to the commission two years later, made him a well-known person in Louisiana by 1928, and already there was a cleavage that would define his entire career: people either revered or reviled him. Yet upon winning the statehouse, Huey promised to work for all of Louisiana, even its most entrenched. "I go into the governor's office as your servant," he promised at a swank New Orleans dinner hosted by both the Uptown elite and the Old Regulars, both suddenly sobered by Huey's potential, only weeks after his startling win.[34]

And in the weeks to follow, Huey made good on his promise. He reached out in particular to the Old Regulars,

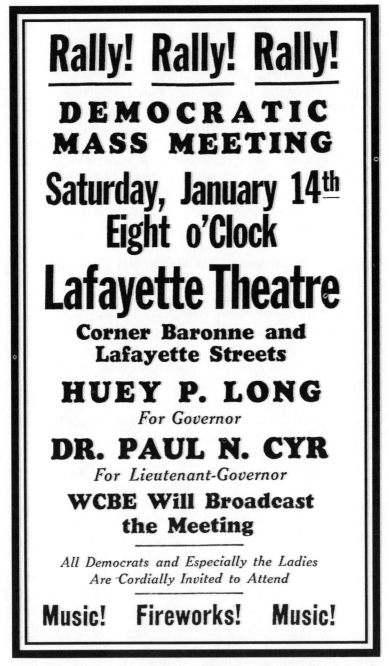

Rally! Rally! Rally!

DEMOCRATIC MASS MEETING

Saturday, January 14th
Eight o'Clock

Lafayette Theatre

Corner Baronne and Lafayette Streets

HUEY P. LONG
For Governor

DR. PAUL N. CYR
For Lieutenant-Governor

WCBE Will Broadcast the Meeting

All Democrats and Especially the Ladies Are Cordially Invited to Attend

Music!   Fireworks!   Music!

Even a larger than expected turnout for this rally, three days before the 1928 election, failed to warn the Old Regulars of the Huey Long tide that was about to sweep the state. (Courtesy the Louisiana National Guard Military Library)

whom he knew he would need to build a reliable majority in the legislature. He sought their help for bills that would bring natural gas to the city and launched one of his greatest dreams, a massive state highway system. Huey even offered to let the Regulars review his picks for leadership slots in the legislature.

But the Old Regulars, too used to winning, demurred. They were the power in the legislature. Huey Long, they were certain, would soon bend to their will.

And there were good reasons for their avarice: for all of their liabilities, the Old Regulars were a highly disciplined organization whose lawmaker members could be relied upon to vote the machine's way. The bloc of votes the Old Regulars controlled in both the state Senate and House had been enough to intimidate most governors in the past, and there seemed to be no reason to believe their experience with Huey would be any different in the near future.[35]

But Huey was different. He managed several times in the regular legislative session of early 1928 to get most of what he wanted passed through a shaky coalition of lawmakers from the rural north and Acadiana. Even in 1929 when the Old Regulars joined in a futile bid to oust Huey by impeachment, he beat them back.[36]

Yet the Old Regulars, at least in public, remained recalcitrant. There could never be a coalition between them and Huey, they said, because of Huey. "No one could merge with Huey Long in anything," Mayor Walmsley observed of the new governor. "He is always trying to trade us a biscuit for a barrel of flour."[37]

But a merger did finally come about because the Old Regulars saw something others did not: Huey could destroy them. Already he had done the unthinkable: he had created, upon the advice of his brother Earl and with the financial backing of Seymour Weiss and Robert Maestri, a city organization called the Louisiana Democratic Association that would now compete for votes in New Orleans. Then in 1930 Huey dramatically announced his bid to run for the U.S. Senate, unseating the hapless incumbent Joseph E.

Ransdell statewide, while Huey received an astonishing vote out of New Orleans: 47 percent. That was up from the 23 percent he won in the city two years before. His raw vote count had improved from 17,819 to just under 40,000.[38]

It was an emergency for the Old Regulars. Never before had so many people in the city of New Orleans defied them. They were the ones with the superb vote-getting abilities— up to 6,000 people working at the ward and precinct level to guarantee a good return for the Old Regulars on election day. They were the ones with the supreme patronage powers and the late-night, flame-lit parades, marching bands, and free food and drink. They had the banners and the flyers and the sample paper ballots all instructing their followers how to vote. And if all else failed they had the likes of Pershing Gervais who would, with his friends, happily disrupt any election to make certain the Old Regulars won. Yet despite all of their advantages, the Old Regulars nearly lost the city of New Orleans to Huey Long.

On the morning after Huey's Senate triumph, the Old Regulars, with a reluctant Walmsley in attendance, soberly weighed their options. They could continue to wage war against Huey. After all, Huey had demonized them as corrupt and the very thing that was wrong with politics in Louisiana, and many of the Regulars were still smarting from the sting. Others noted that Huey was not only a dangerous radical, he also wanted to be the boss. The Regulars would clearly enter into any arrangement with him as the weaker, subordinate partner. And then there was, of course, just the principle of the thing. He had become the enemy; to meet with him now, after Huey had delivered such a public booting, would surely be rank opportunism of the worst degree.

Principle, of course, lost out. The Old Regulars, the tough leaders of all of the city's seventeen wards, and Walmsley, too, soon met with Huey and then released a remarkable proclamation: Huey Long, they now decreed, was really not that bad of a guy after all.

3

"It Almost Turns My Stomach"

HUEY LONG'S OBSESSION WITH THE POLITICAL DYNAMICS of New Orleans extended to the culture and character of the city itself, a place that seemed to forever hold him in its thrall the way it did any out-of-town boy from the country.

And with good reason: in the 1930s New Orleans remained a city of intrigue and imagination, of things showy and seductive, giving to the nation much of its richest and most enduring music and literature.

Guitarist Danny Barker was one among many who lived with the sensations of the city he grew up in during the 1920s and 1930s when he later recalled what it was like to suddenly hear music, floating in from a distant breeze, out of nowhere. "The sounds of the city would be so clear, but we wouldn't be sure where they were coming from," Barker remembered, "so we'd start trotting—'It's this way!' 'It's that way!'—and sometimes after running for awhile, you'd find you'd be nowhere near that music." But it didn't really matter, Barker would add, because there were also other sounds, other songs to be heard. "The city was full of the sounds of music."[1]

Historians Al Rose and Edmond Souchon later documented just how pervasive music was in New Orleans: "Cafes were scattered all over town, bearing names that still set melodies singing in many a jazz fan's heart—the Tin Roof, the Red Onion, the Halfway House . . ." There was also Louis and Leon Prima's Shim Sham Club in the heart of the French Quarter, the Dog House on Rampart Street, and a proliferation of black music clubs, places where white Tulane students went at night: the Tick Tock Tavern, the Rhythm Club, and the Japanese Tea Garden, where according to one contemporary guidebook, "the tunes are loud, but have the 'swing' beat that causes Negroes to move their bodies and tap their feet."[2]

New Orleans also had gambling, and plenty of it, dozens of joints in makeshift stores and at the rear of residential houses where wagers could play poker, a daily lottery, and place bets on horse races listed on large sheets tacked to a back wall. One of the most popular halls was the 1-2-3-Club directly across from the Roosevelt Hotel. And although by the mid-1930s the city's only sanctioned red-light district, Storyville, had been closed for more than a decade, the business of prostitution was still thriving. The houses had moved out of their once-confined neighborhood to quiet locations across the city. Musician Louis Prima was caught by his wife leaving one of the more industrious houses of the French Quarter in 1933 and was promptly sued for divorce. "Beautiful ladies leaned from windows, calling out friendly greetings," the New Orleans writer Lyle Saxon wrote of the Quarter women. "They were all a little fat, it seemed to me, and held their kimonos around them, and they all kept crying out for passers-by to come in and see them."[3]

But hedonism inspires, and in New Orleans emerged a vibrant literature, leading the scholar James Feibleman to later delicately describe New Orleans as "highly conducive to original thought." Sherwood Anderson, who was becoming fascinated by Huey Long and wrote his friends to tell them so, settled into the French Quarter every spring to write and wonder, while William Faulkner "dropped in for a few days at a time." Feibleman added: "Liquor was cheap and plentiful, houses as well as homes were open, and life in general could be good at the sensual level." Another scholar, attempting to explain the city's hold on literary imagination, claimed that it was only "after the ordeals of conquest, occupation, and Reconstruction" that New Orleans emerged as a literary town. "This was accomplished by a self-conscious awareness of the cultural and racial mix that made New Orleans unique in the United States," said Richard Kennedy. The birthplace of Truman Capote and Lillian Hellman, New Orleans in the 1930s would also become the adopted home of Tennessee Williams, who yearned for a place he could be free.[4]

A city of more than 458,000 in 1930, New Orleans was also a place deeply etched by racial and economic woes. "There is no greater comfort to a city housewife with three children than to have a good Negro servant," an Uptown matron, Rachel Violette Campbell, noted in 1935. And for the roughly 110,000 blacks who lived, labored, and played in New Orleans in the 1920s and 1930s, that was about as good as it got. "If you didn't have a white captain to back you in the old days—to put his hands on your shoulder— you was just a damn sad nigger," Louis Armstrong later recalled of his youth in New Orleans, adding that any imprisoned black man absolutely required the sponsorship of a white man to save him. "Get in jail *without* your white boss, and yonder comes the chain gang!" Satchmo added.[5]

There were few blacks of prestige or power with enough influence to change things. Jim Crow laws had disenfranchised the city's black voting so effectively that only a token few dared to cast ballots in either city or state elections. Indeed, only 2,000 or 0.5 percent of the nearly 250,000 black people who lived in Louisiana in 1928 were even registered to vote. Blacks were consigned to their own schools, cemeteries, and churches in their own parts of town, although given the unusual racial and ethnic mix of most New Orleans neighborhoods, segregation was in reality mostly a sometimes thing. Blacks were even prohibited from making music with whites—even on the radio!—and any black person arriving at the front door of the Roosevelt Hotel, Gallier Hall, the Choctaw Club, the Boston Club, or

any other place of commercial, public, or private significance, was put in the direction of a side or rear entrance.[6]

Organized labor, which would emerge in the next generation as the single most important financial and organizing
support for the civil rights struggle in the South, fared little
better in the New Orleans of the 1920s and 1930s. After pre-
cariously maintaining a biracial dockworkers' union during
a time of rampant white supremacy, the Dock and Cotton
Council in 1923 was finally crushed by management. Eight
years later the now-separate black and white waterfront
unions went on strike, hoping to win back many of their lost
bargaining rights. But the struggle proved futile—a federal
judge ruled against the strikers and they returned to the
city's docks busted and divided.[7]

The news was equally dire for the city's streetcar drivers.
Their 1929 strike, popularly supported by the thousands of
New Orleanians who rode the trolleys everyday and saw the
drivers as friends, failed in the face of fierce, almost mind-
numbing opposition from the New Orleans Public Service.
It was such a unbending position that even Mayor Walmsley
seemed like a labor sympathizer, arguing that recognizing
the drivers' union would at least keep streetcars moving
along the tracks. But after two months of violence, the drivers were finally done in, NOPSI emerged triumphant, and
the only benefit to the city was the creation of the po' boy
sandwich, slapped together by John Gendusa, a local bread-
maker, and handed out for free by Bernie and Clovis Martin
from their French Quarter restaurant to the "poor boys" on
the strike line.[8]

New Orleans was also, by the early 1930s, in economic
distress. "On the New Orleans waterfront," historian Joy
Jackson, whose father was a riverboat pilot, later wrote, "the
early 1930s was a stormy time for those seeking employment
or trying to hold a job. The docks were haunted by hollow-
eyed men looking for work and angry union men caught in
labor disputes." A well-known local businessman and president of the New Orleans Pelicans baseball team, Alexander

J. Heinemann, lost $300,000 in the stock market and in January of 1930 shot himself in the mouth at the same park where his team played. He died beneath a sign bearing the message: "A full stomach and a bankroll make a man temperamental." Two months later, a small riot broke out in the French Quarter when nearly 400 men responded to a classified ad for a single job opening. It was no wonder there were too many workers and not enough work: in just a short three years since the crash of the stock market, manufacturing in New Orleans declined by a devastating 50 percent.[9]

Overdrawn accounts, eviction notices, and the bewildered look of hunger in children's faces combined to weaken or destroy even the most buoyant New Orleanian. Dr. George Bel, superintendent of Charity Hospital in New Orleans, noted a marked increase in the number of "whipped, embittered, helpless men, women, and children" entering the hospital's doors, many of whom were "trembling on the brink of physical and mental collapse." Meanwhile, the hospital was treating up to 130,000 New Orleanians suffering from syphilis.[10]

"I think the thing I remember most about the Depression was the lack of prospects," said Howard K. Smith, a young student in New Orleans on his way to national fame as a newsman. "There was no hope. I could work as hard as I wished, but I couldn't get a job, nobody in my family could get a job."[11]

And even having a job was no guarantee of security or a full belly. "There were a lot of people who were not working, and I had some hard times like that myself," recalled Avery Alexander, who would eventually emerge as a premiere civil rights activist and state lawmaker from New Orleans. But with a job on the docks, Alexander had one advantage not enjoyed by everyone in the city: "Bananas were imported through the port of New Orleans at that time. United Fruit Company, Standard Fruit Company. And all you had to do was walk out there and get all of the bananas you wanted. That could be a meal."[12]

"What does it matter then that children in New Orleans are going to school hungry, that families of six and eight and ten people are living in one-room shacks?" asked Louise S. Jessen, a forty-seven-year-old student at Tulane's Newcomb College who advocated a sweeping Socialist response to the city's ills, including a radical redistribution of income and property. The response to Jessen's minuscule Socialist Party, meeting weekly in a French Quarter salon, was underwhelming: in the spring 1934 general election for mayor and city commission, the Socialists got no more than 700 votes citywide. Still, they represented a political and intellectual vibrancy in New Orleans and continually challenged the economic order through demonstrations, pamphleteering, and long, windy speeches. "There was an incredible amount of Socialist and even Communist activity going on in the city then," remembered Floyd Newlin, a Tulane law student in the 1930s who was briefly caught up in the leftist activism on campus. "It was just a very vibrant political time."[13]

Walmsley, unaccustomed to chaos, was alarmed. In March 1930 he noted that the successful conclusion of two pet projects—the new municipal auditorium and the widening of Canal Street—would eliminate the jobs of several hundred people. In response, the mayor asked city employees to kick in up to 5 percent of their already-thin salaries for a fund that would pay those without work to haul trash, grade streets, and mow lawns, an inspiration that would provide at least temporary relief for up to two thousand people. He also personally promoted the New Orleans response to New York's famous Depression apple vendors: orange vendors selling boxes of the Gulf Coast fruit on the street. Within one week after Walmsley announced his idea, more than 500 unemployed women and men were selling up to 500 boxes of the fruit a day. In the summer of 1931, a crowd of jobless men gathered in the front of Gallier Hall demanding something, anything: work, help, relief, attention. Walmsley left his office to greet the men personally and promised a

$250,000 jobs program. Where the money would come from, he wasn't sure. Certainly his banker friends would be reluctant givers. But he would try, Walmsley said. "I don't blame you for coming up here and demanding relief," Walmsley told the hungry, but oddly courteous, gathering. "I've got a kid at home and a wife and if they were hungry, I'd be scraping for help just like you are."[14]

That Walmsley, given his family's wealth, would ever have to scrape for anything was unlikely. But the gesture was appreciated. The men returned to their homes convinced the mayor would at least try. "I think Walmsley was a very sincere man," reporter James Gillis ventured. "He was just in over his head."[15]

Adding to Walmsley's fears was the condition of the city itself: its infrastructure, public services, and police and fire protection. A survey conducted by the National Industrial Conference Board in the early 1930s noted that teachers in New Orleans schools by 1931 were at their lowest salary levels in four years, that nearly one third of the police officers assigned to patrol duty were actually pushing paper at desk jobs—undoubtedly reflecting the department's status as a rich depository of Old Regular patronage—and that those cops out on the beat were ill-equipped to respond to crimes and emergencies. "The burglary problem is particularly marked in the high-class residential area up river from the business section," the report noted of Uptown New Orleans. "Many residents in this area close their houses for periods ranging from a few days to many months, thereby adding to the difficulty of the burglary problem."[16]

The study also noted that at least half of the streets in New Orleans were unpaved and marked by deep, menacing ditches on either side that served as the permanent destination for dozens of broken-down jalopies. Those streets, particularly in impoverished neighborhoods in the French Quarter, the Irish Channel, and Central City, were also frequently filled with refuse, packs of roaming dogs, goats, and even occasional sheep on the lookout for food.[17]

Most of the houses in New Orleans by the early 1930s were still lacking gas heat, the only warmth in bitter damp months coming from small fireplaces or dirty coal-burning stoves, while the introduction of indoor plumbing presented an architectural challenge to the city's many shotgun houses—so called because one could fire a gun through the front door of these narrow structures and see it fly through a string of rooms before emerging by way of the back door. Now these houses, most of them built in the 1880s and 1890s with high ceilings, saw the addition of less sturdy, smaller extensions to accommodate the wonders of the modern age: bathtubs, toilets, and sinks.[18]

Yet for all of its many problems and complexities, the city was a rich plum for Huey Long. Already by 1930 charting his national course—a canvas banner softly blowing in the September wind the morning after Huey's startling Senate triumph said it all: Long for President—Huey wanted for nothing more than a negotiated peace with Walmsley and the Old Regulars. He had spent far too much time and energy battling them, he knew, time and energy that could be better used solidifying his Louisiana base in anticipation of a national run for office.[19]

In the days following Huey's 1930 win, it seemed as though he would get his wish. In a lavish banquet of contrition in the Roosevelt Hotel's swank Venetian Room, Walmsley, the Old Regular captains, and even Huey's most implacable foes, the members of the Uptown elite, gathered to pay their new leader tribute. The smoky hall, stuffed with flowers and food, was filled with more than six hundred men and only one woman—Huey's wife, Rose, who dined next to Walmsley on the dias. "Men who two weeks ago strained the English language to find epithets for their political enemies, sat at the same table, shook hands, swapped jokes [and] lighted each other's cigars," noted Meigs Frost of the New Orleans *States*. Long, in his autobiographical *Every Man a King*, sarcastically noted: "Only a few days previously I was not mentioned in the daily press except where someone had charged graft, corruption, embezzlement, even attempted murder." But now his opponents, the city press, Walmsley, even the gruff ward leaders of the Old Regulars, couldn't say enough good about him.[20]

The evening's peak was reached as Walmsley rose to hail Huey, thanking him, perhaps too profusely, for the roads and rebuilding program he had pushed through the legislature, oddly the same program the Old Regulars had earlier opposed. The mayor also took pains to thank Huey for being a good winner: in return for the pledged Old Regular support, Huey promised he would build for the city its first bridge across the Mississippi River, a modern airport near Lake Ponchartrain, and provide an annual appropriation of up to $700,000 for general infrastructure improvements in New Orleans. "Governor Long made, for a victor, unexpectedly generous proposals to the city of New Orleans, one of the chief centers of opposition to him," even the *New York Times,* which was increasingly emerging as a Huey Long critic, noted.[21]

Walmsley was excited: "Even in the hour of our defeat, we feel that he has stretched to us the hand of friendship for the good of the state," the mayor enthusiastically told the gathering, many of whom still personally detested Huey. But Huey seemed nonplussed, launching into a wild, agitated three-hour address during which he let the Old Regulars know he would be the boss in any partnership as he publicly admonished Walmsley: "I was governor of Louisiana for one year before I learned I had to be governor or get out," Huey said. He argued that all political leaders sometimes had to make painful decisions, even if in this case it meant Walmsley had to lead the Old Regulars into Huey's camp. "Mayor Walmsley is going to learn that he has got to be mayor or get out."[22]

The newfound unity was further cemented in the spring and summer of 1931. With Seymour Weiss frequently serving as Huey's proxy, visiting Walmsley at Gallier Hall or sometimes simply summoning the mayor and the Old Regular ward leaders to the Roosevelt Hotel, the workings of a coalition government gradually emerged. In specific races where Huey identified an opportunity, the Old Regulars would be expected to switch on the power of their machinery to get out the vote. In July 1931, for example, the Regulars agreed to let Huey pick his own candidates in eight state House races and three Senate races, all in the New Orleans metropolitan area, leaving Walmsley and friends to do what they liked with the remaining nine House and five Senate contests. The *Times-Picayune*, now a critic of both Walmsley and Long, reported that the mayor had been a "daily visitor to the governor's suite at the Roosevelt Hotel," where the final details were worked out.[23]

The Old Regulars also promised to dutifully do all they could for Huey's choice to succeed him: Oscar ("O.K.") Allen, who would be facing the voters in early 1932, as they, in addition, endorsed Huey's bid to serve out the term of the late Col. Robert Ewing, publisher of the New Orleans *States*, on the Democratic National Committee for that same year.[24]

The truce was not, however, without its detractors. Good government reformers were instantly alarmed as they contemplated the vast vista of corrupting opportunities in a Huey Long-Old Regular marriage. Others wondered how Huey could get into bed with the very evil, big city political machine he had spent so long previously denouncing. In 1933, author Webster Smith, in his generally critical biography of Huey, which received a wide national response, contended the alliance "looked bad" simply because Huey had spent so much energy and time in the recent past denouncing the Old Regulars "so loudly and long." Gus Williams, a Huey critic in the relatively powerless New Regulars, a small political group drawn up to oppose the Old Regulars, remarked: "By joining forces they hope to secure a policy of political life insurance and at the same time create a monster political machine that will, at the people's expense, supply them and their henchmen with political graft for a generation to come."[25]

But Huey and Walmsley seemed happy with the new arrangement. And for good reason: in the summer of 1931, the *New York Times* reported that Huey had shown a clear "disposition to treat New Orleans generously, and in fact, they [the Old Regulars] argued, had done so since his overwhelming victory last year." In addition, Huey promised to not interfere with the next important Old Regular contest: the January 1934 mayor's race when Walmsley and a slate of Old Regulars would be up for re-election. All seemed bliss.[26]

The first crucial test of the controversial alliance came in January of 1932 as O.K. Allen faced the voters in his bid to succeed Huey as governor. The result was a stunning triumph and potent proof of how things could go when Huey and the Old Regulars worked together. Although Allen won only 51 percent of the vote statewide, he got a thunderous 70 percent in New Orleans, thanks nearly entirely to the Old Regulars' efforts on his behalf.[27]

Now Huey could finally depart for Washington to take the seat he had been elected to more than a year before. In an celebratory journey less than one week after Allen's victory, Walmsley gingerly hopped on board the Huey P. Long Special Pullman coach as it left New Orleans' Louisville and Nashville station for a well-reported victory ride with Huey, Mrs. Long, Seymour Weiss, and a handful of Old Regulars and top Long lieutenants to Washington where Huey would at last be sworn in as Louisiana's new senator. It had been a delayed coronation. Huey had been fearful of leaving Louisiana before because the lieutenant governor was a fierce opponent determined to move into the statehouse on a moment's notice. Allen, however, was an entirely different story: silver-haired, friendly, and calm, he was entirely devoted to Huey and pledged to maintaining Huey's big government, Populist agenda. There were those who said Allen was a little bit too devoted. He suffered through years of abuse at Huey's hands as Huey appeared to enjoy reminding him of his subservient status. Their relationship was devoid of the banter and give-and-take that marked

Huey's friendship with Weiss. But even if others objected to Huey's cavalier treatment of Allen, the only thing that mattered to Huey was getting a new governor set up in Baton Rouge who would respond to his every summons. In Allen, Huey found exactly what he was looking for.[28]

The Long victory train sped through the Deep South by night and into the cold winter wind of Virginia in January the next morning as Huey and company made merry. At the capitol, Huey's Louisiana friends watched him take the oath of office as he also got his first narcotic whiff of attention from the national press: reporters from the *New York Times,* the *Washington Post,* and the *Washington Star* among other papers, thought Huey's arrival into the Senate's august chambers a story of single importance. The following day, as Huey assumed his duties in the Senate, Walmsley and Mrs. Long returned by the same Pullman to New Orleans, where they were met by the New Orleans press. Both seemed entirely taken by their brief Washington sojourn. "There wasn't even a wrinkle in Huey's coat to bother me!" Mrs. Long remarked, as Walmsley reported: "Huey Long is the happiest man in the world. Not only has he achieved his ambition, but he has been welcomed in Washington as a man of the people." Walmsley, it was becoming clear, was now not only a Huey Long man, but enthusiatically so.[29]

By spring, Huey leaned on Walmsley again. Both would be delegates this year to the 1932 Democratic National Convention in Chicago, and both had already decided to support New York Governor Franklin D. Roosevelt's bid for the nomination. That nomination, however, was anything but a foregone conclusion. As the Democrats convened in the Windy City, FDR was still short of the necessary two-thirds delegate vote then needed to win. To make matters worse, two separate delegations from Louisiana had arrived by train in Chicago, both claiming to be the official expression of the will of the people.

Suddenly, if only briefly, Louisiana's political machinations became a national concern. It would be up to the full convention to decide which set of delegates should be properly seated. But for the Roosevelt forces, the Louisiana family feud was of no little importance: both Huey and Walmsley had pledged their twenty-member delegation to FDR's banner. And it was clear that the New York governor would need every vote he could get. But already the Roosevelt forces were wary of Huey. He seemed unpredictable and entirely impervious to the managerial control any national presidential campaign needs to exercise over those who played on its team.[30]

Arriving in Chicago with a trunkload of flannel pants, summer linen suits, and two-toned shoes, Huey headed straight for the nearest golf course—Weiss had introduced him to the game as a way of relaxing, although, Weiss later laughed, Huey spent most of his time talking politics and little putting. Walmsley was there, too, also gaily attired, and the two men plotted their convention strategy. They would first fight for the seating of their delegation before the convention's credentials committee, and Huey's performance before it was not impressive—he made jokes and seemed to regard the entire proceedings as a waste of his time. Although a majority of the committee voted in favor of the Huey and Walmsley faction, a minority challenge to the committee vote meant that it would be finally decided on the full floor of the convention. The big night was slated for Wednesday, June 28. Walmsley and Long together would be allotted 45 minutes to make their case, a case made all the more crucial because it would also be broadcast by all of the radio networks covering the Chicago proceedings. Together, Huey and the mayor decided on their plan of attack: Walmsley would speak first. He would establish the legal framework for the delegation he and Huey led, discussing the intricacies of Louisiana law and how delegates from the state are usually elected to attend the party's convention. He would then relinquish the microphones to Huey for a view of the larger picture, a discussion of the moral obligation of men and women who are legally and rightfully elected to positions of the public trust being allowed to honor that franchise.[31]

As Walmsley and Long took their places on the podium, the delegates responded with a torrent of jeers and cheers, proof that even here, far away from Louisiana, just the appearance of Huey Long was enough to unleash emotions. Walmsley smiled and waved, a happy captain on the *Titanic*. A more wooden, if equally noisy, speaker than Long, Walmsley instantly sparked a round of laughter from the delegates when he began by pointing out: "I am not a henchman of Huey Long." In fact, Walmsley continued, "I tried to keep him from being elected Senator," which prompted even louder catcalls. But Walmsley persisted, he would always persist if booed. He ran through the legal rationale for seating the delegation he led, and then retired, sitting to Huey's left in front of a wooden table stacked with law books. Now it was Huey's turn, and he relished the moment, fully confident he would captivate his huge audience with his superb rhetorical skills. He spoke quickly but calmly, for once not flailing his arms wildly above his head, as Walmsley handed him one law book after another with pertinent passages underlined to bolster the case. What Huey said on that historic night is less important, indeed, he was nearly as legalistic in the intricacies of Louisiana convention procedure as Walmsley, than how he said it. In only a few minutes the convention, even the whiskey-loaded Texas delegation part of it that had booed him roundly when he came onstage, fell quiet. A master was at work, and the delegates recognized one of the greatest speakers they'd ever heard before them.[32]

The outcome now seemed foreordained. By a vote of 638 to 514, the convention's delegates voted to seat the Long-Walmsley faction. Huey responded by grabbing the huge wooden sign bearing Louisiana's standard and waving it wildly over his head. Then he jumped on a chair and waved some more. Walmsley, too, began to cheer, jumping on a chair of his own, as the other members of their delegation crowded around. It was a night to be savored. Not only were Huey and Walmsley victorious comrades in arms, but Huey had impressed millions, including FDR, the famed defense attorney Clarence Darrow, and the humorist Will Rogers, all of whom later remarked on the superb speech, with his reasoned and serene address.[33]

Following the convention, both Walmsley and Long angled to do their part for the Roosevelt campaign. In October Huey was assigned to tour North and South Dakota, Nebraska, and Kansas, states Roosevelt campaign manager James Farley figured he could do little damage in. But the farmers and small-town residents of the dusty prairie were just as desperate in 1932 as people back home in Louisiana. They responded warmly to Huey's speeches, hundreds of them turned out for the briefest address, prompting the Democratic chairmen of each state to jointly wire Farley the good news: "If you have any doubtful state, send Huey Long to it," they recommended. In New Orleans, Seymour Weiss pitched in too, announcing the formation of a businessmen's league for FDR, which won the immediate public support of both Huey and Walmsley. Dues were only $2 per member, but Weiss figured Huey's stature made his membership worth "about three times as much as most Democrats," and jokingly charged him $6, which Huey happily paid. On election day, as Roosevelt won 57 percent of the national vote, his average total in the four states Long worked in for him, four traditionally bedrock Republican states, was 62 percent and as high as 65 percent in several Congressional districts. Walmsley's efforts, on the other hand, were far less triumphant. He was sent to only one state, Pennsylvania, the only large state FDR would lose in November.[34]

The apex of the Long-Walmsley alliance was reached that same autumn with the successful election of John Overton to the U.S. Senate from Louisiana and the passage of a series of constitutional amendments drawn to increase taxes. In both instances, however, the results were more than perhaps either Huey or Walmsley hoped for. Wide-spread voter fraud was obvious in both elections, prompting many to wonder if corruption would be the only child in the Long-Walmsley marriage. Certainly Gus Williams' warn-ings concerning the unchecked activities of an Old Regular-Long alliance now seemed to bear fruit. Hilda Phelps Hammond, one of a group of Uptown women determined to unveil the worst secrets of the Long organization, claimed that the fraud of the Overton election proved Louisiana had descended into a "ballotless state in the hands of political racketeers, who, like all political racke-teers on the route to dictatorship, have convinced simple people that everything they do is in the interest of the pub-lic." Historian Glen Jeansonne later put it simply: "If Long's alliance with the Old Regulars guaranteed his candidates large majorities in New Orleans, it also ensured there would be no restraints on corrupt electioneering."[35]

The Overton election caused no end of trouble for Huey as Hammond and others pushed to investigate not only the incidences of voter fraud, but virtually every dark, mysteri-ous corner of the Long empire itself. With a small group of like-minded Uptown women, Hammond was relentless, and her pursuit of Huey came just as he rose to Washington prominence. He was, by 1933 and 1934, important enough for a Senate committee to meet on just the topic alone of how the Overton campaign was run. Weiss, called to testify on how money in the Long organization was raised and spent, was hardly a cooperative witness; he mumbled, "None of your business," to virtually every question the com-mittee asked him, thereby earning a special enmity among the Uptown women who would forevermore see him as nothing less than a Long henchman. But Hammond and friends were partly successful because they were going after fat game: Huey was now also a Senate sensation, if not among his colleagues, many of whom detested him, then certainly among the visitors who packed the Senate's gal-leries to hear his every speech. "For leading the masses and illustrating your point humanly, Huey Long couldn't be beat," a young Lyndon Johnson, in his early twenties as an aide to a congressman from Texas, remembered. "I was simply entranced by Huey Long." He was so much so, in fact, that Johnson begged the Senate's doorkeeper to call him whenever Huey was about to speak.[36]

Others were far less impressed. Conservative Pat Harrison of Mississippi, a Bourbon Democrat, thought Huey was "less respected by the membership of this body as a whole and by the country than that of any other Senator here." Harry Truman of Missouri, who adored Roosevelt during a time when Huey was beginning to attack the president, told Huey he listened to one of his long speeches only because he was required to as that day's presiding officer in the Senate. He later remarked that he thought Huey was a liar and "nothing but a damn demagogue."[37]

But such detractors did little to dent Huey's rapidly growing popularity across the country. Huey was becoming a lightning rod of dissent because he talked about real things, tangible programs that would help the Depression's many victims: pensions for veterans, federal housing, free education, even at the college level, for all. But by far his most radical and alarming idea—and hence his most popular— was redistributing America's wealth. It was, to some, virtually anti-American, imposing by government fiat a formula determining how much money any one person could accumulate in the private sector. Huey called his idea the Share Our Wealth plan, and it caught fire: a rich man, he said, would be permitted to bank as much as $1 million, but anything over that amount would be heavily taxed on a graduated percentage until an income at the $8 million level was entirely absorbed by a 100 percent tax rate.[38]

The revenue gathered from these taxes, Huey's program made clear, would then be used for the most attractive part—that is, if the simple taking of money from millionaires wasn't attractive enough—of the Share Our Wealth plan: income redistribution. Every citizen of the country would get a proportional share of the funds netted under Huey's program, guaranteeing them, he promised, enough for the essentials: "a home, an automobile, a radio, and the ordinary conveniences." In a nation where many were now reduced to scraping meals from garbage cans and calling flimsy temporary structures of cardboard and tin home, the Share Our Wealth plan was wildly popular. More than 7.5 million people would become members of Share Our Wealth societies, sometimes joining at the rate of 20,000 a day. The societies, not incidentally, created for Huey a powerful network of supporters and volunteers he could use for a possible presidential campaign.[39]

Huey's national ambitions were also, by 1934, increasingly defined by his rancorous relationship with Roosevelt, the man he helped elected president only two years before. Throughout 1933 Huey's comments concerning his opinion of the new president and the methods FDR took to get rid of the Depression were critical. By 1934 it was evident to nearly everyone in Washington that it was only a matter of time until Huey would make a final public break with the White House as the first step in his own bid to become president. No one, either in Washington or Louisiana, was entirely sure why Roosevelt and Huey seemed destined to break. Certainly ideology was part of it: In the first years of his presidency Roosevelt was dedicated to balancing the budget and spending only as much as the federal government had in reserve on public works programs to help the nation's starving jobless. Huey was horrified by FDR's hesitancy. When he needed to help those without work in Louisiana, Huey simply had the legislature pass an appropriations bill, even if it meant running up a budget deficit for that year. Food on the table, Huey reasoned, was always more important than red ink on the state records. But Huey may also have broken with Roosevelt for a more fundamental reason: Unlike the corrupt Old Regulars and the sometimes self-serving Democratic leadership in the U.S. Senate, Roosevelt simply could not be outfoxed. He was every bit Huey's political equal, and Huey knew it. "He's so doggone smart," Huey said of Roosevelt after one 1933 meeting with the president in the White House, "that first thing I know I'll be working for him—and I ain't going to."[40]

In order for Huey to pursue the his ambitions, he frequently returned to Louisiana in 1933 to mend his political machine—only to find new rifts between the state government and New Orleans and a growing reluctance among the Old Regulars to do what they had earlier promised: to carry out Huey's every order without complaint. Inevitably he began to realize how much easier it would be to simply destroy the Old Regulars and Walmsley altogether, replacing them with entirely loyal Long men. Huey dwelled upon the benefits of creating, as historian Allen Sindler later concluded, "a base of unchallengeable state power, independent of any deals with the state machine." A circular authorized by Huey and distributed by his men in the fall of 1933 was portentous. Just as the sternly worded wall banners in later-day Peking would tell the Chinese of the latest drift in Mao tse-tung's thinking, so would the wordy circulars, usually reckless with facts and reputations, give Louisianians a taste of who was saved and who was about to be excommunicated in the kingdom of Huey Long. "No combination with lice and rats who have mulcted our people," the circular colorfully declared, as the text below described in detail how the Old Regulars and Walmsley had continually betrayed Huey in the course of the past year. Walmsley saw the direction the wind was blowing and began to publicly distance himself from the man he only months earlier had extolled. "That's all bosh," Walmsley snapped when a New Orleans reporter asked if it was true that without Huey's endorsement the mayor would be hard-pressed for re-election in the January 1934 mayoralty race. "Huey has nothing to do with it."[41]

But all was not lost. In December of 1933 Huey and Walmsley made one last stab at keeping their coalition together. Meeting nearly every day for the week before Christmas at the Roosevelt Hotel, the two men played political poker: Huey, demanding to name at least half the candidates running for office in the January election, upped the ante on his continued truce with the Old Regulars. Walmsley, knowing fully well what the Old Regulars would and would not agree to, folded. If the sweet strains from Cole Porter's "Just One of Those Things," could have been heard from the Blue Room below, the final parting could not have been more dramatic. Walmsley strolled out into the brisk December air with a dark hat protecting his bare head, and arrived next at the Choctaw Club, where the all-powerful 17 ward leaders of the Old Regulars, like a pontifical college of cardinals, voted 12 to 5 to officially sever their relationship with Huey. They left it to Walmsley to dutifully announce their decision to the press, and upon doing so the mayor's customary gusto was back in evidence as he called the action great news and said now, finally, the Old Regulars could go about their business without any "outside suggestion or dictation."[42]

Huey's immediate reaction was more gastronomic: "It almost turns my stomach to have the matter even mentioned to me," he ruefully said of a breakup he precipitated. The New Orleans press, never accurate predictors of the future of Huey Long, now almost unanimously predicted his career was over.[43]

It was hardly that. But, unknown to all, was how truly bad the end of the Long-Old Regulars alliance would soon be for the city of New Orleans, ushering in an era of violence and anarchy the likes of which had not been seen since Reconstruction. For his part, the morning after the Old Regulars decree, Walmsley was cheerful. "Yes, sir, it looks like the beginning of a new deal from now on," he chirped, straining credulity by adding, "now everyone will be able to go forward with his head held high, knowing that we have not sacrificed our principles so the fight would be easier."[44]

Huey was petulant. Annoyed by Walmsley's refusal to

CHIEF PUSHMATAHA CALLS ON THE CHOCTAWS TO ASSEMBLE AT HIS WIGWAM ON LAKE PONTCHARTRAIN AT THE RISING OF THE SUN OCTOBER - NINTH - THIRTY THREE AND TO REMAIN UNTIL FULL MOON TO DO HONOR FOR HIS FAVORITE WARRIORS

Walpraskeeargom

SYERHPMUH MIJ ⟨ HEAP BIG CHIEF ⟩

- GRELLE -33-

Their break with Huey only weeks away, Walmsley and the Old Regulars throw a party. The bottom signature is an amalgam of the ruling Old Regular City Commission: Walmsley, A. Miles Pratt, Joseph Skelly, Fred Earhart, and Frank Gomilia. (Courtesy New Orleans Public Library, Louisiana Division, Rare Vertical File)

capitulate and perhaps additionally irked by a cartoon in the afternoon *States* depicting him as a crawfish—a play on his self-imposed Kingfish moniker—vainly attempting to enter the Old Regulars' Choctaw Club, Huey played the game of 'Who needs ya anyway?' "I don't need the help of this city in politics," he was sure. Reminding New Orleans that he still had plenty of friends elsewhere, all across the state, in fact—people who would come out of the forests and fields to respond to his banner time and again. "I have," Huey flatly declared, "enough friends to get me elected."[45]

Although publicly continuing to deny he had any intention of becoming involved in the upcoming mayor's race, Huey privately made quick work of putting together a ticket, against the advice of Seymour Weiss, who warned him: "Now look here, partner, you are about to make one of the biggest mistakes I've ever seen you make in politics . . . all I want you to do is come out and say to the people of New Orleans 'I am busy. I am looking after your best interests in Washington; my friends are free to vote for whomever they please for the mayor of New Orleans.'" But Huey had his own ideas.[46]

By New Year's Eve he had slated John Klorer, Sr., a colorless but well-regarded New Orleans engineer, to oppose Walmsley. In addition, there were four candidates who would battle the Old Regular incumbents on the city commission. And, improbably, Gus Williams, a longtime critic, was his man for city attorney.[47]

Two days later Walmsley, smartly attired in a dark three-piece suit, posed for photographers in his Gallier Hall office as he qualified for the election and declared that the upcoming battle would be in essence a referendum on two men: Huey P. Long and Franklin D. Roosevelt. "To my mind, and I am sure in your mind, no greater crime could have been committed by any Democrat of the nation than the betrayal of President Franklin Delano Roosevelt," Walmsley charged in an obvious reference to Huey's now-bitter

Public
Choices

FRANKLIN DELANO ROOSEVELT
President
of the
United States

T. SEMMES WALMSLEY
President
of the
United States Conference of Mayors

MAYOR T. SEMMES WALMSLEY supported Franklin Delano Roosevelt for the Democratic nomination for the Presidency. Mayor T. Semmes Walmsley worked for the election of Franklin Delano Roosevelt to the Presidency, spoke in his behalf and raised a considerable contribution to his campaign.

Immediately following President Roosevelt's election and inauguration. Huey P. Long, charged with the duty of representing the people of the City of New Orleans and the State of Louisiana at Washington, broke with President Roosevelt. opposed and betrayed him.

In this act of treachery, Senator Long was followed by his two hand-picked Congressmen, Maloney and Fernandez, who were likewise supposed to support the interest of the City of New Orleans at Washington.

In the huge program of public improvements which was planned by our President, there was no representative from this City at Washington until Mayor Walmsley took it upon himself to secure for New Orleans what it was justly entitled to.

While Mayor Walmsley was engaged in frequent trips to the National Capital in conferences with the President and members of the Federal Government, Senator Huey P. Long, Mr. Francis Williams and Messrs. Maloney and Fernandez were engaged in peanut municipal politics here in New Orleans.

Mayor Walmsley, as President of the United States Conference of Mayors, called the Mayors of all great cities to Washington and impressed upon the President of the United States and his advisors the necessity for spending thousands of dollars in the great cities of this country in public work to relieve unemployment.

Mayor Walmsley takes no credit and seeks no political vantage as the result of his work with the President in the matters referred to above.

Mayor Walmsley feels that he is sufficiently rewarded for he has done everything humanly possible to contribute to the relief of our citizens.

While Mayor Walmsley was engaged in this work. Huey P. Long, Francis Williams, Maloney and Fernandez were busy at home in New Orleans sniping Mayor Walmsley in his efforts.

Thousands of dollars are still to be expended in the work of the CWA, PWA and under other Boards and Commissions. Mayor Walmsley's contacts at Washington are invaluable to the people of this city.

Huey P. Long has no contacts to advance our interests. Francis Williams has no contacts to advance our interests. Maloney and Fernandez are discredited representatives. To vote for your own interests, vote for Walmsley and the Regular Democratic Ticket.

This Space Paid for by Friends of the Administration

In the midst of the angry January 1934 New Orleans campaign for mayor, the Old Regulars remind voters that Walmsley is not only a Huey Long foe but a friend of the hugely popular Franklin D. Roosevelt. (Courtesy the Times-Picayune)

attacks against the president. Soon Walmsley's advertising would reflect the same theme: one full page ad in the New Orleans *Item,* with companion photos of Walmsley and Roosevelt, noted that the mayor not only supported FDR in 1932, but "spoke in his behalf and raised a considerable contribution to his campaign." By contrast, the same ad continued, Huey Long "broke with President Roosevelt, opposed and betrayed him."[48]

In a city where Roosevelt had won more than 93 percent of the vote in 1932 and was by any measure still immensely popular with New Orleanians two years later, Walmsley's pronounced public support for FDR could only be smart politics. If there was one man who united the Uptown elites, the Old Regulars, and just about everyone in between in their devotion to him, it was Franklin D. Roosevelt. Indeed, upon the anniversary of the president's first inauguration, the New Orleans *Item-Tribune* would publish a special issue that paid fulsome tribute to the president's first year in office and gave him thanks for his service. More than fifty local businesses would run ads in the publication to specifically salute the president's program in a manner unimaginable in future years with future presidents who were far less adored. It was only the latest, albeit New Orleans, evidence that, "for the time being," said critic Alistair Cooke of Roosevelt, "the entire country had decided he was their savior."[49]

But Walmsley and the third major candidate in the mayor's race, fiery independent Francis Williams, were wise to make Huey the main issue of their campaigns simply because the same man who had swept the state and nearly won the city in his successful 1930 run for the U.S. Senate was, by early 1934, not nearly as popular. Huey's slide from favor might have started with his increasingly venomous attacks on Roosevelt, beginning in the spring of 1933. But in August of that same year he became embroiled in an embarrassing controversy that would have probably finished for good a less determined public figure. Attending a charity revue at a club in Sands Point, Long Island, a small beach village where the settlers once tied bothersome slaves to huge rocks at low tide and left them to drown as the ocean swept over them, Huey entered the men's room of the exclusive Sands Point Bath Club his normal self, but left with a prominent black eye. The accounts of what happened in between naturally varied widely, but speculation eventually settled on the probability that Huey, perhaps not for the first time, urinated on another person, in this case a man at the next urinal. It was worth a black eye. But Huey's shiner was nothing compared to the beating he soon took in the nation's press from the incident. For the *New York Times*, Huey's bathroom antics were a front-page story, while the far away London *Times* informed its readers that in the peculiar states an organization calling itself the American Nusimatic Society was minting a medal paying tribute to the "unknown hero who hit Huey Long." The medal depicted a fist pounding Huey's head with a backdrop of flowing water taps in a wash basin.[50]

Two months later, Huey was repeatedly heckled by rowdy audiences on a speaking tour of southern Louisiana. In Alexandria he was roundly pelted, like a failing vaudevillian, with rotten vegetables and eggs. "He finds himself with his back to the wall in the most desperate fight of his career," the aptly named Southern journalist, Mason Dixon, wrote, arguing that Huey's 1933 misfortunes were threatening the loss of his "political czardom in Louisiana."[51]

In reality, it was not as bad as all that. Huey still, as 1934 dawned, had a tenacious grip on Louisiana. But his political momentum had been stalled. His big 1930 U.S. Senate win, his triumphant campaigning for FDR in 1932, and the explosive national press he received throughout 1933, gave palpable evidence of that momentum over a four-year period. Now Huey looked towards New Orleans and a crusade to finally unseat Walmsley and destabilize the Old Regulars as a way of demonstrating he was still on a roll, once and forever the Kingfish.

4

"Poor C. S. Barnes"

AT THE END OF THE FIRST WEEK OF 1934, Hermann Deutsch, his shiny straight black hair slicked back, his face habitually mournful, bellied up to his typewriter in the littered newsroom of the *Item-Tribune* and clanked out a sentence of wonder: "Instead of becoming, as might have been surmised, one of the most fiery campaigns of recent political history," he wrote, the January New Orleans mayor's race is "receiving less interest at the moment from the general voting public than any other feature of the general public scene."[1]

First paragraph written, Deutsch, who in his more than four decades as a New Orleans journalist would demonstrate an uncanny knack for accurately forecasting political earthquakes, went on to ponder how anyone in New Orleans could resist the essential drama of the January election: a titanic struggle between two powerful forces, a rural radical with a huge state and national following versus the nominal head of one of the most powerful, if ancient, political machines in the country.

But as 1934 introduced itself with a gust of arctic air, many New Orleanians had their minds on other things. This was, after all, the first week in more than fourteen years in which any kind of liquor could be purchased legally. By December 1933, a required two-thirds of the states had ratified the Twenty-first Amendment, finally ending the failed experiment in social engineering known as the Prohibition and launching a new era of sodden revelry.

And New Orleanians responded in kind, celebrating not only the reappearance of legal hootch, but its industry: one local report predicted that up to one thousand people would soon have new jobs as some six New Orleans liquor plants reopened their doors.[2]

"New Orleans really did make more than merry on New Year's Eve," the amiable entertainment columnist Mel Washburn reported. Washburn, who could announce the opening of a Louis Armstrong show or the death of a friend's dog with equal gravity, went on to reveal what New Orleanians were drinking: mixed wines, of both old or new vintage, seemed to be the most in demand. Not surprisingly, the number of arrests for public drunkenness jumped in the weeks after January 1934, from 996 in the first six months of the year before to 2,899 for early 1934.[3]

Prohibition's end sparked hope in New Orleans that dark days were over, with the promise of something better beaming brightly ahead. All over the city, at clubs like the Club Plantation and the St. Charles Bar—where Pinkey's Radio Orchestra provided the dance music—New Orleanians refused to go home. Among the celebrants was the darkly attractive daughter of Mayor Walmsley, Augustus, who spent the evening with her fellow Newcomb coeds at the swank Beverly Gardens nightclub in adjacent Jefferson Parish. "As late as 9 A.M.," on New Year's Day, Washburn continued, "many of the parties were still going strong." At the Roosevelt Hotel's Blue Room, the same club where Huey several days before abruptly stopped dancing to complain about the attire of two musicians sporting mustaches—"misplaced eyebrows," Huey called them—Seymour Weiss was elegant in evening wear while surveying a mixed crowd of Tulane students, Uptown businessmen, and downtown political cronies. But finally even Weiss could take no more. His watch reading 5 A.M., Weiss signaled the Blue Room's 16-member orchestra to play "Let's Call It a Day," as the club's seductive dark blue lighting gradually turned bright.[4]

The celebrations, of course, were not confined to just

New Orleans. Prohibition was given a moist send-off across the country. And almost everywhere boarded-up, dark, and vacant nightclubs suddenly came to life again. By summer, *Variety,* the national entertainment weekly, would count "more niteries, pubs, taverns, roadside inns, large and small cafes, hotels, and nite spots offering entertainment today, than there were speakeasies" the year before.[5]

But in New Orleans, as always, there were plenty of other diversions as well. On New Year's Day morning, more than two thousand black residents of the city, regular churchgoing people, crowded into Shakespeare Park after walking miles down the tree-lined streets of Central City, to pay worshipful tribute to the seventy-first anniversary of the Emancipation Proclamation. Half that many Jewish people, meanwhile, showed up for a dramatic recreation of Moses delivering his people from slavery as the Uptown Jewish Children's Home celebrated the founding of its center, in the decade before the Civil War, nearly 80 years before.[6]

The specter of budding womanhood also captivated the city as local debutantes, promising to present themselves to society in blankets of red, purple, and white flowers, announced their intention to do things differently this year: coming out on horseback at the New Orleans Fairgrounds for the annual Flower Carnival. Femininity of a different kind, however, would be displayed at the midnight Municipal Auditorium opening, one week after New Year's, of "La Vie Paree," a burlesque of scanty suggestion bringing the revelations of the Folies Bergère to New Orleans.[7]

There were, by 1934, more than thirty theaters in New Orleans, many one-time vaudeville palaces, now offering mixed menus of live entertainment and movies continuously from morning to midnight. Some of the most opulent theaters were in the downtown core of the city, but many others dotted the New Orleans map in residential blocks, in neighborhoods where there were also typically corner grocery stores and small family-run taverns. The theaters had colorful names: there was the Liberty, the Isis, the Escorial,

the Arcade, and the Grenada. And the promotions to snare
viewers to the city's theaters seemed endless. Not only did
major movie stars visit New Orleans throughout the 1930s,
so did a delegation of mannerly penguins and huskies get
trucked in for a round of school appearances to promote
the eerie MGM film *Eskimo,* a startling graphic movie that
promised to reveal "a strange primitive people who practice
an even stranger moral code."[8]

At the same time, George's Tavern in downtown New
Orleans, a pleasant, quiet hideaway for the Central Business
District's businessmen, banked on the mysteriously exotic
Prince Ibraham, billed as a "noted Oriental astrologer," to
increase business. He would give free personal readings
with each 35-cent meal. But the Monteleone Hotel in the
French Quarter figured the annual gathering of the Canary
Breeders and Fanciers Club, this year with birds named in
honor of President Roosevelt, Fu Man Chu, and Huey
Long, would be an even better crowd-pleaser.[9]

The real Huey Long, after a brief, harried week in Washington, returned to New Orleans on January 10, determined to make a difference in the city's election. Before
leaving his Washington office, Huey phoned Seymour Weiss
and told him: "You almost made me sell my birthright," he
began, reminding Weiss of his earlier advice to stay out of
the mayor's race. "My friends have been up here and they
have convinced me that Klorer [Huey's choice to run
against Walmsley] is a cinch."[10]

Weiss gave up, knowing how headstrong Huey could be.
"Partner, I have nothing more to say," he replied. But by getting involved, Weiss continued to insist, "you are guaranteeing Walmsley's election."[11]

If he wasn't guaranteeing a Walmsley victory by his decision to actively participate in the New Orleans election,
Huey was at the very least making it certain that what might
have been a routine city election (if, indeed, any election in
New Orleans could be so described) would now be a sensational battle to the finish by two determined political foes.

The election was set for January 23, but as early as January 2 Walmsley had made the announcement of his candidacy official and declared he was overwhelmingly confident of victory. The mayor had good reasons for being so sure. There were two factors in the city now who were implacably opposed to Huey: the Uptown elites and the Old Regulars. As long as Walmsley could keep those two groups united in their hatred, he was certain to win. Naturally he began his campaign with a broad anti-Huey theme: "We find ourselves in a campaign, the main issue of which is the elimination of Senator Huey P. Long from the political and public life of Louisiana," Walmsley proclaimed to murmurs of approval after the Old Regulars surprised no one and officially endorsed the mayor for re-election.[12]

The Regulars also moved swiftly—the seventeen ward leaders could be very swift when they got the notion—to adopt a resolution in the same January 2 meeting promising they would never rest "until Senator Long has been retired to private life and the machine he has set up in this state is destroyed."[13]

Could things get more personal? The answer came five days later near the end of an otherwise conventional political address before a luncheon of the Young Businessmen's Association meeting at the Roosevelt Hotel's Tip Top Inn. Suddenly all the years as the target of Huey's invective welled up in Walmsley and created a splendid explosion. Huey had taken, once again, to calling the Mayor "Turkey Head," an appellation, it seemed, that would follow Walmsley to his grave. But now word had gotten back to Walmsley that Huey was also about to accuse members of Walmsley's family of misdoings. Contending that the mayor's mother, Myra E. Walmsley, attempted to bribe a local printer for her son by promising that cooperation now would produce a lucrative city contract later, Huey was going to say as much in one of his wordy, sensational circulars. "This will cinch the election," Huey, with delight, told Weiss. But Weiss was not amused. "I know, but every man's got a son. Here's a mother trying to help a worthless son. You just can't do that." Huey, reluctantly, agreed. Meanwhile chief of police George Reyer, an Old Regular loyalist, also heard rumors of Huey's circular attacking Walmsley's mother and decided what he would do the moment he read one: he'd arrest Huey for libel. "After all, it was the man's mother," Reyer exclaimed. Incredibly, after the election, Huey even took credit for not publishing the circular when he ominously told a group of supporters: "I did not have the heart to publish a document which fell into my possession which would have turned the stomach of humanity against such a man as Walmsley."[14]

It was finally all Walmsley could take. "There comes a time in every man's life, whether in public or private, when he must refuse to take any more insults," Walmsley was suddenly yelling, as he departed from his written address, startling the dining YBA audience. "That time has come now for me."[15]

"He clenched his fist and shook it in the air," a reporter for the *New Orleans States* noted in his dispatch later that day. Hermann Deutsch, who was also in the audience, was also surprised, calling Walmsley's outburst "blazing" and "unrehearsed." And everyone heard something they had never heard before in conventional political discourse: the Mayor of New Orleans promised to beat up Louisiana's senior Senator the next time the two men met. "He has attacked my family," Walmsley continued, his fist in the air above his head. "I am going to choke those words down his cowardly throat the next time we meet."[16]

Oddly, Harry P. Gamble, a blunt-speaking supporter of third-party candidate Francis Williams, had earlier made light of the falling out between Huey and Walmsley and sought to remind voters that the two men just weeks before were supposed to be friends. "Let Mr. Walmsley and Mr. Long stage a genuine fist fight on Canal Street and take real delight in blacking the eyes of oneanother," Gamble cynically suggested. "They could and would get together 10 minutes afterward."[17]

But a brawl, if it should ever come to that, could easily have become a slaughter. Although the mayor's shiny noggin was the first thing people noticed about him, Walmsley, at forty-four, was in impressive physical condition, a hangover from his frenetically athletic days at Tulane. His six-foot-plus frame bore the countenance of discipline. His bearing was erect, his stomach flat, and his fists skilled in training as a boxer. The mayor, in addition, still liked to work out regularly, sweating off the worries of the day at the nearby New Orleans Athletic Club.[18]

Huey was quite another matter. Although only forty, he was several inches shorter than Walmsley and a fleshy two hundred pounds—up from the 175 he weighed when he became governor in 1928. His was a life full of rich plentiful foods that he gulped down, and occasional bouts of drinking. Also a member of the marble-columned NOAC, Huey tried to train, but quickly bored with the idea, instead mugging for onlookers when he lifted weights and, like a champion boxer entering the ring, eliciting cheers while wearing a sweatshirt, trunks, and shoes—all bearing his name. It made no difference that the staff of the athletic center genuinely enjoyed Huey and his antics, he was one of NOAC's worst walking advertisements.[19]

It was not without good reason, then, that a rural supporter sent to Huey a good luck charm just as the mayor's race was getting under way. This particular rabbit's foot was snared in a Negro graveyard, the farmer reported, under the light of the moon at midnight, thereby enhancing its magical potential. Entering a maelstrom of opposition, Huey would need all the good fortune he could muster.[20]

His first problem was the candidate Klorer, a well-intentioned, lackluster candidate who was the quietest person in a loud campaign. "Let me say—Senator Long is not running for office," Klorer weakly argued in yet another luncheon of the Young Businessmen's Association, who, if nothing else, were among the most regularly fed men in the Great Depression. "If you disapprove of him, record

your disapproval when he offers himself for reelection."
But Klorer and Huey were, for better or worse, engaged,
and each man's liabilities would weigh on the other during
the campaign. For his part, Huey was stuck with a candidate singularly incapable of exciting a political following.
But Klorer was also burdened by Huey: "For the first time
since 1928, when Huey Long became governor, his support
is being publicly proclaimed a definite liability instead of
an asset," thought Deutsch, as he surveyed the overall weakness of the Klorer effort.[21]

In response, Huey decided to do what he had done
countless times before: turn around a seemingly hopeless
campaign through sheer superhuman effort. On January
13, with only ten days to go before the balloting, Huey
made his first appearance for Klorer, speaking in the still-
cold night air before a rally in McCarthy Park in the middle
of a working-class neighborhood. Thousands of supporters
turned out in their winter clothing, but instead of hearing
the reasons why they should vote for Klorer, they listened
instead to a protracted, blistering attack on Walmsley and
the Old Regulars from Huey. "You people of New Orleans
and the state of Louisiana don't owe me a cent," Huey
began, speaking, as usual, without any notes. "But Turkey
Head Walmsley does."[22]

The crowd immediately howled as they heard the words
"Turkey Head." But Huey was hardly through. His arms waving wildly in the air—he didn't seem cold at all—he
launched into a detailed account of how much money he
had given New Orleans since he signed his truce with the
Old Regulars in 1930. How he had always been fair to the
city, and even to the Regulars, and don't forget the time,
Huey continued, he really had the goods on Walmsley, he
could have had the mayor thrown in jail for his corruption—Huey was now rolling. Walmsley then was a "poor,
downtrodden thing." Huey shook his head sadly, recalling
how Walmsley begged to be saved. "He came to me on
bended knee," Huey added. It did not matter if the story

was untrue—Huey gave no specifics—the crowd, laughing at the vision of Walmsley crawling, loved it.[23]

In the next week, Huey continued his assault against Walmsley and the Old Regulars in both daily radio speeches and night-time campaign appearances. The attack never varied: the Old Regulars were corrupt, and Walmsley was even worse, incompetent and corrupt. Meanwhile, Long's Louisiana Democratic Association sought to duplicate the intricate neighborhood vote-drives perfected by the Old Regulars by holding nightly meetings with block leaders virtually everywhere: at Vaughn's Garage in the Ninth Ward, the Italian Hall in the Sixth; the Little Flower of Jesus Hall in the Seventeenth, and the grand old Loyola University gym, decked out in patriotic bunting, in the heart of enemy country—the Uptown elite's Fourteenth Ward.[24]

It was a heroic effort. His throat growing harsh, Huey spoke for hours, promising to fight for lower utility rates in his speeches around the city and for expanded relief programs once he returned to Washington. Give me men in New Orleans I can rely on, Huey said, so that I can go back to the Senate and pay attention to your needs. In addition, Huey denounced Walmsley for allowing gambling to flourish in the city, a sin that had not seemed to bother Huey before. And he predicted an unceremonious end for Walmsley come election day: "You know the turkey head usually goes on the block," Huey declared with relish, "and we're fixing to have a little execution here on January 23."[25]

Huey even made light of Walmsley's threats to physically fight him, threats that had become the talk of the town. "Turkey Head says he is a great prize fighter," Huey pondered during yet another rally, this one near the city's "Little Warsaw" neighborhood off of Dryades Street, where mostly Jewish merchants sold to mostly black customers. Walmsley says, Huey continued, that he wants to "mess me around." "My friends,"—Huey was on a roll—"I hope he changes his mind about that, because I don't want that to happen to me." Huey was superbly sardonic, and the audience cheered his performance. Klorer, on the same platform with Huey, no longer spoke much at all.[26]

Always a music lover, Huey finally took to singing before the campaign reached its final days, breaking into the old country tune "The Whole Damn Family" after charging Walmsley with nepotism, then adding his own lyrics to the simple folk song "Git Along Little Doggy." Huey's version had it: "Anti-Long, little bogey, anti-Long, little bogey . . ."[27]

But removed from Huey's antics and Walmsley's taunts, the unlikely figure of C. S. Barnes, a bespectacled bureaucrat given to tweed suits and vests, was now about to emerge as a major, if unwilling, figure in the campaign. On the night of January 16, with just one week to go before the election, Barnes was in his office at Gallier Hall. All of the other offices in the building were closed, including Mayor Walmsley's. But Barnes and a group of determined men, some carrying revolvers, were busy at work. Laid out before them were the voluminous, worn poll books containing the names of thousands of people in New Orleans who were registered to vote. Open bottles of red ink, blotters, and pens were also in evidence.[28]

An Old Regular loyalist, strolling by Gallier Hall, noticed the late-night light burning in the registrar's office and became alarmed: who would be up there at this hour? Was someone tampering with the registrar's books? Was that someone under Huey Long's orders? Minutes later, a squad of police, all Old Regulars if they wanted to have a job, forcibly entered Barnes' office and arrested him and the men with him. Driven to Central Lockup and thrown in what Barnes, who was a stranger to this world, later described as "filthy, dirty cells," the men watched uneasily as the police also seized the open books and stacked them in the same jailhouse tier occupied by Kenneth Neu. Awaiting death by hanging, this celebrated "Sabbath Killer" of two people regaled his fellow prisoners and the guards with popular ballads of the day sung in a deep, pleasing baritone.[29]

"Poor C. S. Barnes," reporter James Gillis later recalled.

"He was only carrying out Huey's orders. He was no criminal or tough guy. But *he* was the one in jail."[30]

Although no one could prove that Huey was involved, it was certain that any tampering with the registrar's books— Barnes himself had recently suggested that many names on the lists, put there over the years by the Old Regulars, were fraudulent—was a direct violation of a restraining order handed down by the Civil District Court of New Orleans only three days before. And now Barnes, a state appointee, was at risk of a criminal indictment and a possible jail sentence for the whole affair.[31]

"My assistants and I were just finishing up the work of checking up on the registration books," Barnes nervously explained to a reporter from his jail cell. "A crowd of us were just sitting there talking." Walmsley, however, understandably saw things differently: "They stealthily entered in the middle of the night and without one whit of legality began their reckless misconduct," the mayor charged in a typed statement handed out to reporters only hours after Barnes' arrest became known. He had suddenly been given a great political gift, a perfect weapon, in the last days before the election, to prove how corrupt and dangerous Huey Long and the men who did his bidding were. And Walmsley made the most of it. It is, Walmsley concluded, "an outrage that must be condemned in no uncertain terms."[32]

Years later the Old Regular leader Joe Cangiamilla said that the Old Regulars were "notorious for padding the voting rolls, and wouldn't have been above adding fake names to the books if they got them first." Reporter Gillis agreed: "Both sides did it blatantly. In this case it just happened to be that Long's side got caught."[33]

"I want you to get me out of jail!" Barnes pleaded with Huey, using up his one phone call. "Get you out of jail, they can't put you in," Huey replied. Several hours later, Barnes was a freed but shaken man. A Long loyalist who owed his job to Huey, Barnes may have began wondering what he had gotten himself into.[34]

Walmsley, naturally, refused to let the matter die; it was just too good of an issue to let go of. He began to talk about it in all of his campaign addresses until election day. But at a rowdy, well-attended rally at Loyola University's main auditorium, Huey and Klorer sought to make the arrests an issue for their campaign. "I never dreamed citizens would be thrown into jail and denied bond until they were heard in court," said Klorer, momentarily regaining his voice, "and yet it has happened." Huey was more sweeping in his indictment. The arrests, he charged, were another sign of the way Walmsley did business. "He is not only not fit to be the mayor," Huey continued, before adding an unique denunciation, "he's not fit to be the lackey boy for a coyote."[35]

But even if Barnes had managed to do what he claimed he was not doing—removing names, hundreds, thousands of names, put there by the Old Regulars, from the lists— Huey's men still would have faced another obstacle far greater than Walmsley, and his name was Franklin D. Roosevelt. As Huey's rift with the White House grew ever more rancorous in 1933, millions of federal dollars earmarked for relief under programs like the Civil Works Administration and the Federal Emergency Relief Administration made their way to Louisiana, but specifically to those who were reliably anti-Long. Naturally, Walmsley and the Old Regulars were first in line. And public knowledge that, at least in New Orleans, federal jobs were coming through Gallier Hall was of incalculable political value. "The big pocketbook vote," said Marshall Ballard of the New Orleans *Item* after the election, "was in the hands of the Regulars. It counted still bigger than ordinarily because jobs are harder to get than ever."[36]

On election day Walmsley—glowing after a downtown rally bathed in fireworks, flares, and illuminated signs bearing his name—scored the most satisfying triumph of his career. His ticket fell short of a majority with 45 percent of the vote, but he ran far ahead of Klorer, who came in with a distant 29 percent, and independent Williams' 26 percent.

Klorer visited Huey at the Roosevelt the following morning and got his instructions. Although he could, as the second-place finisher, demand a runoff with Walmsley, he was too far behind. Huey told him to drop his challenge, which Klorer did, thus ensuring Walmsley's re-election.[37]

For his part, Walmsley ended the angry campaign where it had begun for him nearly a month ago. The election had nothing to do with him, Walmsley figured; it was all about Roosevelt and Long. The president, Walmsley declared in his victory statement, was "a great humanitarian," and the mayor pledged to "work with him in bringing prosperity back to this city of ours." But Walmsley had no gracious statements for Huey, none of the conventional bromides candidates usually utter regarding their defeated opponents on election night. Calling Huey a "crazy man," Walmsley promised "the fight against Senator Long shall be prose-cuted vigorously." Their battle would continue, he said. What had started out as a grudge match between the two men now would become an obsession.[38]

Yet for all of the hostility and rancor between Huey and Walmsley, lieutenants from the two men's offices were able to hammer out an important cooperative agreement in the final days of the campaign, an agreement that may have pre-vented violence and bloodshed on election day. After Barnes' arrest, Huey was worried. The Old Regulars, he thought, might physically take the registrar's office. Perhaps he should send in the state militia to prevent them. Walms-ley, in turn, publicly declared he would swear in and arm enough police, up to 10,000 if necessary, to check any mili-tary move on Huey's behalf. Tensions were only heightened when Col. Guy Molony, a former, tough city police chief and die-hard Old Regular now living in Honduras, suddenly reappeared in New Orleans. Molony enjoyed a fearsome reputation as a man who was not afraid to use physical force to get what he wanted. He was, in fact, a mercenary (a job description he himself gave) willing to fight anyone's good battle for a good price virtually anywhere in the world. He

was not a man to be trifled with, and he loathed Huey Long.
Holing up at the St. Charles Hotel, where virtually all of
Huey's foes eventually ended up, Molony was said to have
with him a cache of weapons and a small band of eager
recruits who were anxious to do battle with Huey. Violence
hung in the air. But on the very night before the election,
men representing Huey and Walmsley agreed to the creation of a special arbitration committee that would hear any
and all election-day disputes, thus making the presence of
either the police or the militia purposeless.[39]

Still, the concerns that there might be violence—there
had been before, in elections that were far less hotly con-
tested—seemed to be on everyone's mind. At Tulane University, the *Hullabaloo*, the weekly student newspaper, called
upon its readers to volunteer as neutral observers. Socialist
Louise Jessen and her like-minded activists suggested the
same thing. The reasoning was simple: the more people
there were to neutrally observe the proceedings at the city's
polls, the less likely it was that there would be either fraud
or violence. On election day, more than sixty students from
Tulane came out to observe. "We were full of idealism then
and really concerned about the excesses of the Long
machine," recalled Lindy Boggs, at the time a junior at
Tulane's Newcomb College who would someday serve in
Congress. "It was Long's methods that so many of us dis-
agreed with."[40]

But even with the presence of neutral observers, the election, Huey thought, had been a fraud. "They stole the election," Huey confided angrily to Seymour Weiss at the
Roosevelt Hotel as the two men went over the precinct-by-
precinct returns. Weiss, trying to calm Huey, pointed out
that fraud was not the exclusive province of the Old Regulars. "Maybe we stole a few elections, too." But Huey was in
no mood for charity or reason. "He was very frustrated by
the whole thing," recalled Huey's son Russell, who was fifteen at the time of Walmsley's re-election. "The rank and
file would turn out in mobs and hordes to hear him talk,

and they would cheer what he had to say, and laugh at his jokes, and you'd think you were going to carry this thing by an enormous majority. But when the election came, the Old Regulars had it under complete control."[41]

Huey vowed revenge: something had to be done about the registrar of voter's office. It was a thicket of Old Regular corruption, even though his own man, Barnes, was the nominal head of the office. By his own reckoning there were at least 40,000 fraudulent names on the books, names the Old Regulars could manipulate whenever they needed to win an election. He needed to gain complete control of the office and the big, bound books it contained.[42]

Meanwhile Barnes, the registrar who had held that position since 1926, weaving through treacherous political seas filled with Old Regulars, New Regulars, the Uptown elite, and now the Huey faction, finally ran out of luck. Facing a criminal indictment with possible jail time for tampering with the voter's list, Barnes was also facing the wrath of Huey for tampering badly. On March 29, just two months after Walmsley's win, Barnes suffered a massive cerebral hemorrhage that left him partially paralyzed and confined to his Irish Channel home. Three weeks later, Huey fired him from his job. An invalid for the next five years, Barnes died in 1939 at the age of sixty-six, unnoticed as the first casualty in Huey's war against New Orleans.[43]

5

Dreams of Dust

EVEN BY WALMSLEY'S STANDARDS, the dawning days in the wake of his re-election triumph were curious ones. Tracking Huey's return train ride to Washington on board the Crescent Limited, the mayor and his wife, Julia, registered at the old Mayflower Hotel in the nation's capital at the end of January. There he proceeded to prowl, hoping to find Huey so he could hit him.

"If I see Long, I'm going to beat him up," Walmsley proclaimed to the reporters of Washington, who suddenly began to see how Louisiana politics and politicians were somehow unique. Noting that Huey often made the Mayflower, a busy and popular hotel frequented by presidents and members of Congress some six blocks from the White House, his home away from home, Walmsley explained: "I understand this is his hotel and I selected it deliberately. If I run across him I am going to do exactly what I said—make him take back the things he said." That Huey was usually on frequent prominent display in the hotel lobby as he hailed reporters and politicians and almost always introduced himself as the Kingfish, a nickname he lifted from radio's popular "Amos n' Andy" show, only made Walmsley's arrival there more portentous.[1]

In the days to follow, sometimes for hours on end, Walmsley sat regally in the lobby, his back to a colonnaded pillar, as he yarned out the details of what he planned to do to Huey when he got him. Sometimes he said that all Huey really needed was "a good thrashing." Other times he promised to simply smack Huey in the face or punch him in the nose.[2]

The prospects of pugilistics between Louisiana's two most excitable politicians likewise excited the nation's press. Several papers even assigned sports reporters for the presumed Mayflower bout. Two nights after Walmsley's highly publicized arrival at Washington's Union Station, he and Julia were trailed by more than a dozen reporters, photographers, and even the newsreel camera boys in the Mayflower's restaurant who came to watch the mayor and his wife dine on grilled squab. The press prayed for an entrance by Huey. Harry Ferguson, a correspondent for United Press International, was ringside: "Walmsley entered promptly at 8 P.M. wearing a tweed suit and a fighting face. Friends rushed forward to shake his hand." "The place was packed," noted Roland B. Howell, an anti-Long aristocrat hanging around the Mayflower in hopes of seeing Huey pounded. The press attention was so intense, Howell continued, that whenever the Mayor goes for a stroll, "he is immediately followed by a long string of newsmen and photographers."[3]

But for the entire week of Walmsley's Washington visit Huey was nowhere to be found. To break the monotony, Walmsley took in the capital, called the White House, and even met with Harry Hopkins, perhaps the most influential New Dealer in the Roosevelt administration. Then Walmsley announced he was going home. He had duties to attend to in New Orleans, he said, and besides, Mardi Gras was just around the corner. But on the morning before his departure, Walmsley received an alarming telephone call. He was needed at the White House immediately, a voice said. All federal aid to the South was about to be cancelled! "I couldn't understand it," Walmsley later admitted. "But I grabbed my hat and coat and dashed for a car."[4]

With the Mayflower's lobby finally emptied of Walmsley's noisy presence, Huey suddenly materialized, claiming he

had been looking for the mayor all along. Where was Walmsley now? Huey asked onlookers, just as Walmsley himself
must have realized the mysterious call was nothing more
than a ruse to get him out of the Mayflower long enough to
give Huey strutting rights. "A typical Huey trick," Walmsley
admitted, even managing a smile, as he told the story to
reporters back in New Orleans.[5]

If Walmsley's hatred for Huey now seemed excessive, he
could be excused, at least, in a winter of rancor for not
being alone. In the aftermath of the mayor's race, Huey's
opponents seemed more numerous and vocal than ever,
perhaps giving comfort to what they hoped would be the
beginning of many more defeats to come for Huey. In two
more years, predicted Gabe Mouledoux, former president
of the elite Board of Trade, "Huey Long will be a forgotten
man in this state." "We have just succeeded in burying the
'Crawfish' Huey Long beneath an avalanche of votes,"
Lavinius Williams wrote to his fellow anti-Long legislator
Cecil Morgan on January 27. "We, here in New Orleans,
believe he is politically dead, and we know he has lost much
strength throughout the parishes." Three days later, Morgan received another piece of correspondence, this one
from Burt Henry, a New Orleans attorney and chairman of
the Honest Election League, a group composed of wealthy
city businessmen who never complained before about
fraudulent elections until Huey won a few. "The one great
effort here was to destroy Long," Henry wrote Morgan, "and
we believe he is on the road to the end."[6]

Even Morgan himself, who had played a prominent role
in the 1929 effort to impeach and convict Huey, saw the
beginning of 1934 as an ominous time for Huey. "It was the
first time in a long while that he was on the defensive," Morgan later reflected, "and a lot of people who by then had
come to dislike him saw his defeat in the mayor's race as a
sign that voters were finally tiring of him."[7]

Other foes becoming more prominent in 1934 included
Hilda Phelps Hammond, the wife of an Uptown attorney

Huey had fired from two state jobs as he gleefully sought to prove he would not tolerate "double dipping," a sin his own employees had been charged with often in the past. Hammond nurtured a seething grudge against Huey, claiming he represented "pure evil." Her zealous hatred of him led her to a virtually one-woman effort to convince the U.S. Senate to investigate Huey's organization, an investigation that did eventually occur, although it did not bring Huey down. But Hammond was also responsible for the formation of the Louisiana Women's Committee, a group composed almost entirely of Uptown bluebloods who found nearly everything about Huey objectionable.[8]

Huey was additionally opposed by a newly formed group of anti-Longs called the Square Dealers, who included in their membership Walmsley, former governors John Parker and Ruffin G. Pleasant, and a number of lesser-known Huey-haters who nourished thoughts of a militia uprising against Huey's rule.[9]

Another foe came in the form of an increasingly hostile young journalist who seemed every bit Huey and Walmsley's rhetorical equal: Hodding Carter, the editor of the Hammond *Daily Courier* who had begun cutting Huey up in front-page editorials as early as 1931. Now in January of 1934 Carter was getting his first taste of national fame with the publication of an article he wrote in the *New Republic* arguing that Huey, because of a string of reversals, was "on the spot" and in more political trouble due to the coalition of opposition forces gathering in Louisiana than perhaps he realized.[10]

"The small-town day laborers and indigent farmers who built Huey's roads and swelled Huey's majorities are now chopping wood for the NRA and registering for the CWA," said Carter of the New Deal relief programs giving work to thousands in the state. "Though there is an honest effort to keep these organizations nonpolitical, it isn't dishonest to tell the workers that the man Huey is fighting is the man who made their jobs possible."[11]

Carter added that Huey had fallen "into an extremely deep hole," which may have been more wishful thinking, but the national press thought he was right. A February *New York Times* headline: "Huey's Star Is Seen As Setting," was followed by a report that said, "It is the view of astute politicians that Senator Huey P. Long, self-styled Kingfish of Louisiana, is on his way out." The *Literary Digest* declared Huey's recent defeats had "encouraged his enemies to believe they can change his self-conferred title of Kingfish to crawfish—and make it stick." While the *Washington Post*, revealing an ignorance of the New Orleans political scene, reported, "Two years ago it would have been folly to think of smashing the Long machine in New Orleans. Today it is in ruins." In reality, Huey had never had a machine in the city.[12]

But because Huey and his times were extraordinary, he now inspired the same in his opposition. Angry foes paid peculiar homage to the burning fires of protests past. Their lips sang with the hot rhetoric of revolt and liberty, they summoned up apocalyptic visions of knights and Klansmen who rode against the dark skies to defend honor and a way of life now nearly dead. Soon even the Ku Klux Klan itself— of what still existed of its murderous membership in 1934— promised to invade Louisiana and remove the state from the yoke of Longism.[13]

"People detested Huey Long because he was detestable," contended reporter James Gillis, who stomped his foot on the floor for emphasis. "He was . . . amoral," Gillis whispered.[14]

The anti-Long hatreds produced a garden of responses. The gifted New Orleans sculptor Enrique Alferez, whose sleek modernistic friezes, artworks, and murals decorated a variety of state public buildings in the 1930s, concluded not only that Huey was crude and inconsiderate, but that he had the unappealing habit of scratching himself in public. "He would scratch his privates and then reach around and start scratching his rear end," Alfarez recalled, mortified. "It didn't seem to make any difference to him if anyone was watching."[15]

Huey's buttocks were also discussed by Betty Brunhilde Carter, wife of Hodding, who contemplated nailing a sharp projectile dipped in tetanus toxin onto the seat of the chair Huey would wildly plop in after giving a speech. "He'd sit on it," the otherwise genteel Mrs. Carter anticipated, "he wouldn't know it, and he'd die the death of a mad dog."[16]

Within this miasma of malice it seemed perfectly natural that Walmsley would devote most of his administration's energy in the spring of 1934 to destroying Huey. For the mayor, two compelling goals had now become enmeshed in his mind as one: his personal desire to ruin Huey, to somehow or other finish him off for good was now joined with the Old Regulars' desire to reduce Huey to either an equal or subordinate political position.

To that end, Walmsley enjoyed a calm, confident spring as New Orleans' mayor, his last, as it turned out, season of great popularity. He presided once again over Mardi Gras, returned to Washington to secure yet more federal funds for New Orleans' relief, and sat serenely satisfied as the women of the Old Regulars' women's chapter praised him in song and rhyme at a special luncheon fete at the Jung Hotel.[17]

By May, as the state legislature was set to convene, Walmsley, the Old Regulars, and anti-Long lawmakers from around the state, like Napoleon, had it all worked out: Huey could be ambushed in his own legislature. First House Speaker and Huey supporter Allen J. Ellender would be replaced in a surprise vote by George K. Perrault, a reliable, rotund friend of the Regulars from St. Landry Parish. Then the anti-Longites would go to work on the next most devoted Long man, Lieutenant Governor John Fournet, removing him by the required two-thirds vote of the legislature for transgressions not yet decided. Finally, Gov. O. K. Allen would fall victim to the same kind of impeachment bid made against Huey in 1929. It could have been Havana or San Salvador for the manner and style with which the

Three months before the invasion, Walmsley—white linen suit, white fedora, and spats—followed by Old Regular Police Chief George Reyer, inspects his first line of defense. (Courtesy Joyce M. Zaffuto)

Regulars and anti-Longites hoped to execute their coup. They would be the caudillos now, calling the shots to determine the new direction of Louisiana. There would be no election, no debate, but by the time it was over, the state government would be returned to the eager hands of those Huey had pushed over long ago. Walmsley would emerge as a kingmaker, and Huey, bewildered back in Washington, would suddenly be deprived of any state machinery to return to.[18]

"Hotel rooms, lobbies [and] office buildings . . . swirled with activity here today," wrote the *Times-Picayune* reporter George Vandervoort as the sun rose on the steamy opening day of the spring legislature. "Hotels, apartments, and private homes are crowded with legislators, lobbyists, and politicians," the New Orleans *States* reporter noted in a similar dispatch the same day.[19]

Attracted by the prospect of battle and bloodshed, thousands filled the marble elegance of the state capitol, crowding the lobby with a mixture of sweat and smoke and hanging like so much moss from the grand assembly galleries. But the anticipated crucifixion was swiftly transformed into a resurrection as Huey bounced into town with a net wide enough to round up stray and uncertain legislators. In a body of one hundred members, those searching for the head of Huey Long claimed to have a certain 52 votes, while dreaming of perhaps even more. In less than three dizzying days, Huey made dust of those dreams, working as he did on the lawmakers he felt were most likely to cave in. Some he threatened, others he cajoled, and still others he gave money to. Alarmed, the Old Regulars and the anti-Longites watched their numbers dwindle until it was obvious they were beaten and the chance to hurt Huey had gotten away from them. The vote to reorganize the House and topple its leadership, in fact, never even came to the floor. Huey's brilliance, his eerie ability to size up any opposition and instantly discern its weakest link, had turned the trick. "He could always outsmart the opposition, no matter how hard they tried," Russell Long remembered with admiration. "He was just much more politically astute than they were." Even Cecil Morgan, some sixty years later recalling the frustrations and anger of another time now distant and murky, remembered the futility of trying to do battle with Huey. "He continually had his enemies off guard," Morgan said in what could be best described as a quiet seethe. "He was very, very clever."[20]

Had the 1934 legislative session concluded its business here, indeed, had Huey's career ended here, putting down an ill-conceived putsch, the record against Huey in the daunting court of historical opinion would today be far less damaging and compelling. On the negative side of the fading ledger, critics could rightly point to Huey's abusive, confrontational ways, the excesses of his political machine and the coercive way it was funded, the blatantly dishonest Overton election of 1932, and a handful of other symbolic and substantive sins as evidence of the things they had for some time now repeatedly and wildly accused him of being: a dictator. But he was not, certainly not entering the spring of 1934, a dictator. He was instead only an overpowering, eccentric, ambitious, and wickedly clever boss, a machine boss, of which many existed—for better or worse—across the country in 1934, providing needed jobs and services to mostly laboring and sometimes illiterate constituencies as they sometimes circumvented laws and convention to get what they wanted done.

But Huey's next move, executed with what he expected would be the smooth efficiency of his underlings responding to his smallest order, forever altered his course and precipitated a lengthy decline into darkness that produced the stuff that dictators are made of.[21]

In short order Huey unveiled a series of measures that stunned even his most implacable foes. He would take from New Orleans the $700,000 appropriation it was getting annually from the state in a bill known as the Tugwell Measure, in honor of A. G. Tugwell, the chairman of the

Louisiana Highway Commission and a Long loyalist. The loss of the money would cripple New Orleans, already struggling in the sixth year of the Great Depression.[22]

But the assault had just begun. New Orleans would also be stripped of its right to grant liquor licenses to bars and stores—there were more than one thousand bars currently operating in the city—a process that netted New Orleans tens of thousands of dollars each year. Now only Huey would be in the booze business, with the state as the sole authority determining who would and who would not be in possession of said licenses. Huey also moved to gut Walmsley's police force, one of the mayor's most important departments and a rich source of patronage for the Old Regulars, by putting the city's cops under the direct control of the state. Taxes would be raised on the New Orleans Cotton Exchange, a den of linen-suited bluebloods who detested Huey, while, finally, a separate tax would be slapped on newspapers in the state with circulations of 20,000 or more—papers from New Orleans to Shreveport qualified. "It's a tax on lyin'," Huey told lawmakers. A Long-printed circular said the tax would work out to roughly "two cents a lie." Huey took particular delight in this measure, aiming a dagger at the heart of his most persistent foes. "I'm going to help these newspapers by hitting them in their pocketbooks," Huey explained. "Maybe then they'll try to clean up."[23]

The fiasco of the January attempt by Huey's man in the New Orleans registrar of voters office to alter the voting lists was the inspiration behind another bill, this one making it impossible for any court to impound records in the possession of a state official. Had this law existed during the January mayoralty campaign in New Orleans, C. S. Barnes may have still been discovered late at night going over the books with a bottle of red ink in the registrar's office. He may have even still been arrested and sent to jail. The fate of C. S. Barnes was of little concern to Huey. What mattered instead was possession of those all-important voter registrar books. Huey now made certain to never lose control of them again.[24]

A final measure was the final nail in the coffin for Walmsley and the Old Regulars: a special committee would be established to investigate charges of widespread corruption in New Orleans' city government. Every aspect of City Hall would be examined, from the inner workings of the police and water departments, two of the Old Regulars' biggest patronage pools, to Mayor Walmsley's office itself. Whether the investigation revealed wrongdoing, which would almost be inevitable given the Old Regulars' penchant for installing cronies in favored positions, was less important than the fallout Walmsley would face from months and months of a protracted inquiry into the innermost workings of his administration. The Old Regulars could not decide what about this bill in particular annoyed them more—its contents or its sponsor—Rep. Joseph Weber of the city's Eleventh Ward, elected to his seat with Regular support only to join ranks with Huey after taking office.[25]

In response to Huey's assault, his opponents seemed stunned, their arguments reduced to vague generalities or obscure legalisms. "Some of the bills are of the most vicious character," Mayor George Hardy of Shreveport, emerging as a vocal Huey foe, weakly responded during the annual meeting of the Municipal Mayors' Association. Walmsley, gray, told his even grayer commissioners that taxes would now almost certainly have to go up. While Rep. Frank Stitch, an Old Regular from the Fifth Ward, mysteriously divined that one Long measure was illegal because "the constitution of 1921 does not contain the specific language which was placed in the constitution of 1913 by the amendment of 1916, and simply gives to the Louisiana Tax Commission authority in respect to assessment, etc., as 'now is or hereafter maybe, prescribed by law.'" There was no reaction to this latter pronouncement, quite possibly because no one knew what Stitch was talking about.[26]

Gradually, however, a unified response did emerge, but it

doomed itself to defeat by offering nothing except opposition. Huey was a champion in Louisiana in the hearts and minds of most people in 1934 because he gave them things: work, roads, books, and hospitals. The opposition, showing, as the *New York Times* correspondent George Coad pointed out, "no signs of having learned anything from its many defeats," made no attempt to present alternative programs of their own. Instead they waxed poetic over the merits of liberty and honor to a people far more in need of bread and beefsteak.[27]

A separate flaw in the opposition's thinking was instantly seen in the symbols they embraced, specifically the conscious attempts to recall the halcyon days of September 1874 and the uprising of the White League at Liberty Place in downtown New Orleans. For some, conveniently overlooking the oppressive and racially genocidal ways of the white, aristocratic, conservative Bourbon Old South, the 1874 revolt against Reconstruction rule had become an event worthy of memory and tribute. Hilda Phelps Hammond was either unconscious or purposely ignorant of the White League's evil underpinnings when she recalled the romantic stories her father told her about the League: "He would go on, telling me the tale of how New Orleans boiled like a kettle under insults and indignities, of how the heroic White League was formed by those citizens who decided that life without liberty is no life at all," Hammond wrote, not mentioning the White League's equal reverence for violence, racial oppression, and class hegemony.[28]

But now Hammond, Walmsley, and John Wegmann, president of the local chamber of commerce and suddenly a very active Huey foe, all sought to summon warmly nostalgic views of the White League, painting the battle against Huey Long as an extensive of the battle against the oppression of Reconstruction. And the New Orleans press cheered them on. In a front-page editorial, the *Item-Tribune* encouraged its readers to attend a rally to protest Huey's slate of bills and argued that New Orleanians must respond as did the White Leaguers who "shed their blood and their lives to free themselves."[29]

At that rally on June 7, more than one thousand people filled the city's Municipal Auditorium, cheering two elderly veterans of the 1874 White League uprising before standing in solemn silence as a band served up a rousing rendition of "Dixie." "Repeated reference was made to the bloody September 14 [1874] which ended carpetbag rule in the city," one journalist at the rally reported. The speakers, too, waved the same flag of resistance with Walmsley bringing the spirited crowd to its feet when he declared: "The time is coming when the people of the state will no longer bear the yoke that has been placed around their necks by the state administration." When that time comes, the mayor added ominously, "they will take action such as was taken by Orleanians on the famous September 14."[30]

So it was now in the open. The suggestions could be taken no other way. Walmsley said the patriots of the White League turned to violence only when it became apparent they "could not get what was theirs peacefully." As Walmsley drove the auditorium audience to a frenzy of remembered past and imagined future glory, a spokesman for a newly formed militia group headquartered in Baton Rouge handed out a statement to the press, claiming he already had up to five thousand armed men across Louisiana and five hundred in Baton Rouge alone, "ready to serve at a moment's notice" against Huey's government. Would that moment come on June 12? That was the day Walmsley and virtually every other visible leader in the anti-Long movement would mass at the state capitol for what they promised would be the largest public anti-Long demonstration in the history of the state.[31]

But even before the rally became reality, its limitations were revealed by its leadership: the exclusive Boston and Pickwick clubs, the Chamber of Commerce, and the Cotton Exchange pitched in to underwrite the costs for the five trains carrying the more than seventy coaches that would be needed to cart the angry anti-Longites of New Orleans. The laborers of the city, with their faded newspaper photo cutouts of Huey on prominent display in their shotgun houses, were left behind.[32]

"This is the most disgraceful scene that those of us of this generation ever had the misfortune to witness," bellowed state senator Coleman Lindsey, a Long leader who claimed the trains were packed with hard-drinking celebrants who got their liquid replenishment free from young barmaids servicing the coaches. "Give me a set-up like that and I can take 5,000 people to any part of the United States to protest against anything in the world." Although the protestors would deny it, K. T. Knoblock, a correspondent for the New Orleans *Item,* claimed to see "rivers of beer" sold on the train he sat on, the same train where "hips with flasks" were in abundant evidence while "hoots and catcalls and the inelegant 'razzberry'" filled the close air.[33]

But the organizers for the Baton Rouge rally made one strategic error—they forgot that incendiary rhetoric incites. As soon as the Illinois Central pulled into the state capital, hundreds of men, some with guns, began roaming about the city. "We came for action, not to hear speaking," one hunter explained to Knoblock.[34]

The crowd at the day's rally, meanwhile, was massive. "For blocks in every direction men and women were assembled in the streets, on lawns, on the galleries of nearby houses," wrote Hermann Deutsch, who estimated that up to thirty thousand people were there. Repeatedly, the speakers bellowed wartime chants bathed in the rhetoric of violence. "If it is necessary to teach those who misgovern us fair dealing at the end of a hempen rope," Mayor Hardy of Shreveport yelled out, "then by the eternal, I for one am ready to swing the rope."[35]

Perhaps sensing the rally could at any moment give birth to carnage, Walmsley kept his remarks relatively level. As soon as his name was announced before the rally, which was also broadcast over statewide radio, Walmsley received a thunderous ovation. Hundreds of people stood on their feet to get a better look at the man who had now become Huey's most prominent foe in Louisiana. "Other hundreds shouted 'louder' and 'turn on the microphones,'" observed Knoblock. "Radio technicians ran to bring their instruments nearer. Flashbulbs and trays of flash powder popped and exploded."[36]

But Walmsley made the briefest speech of the day. He did not, this time, talk about the White League or armed insurrection or even his own attempt to personally assault Huey several months earlier. Instead he appeared to cool burning passions, promising that the partisans of New Orleans would not act without the cooperation of their patriotic brethren from the country first. The anti-Long movement, the mayor reminded all, was a statewide phenomenon. "Tell us," when you want to march, Walmsley offered. "We pledge that we'll be with you."[37]

Walmsley's sudden appeal to reason could have had several explanations. He may have genuinely feared that the enraged crowd, littered with drunken, armed men, was on the verge of becoming an unruly, violent mob. There was no telling what could happen. But Walmsley was also a canny politician, he had fenced with Huey, the Uptown elites, and even his own Old Regulars long enough to be confident in his own political skills. If this huge outpouring could actually be transformed into a working, coherent movement, Walmsley would be in its leadership, giving him for the first time real influence far beyond New Orleans. He needed to proceed with caution: a rousing speech inciting the crowd to mayhem would be a disaster, and one easily put out by Huey's militia. The day needed to end on an angry, energized, but nonviolent note, with the thousands of people there assembled confident in Walmsley's ability to wave the banner for them any way he saw fit.

Walmsley may have also restrained himself because of his instincts. He was never an outsider, a street agitator. Such creatures, in fact, horrified him; they were threats to the very social order he swam in. Instead, Walmsley would have been more prone to see the demonstration as nothing more than a means of influencing legislation, of impressing lawmakers that he spoke for huge numbers of people. The mayor would then work the backrooms and the committee rooms of the legislature as a gentleman, hoping to ameliorate Huey's anti-New Orleans proposals through reason and barter. After all, even the provincially powerful Leander Perez of Plaquemines Parish—usually a stout supporter of Huey—was in Baton Rouge to do the same thing, telling lawmakers that "neither Plaquemines nor St. Bernard Parish will give up its right to local self-government," in response to Huey's proposal to permit the state to take control of the local functions of government.[38]

Walmsley's hunch that the massive Baton Rogue protest could be used to impress or scare lawmakers proved correct, at least initially. With Huey again back in Washington for last-minute business before Congress adjourned, his measures in the state legislature were suddenly dying for lack of action. His lieutenants seemed confused and unable to marshal the support needed for passage, while anti-Long lawmakers bottled up several bills in committee. But once Huey returned on June 21, everything changed. "One could almost hear the disjoined members of his machine click back into place, one by one," reported an impressed Deutsch. The force of Huey's personality and power was on particular display on June 27 as he stormed into an Appropriations Committee meeting. "I'll give you the benefit of the experience I had during the four years I was governor," he told the arguing lawmakers, who were perplexed over how to spend a $78,000 education package. "The schools are objecting because one is getting more than the other," explained Sen. Hugo Dore, the committee's chairman, to Huey. "We propose to give Normal $8,000, Tech $20,000, and Southwestern $50,000." Huey thought for only a moment: "Just reduce the $78,000 to $75,000 and give each school $25,000 and none of them can object. They would all get the same." In his dispatch back to New Orleans that day, Deutsch added, "Senator Long's suggestion was followed instantly by the committee and this vexing argument that had involved 30 minutes of argument was settled."[39]

Huey's presence in the state capitol and his undiminished capacity for work—rushing into this and that committee room, yelling his instructions to startled lawmakers, rushing out again—showed in the results. By the end of the session on July 12, lawmakers in both chambers were not only passing whatever measure Huey told them to, they were also allowing him to doctor legislation with last-minute and sometimes unrelated legislation, thus resurrecting bills his opponents had defeated during his absence. The opposition, noted historian Glen Jeansonne, "melted away before the Kingfish's onslaught." In both the House and Senate, Huey's cushion of support was now double the size of the opposition's.[40]

In the waning days of this session, as the Louisiana sun baked the white limestone of the state capitol, an unusual, eerie silence descended upon a hall more accustomed to discourse. The lawmakers were only going through the motions, and some were incapable of even that. When Walmsley, in one last valiant effort to defeat the damaging liquor control license legislation, appeared before the House Appropriations Committee he found a group of men not only resigned to doing Huey's bidding, but to doing it blindly. "It has been said that members of the committee have not even read the bill," Walmsley noted with alarm. A Huey supporter, Rep. Smith Hoffpauir of Crowley in Acadiana, blithely responded: "Possibly we won't ever read it."[41]

Chastened and incredulous, Walmsley returned to New Orleans the second week of July to a city facing financial and even political doom. So masterfully had Huey manipulated the legislators that now nearly one third of the Old Regular New Orleans bloc was regularly voting Huey's way. Things had never looked worse. Cancelling a planned trip to Paris where he was scheduled to attend the International

Conference of Local Officials, Walmsley promised he was
not going to leave New Orleans any time soon, not, at least,
until it's "disturbed condition" created by Huey's legislation
could be fixed.[42]

But Walmsley knew he was running out of options. Without money, the city under his rule could only survive for so
long, and Walmsley's staff, the city attorney, and various
Old Regulars were now consumed with a miasma of injunc-
tions filed by the anti-Long and Long forces testing the
constitutionality of Huey's laws. Soon those around the
mayor, even the somber Old Regular leaders of the city's
seventeen wards, began to wonder where they went wrong.
How could they have beat Huey so decisively in the mayor's
race in January only to emerge almost entirely under his
thumb by July?

The answer, of course, came from Huey himself, if only
Walmsley and the Old Regulars had been listening. On the
morning after that bitter January race, Huey issued an
oblique warning that his political humiliation would soon
be revenged. New Orleans, the Old Regulars, and Walmsley
would all pay for what they had done to him, Huey said—
only this time it would not be like before, when Huey, after
doing battle with the city, signed a truce with Walmsley and
the Regulars at the moment of his triumph, a truce that led
to a series of gifts for the city, including that $700,000 state
appropriation. This time, Huey said, he would reap revenge
and Walmsley would seek forgiveness in its wake. "But I
want to tell him now that never again will I listen to the
pleas of Walmsley and his civil leaders of New Orleans.
There'll be no quarter this time."[43]

In fact, Huey Long's assault against New Orleans had
only just begun.

6

"He Can't Do That"

IT WAS A MEASURE of the nation's fascination with Huey Long—of the notion that here was a leader, for better or worse, who was entirely different: a pulsating, impulsive, and explosive figure who drew contention and controversy around him like a magnet to steel—that so many noted authors of the day and beyond found him worthy of comment. It could be, to turn a tired phrase, that Huey really was a fact stranger than fiction. In turn, fiction was inspired by his fact.

"If I had never gone to live in Louisiana and Huey Long had not existed, the novel would have never been written," Robert Penn Warren once said of his powerful *All the King's Men,* a 1946 book centered on the flamboyant countryboy Willie Stark, who rose to unanticipated heights of power in a backwater state. Warren, who moved to Louisiana during the summer of 1934 to become a professor of English and edit the *Southern Review* at Louisiana State University, always maintained his novel was based on Long the myth, not Long the man. But he nevertheless remained personally fascinated with Huey decades after the 1930s. As late as 1985, Warren was still discussing Huey, recalling for film documentarian Ken Burns snippets of Long's life, and at one point exclaiming: "That man went to freshman English at Oklahoma, one year of law school at Tulane for a three-year course and then applied for the bar examination. That's first-rate brains."[1]

H. G. Wells, on one of his periodic forays across America, was also captivated by Huey and wrote in *Collier's* that Huey was like a "Winston Churchill who has never been at Harrow. He abounds in promise and is capable, I suspect, of the same versatility." Wells also thought Huey was, "for a prominent political figure, very young." James Thurber, writing for the *New Yorker* in the fall of 1933, visited Huey while Huey was in New York and hardly needed to apply his comedic skills to the scene: Huey, Thurber suggested, was funny enough as it was. Noting that Huey had booked four suites at the Hotel New Yorker, Thurber observed, "He needs a lot of space." Thurber also judged that Huey was a much better talker than listener. But Thurber's description of life in Huey's suite could have been Huey anywhere: "The phone rang every minute or so while we talked," wrote Thurber, "and he would get up and walk through a couple of rooms to answer it and come back and fling himself heavily on the bed again so that his shoulders and feet hit at the same moment." Even in repose, Thurber noted, Huey was noisy, repeatedly tapping the bed's headboard with his stubby fingers while moving side to side like a beached whale longing for water.[2]

Gertrude Stein, meanwhile, expressed both a general approval of Huey's program as well as an abiding attraction to him as a person. Although Stein never met Huey, she did encounter a photographer from the Associated Press in New Orleans, "and he told me a lot about him," Stein wrote to novelist Cal Van Vechten in early 1935. "I am still interested in him and when we get back I'll tell you all I heard." Several weeks later, Sherwood Anderson recalled watching a young man posted in front of the Roosevelt Hotel selling for 35 cents each pamphlets entitled "Why Huey Long Should Be President." Although Anderson found the scene amusing, he did view Huey soberly: "He isn't, as a lot of people have begun to think, a superman, or superdevil, but he has, hidden away in him, a real feeling, I suspect, for the underdog."[3]

Far more critical was Katherine Anne Porter, who although published in the *Southern Review,* which would not have existed without Huey's largesse, nonetheless viewed Huey as "the worst sort of Fascist demagogue." John Dos Passos meanwhile openly admitted his creation of the fascist dictator Homer T. ("Chuck") Crawford was "the nearest I ever came to a character completely from life"—Huey P. Long—and called Huey one of the "smartest aspirants" for the title of dictator in American history.[4]

But perhaps the most chilling and uncanny treatment of Huey by a writer came with Sinclair Lewis's *It Can't Happen Here.* A Lewis scholar, James T. Jones, noting that Huey's political peak and Lewis's literary peak were reached at the same time, later claimed the author was "fascinated by the power of rhetoric—think of Babbit's speech—and the oratory of Huey Long combined with the novelist's own familiarity with American populism (upper-Midwest style) to convince him that a dictatorship could, indeed, happen here."[5]

In Lewis's book, Sen. Berzelius Windrip is Huey, a man of copious energy and wild faith who rises to unprecedented power in America and in so doing transforms the country into something else, something dark and unforgiving: he becomes America's first dictator. The Windrip-Long similarities are clever and unmistakable. Windrip as a young man sold a bogus wonder drug called the Chinook Consumption Soother to unsuspecting country folk, Huey dispensed Cottolene, a lard substitute, in his early years. Windrip extolled the virtues of wheat cakes covered with maple syrup, while Huey won national headlines in 1931 as he proclaimed the healthy effects of potlikker. And in an act of effrontery, Windrip further endeared himself to his nativist public by purposely refusing to appear at an embassy dinner for the Duke of York, "thus gaining," Lewis wrote, "in all farm kitchens and parsonages and barrooms a splendid reputation for Homespun Democracy." Huey, of course, enraged the visiting German consul at the Roosevelt Hotel in 1930 by greeting him clad only in colorful pajamas, an episode that served to amuse Huey's "country followers," historian T. Harry Williams has written. "They relished the spectacle of their hero embarrassing the dignified Germans."[6]

Windrip also "preached the comforting gospel of so redistributing wealth that every person in the country would have several thousand dollars a year," and did so in his book *Zero Hour*, a gospel made up in part from the ideology of Hitler, a press agent in Windrip's hire, and the musical revue *Of Thee I Sing*. Huey's well-received program for wealth redistribution saw its greatest circulation with his 1933 book *Every Man a King*, a program he said he lifted in part from the Bible, the speeches of William Jennings Bryan, and an article he once read in the *Saturday Evening Post*.[7]

But the most disturbing similarity between Windrip and Huey came with their use of militiamen to further their political aims. For Windrip it was the Minute Men, soon known as the fearsome MMs, "stray imitation solders," with blue tunics and trousers, boots of sleek black leather, who "swaggered so brazenly, shouldering citizens out of the way." The MMs kept Windrip in power, exhibiting their brutality throughout *It Can't Happen Here*, breaking up the opposition's political rallies, arresting Windrip's foes, and showing a stupid contempt for thought when they burst into the home of a Vermont editor critical of Windrip, "yanking the volumes of Dickens from the shelves, dropping them on the floor, covers cracking."[8]

When Huey's men moved, it was no less dramatic: just minutes before midnight on July 30, only two weeks after House Speaker Allen Ellender gaveled to an end Huey's triumphant 1934 regular session, at least three dozen helmeted young boys in knee-high boots, jodphurs, and steel helmets filed into enemy territory—Lafayette Square in downtown New Orleans—a pretty, tree-lined park surrounded by the last vestiges of resistance to Huey's rule in New Orleans. The city's three largest papers were housed in concrete and marble buildings bunched at one end of the park. The Old Regulars conspired in their balconied Choctaw Club headquarters a block away, while fronting the park was the stately Gallier Hall, a Greek Revival building where the body of Jefferson Davis once lay in state and Mayor Walmsley maintained his elegant, airy offices.[9]

Marching up the steps to the red-bricked Soule Building across the way from Gallier Hall, the soldiers—Depression-era farm boys and city kids looking for work—were under the supervision of Raymond Fleming, a Long appointee who had greatly expanded Louisiana's National Guard after he became adjutant general in 1928. "Huey had great faith in military people," Fleming later recalled. With Huey's support and ever-larger appropriations, Fleming soon recruited hundreds of boys from across the state, and, according to historian Evans Caso, "accelerated its training program, improved its armories throughout the state." At just Camp Beauregard alone, "a new target range was built, twelve new mess halls were constructed, new roads were laid giving access to all areas by motor vehicle, and part of the area was reforested." The major general of the entire U.S. Guard, visiting New Orleans in April 1934, was moved to laud Fleming as he inspected the 750 men in their full regalia who made up the New Orleans unit: "You have taken a broken down plant and developed a great thing for this state," he said. Maj. Gen. V. H. Mosely also thought the guard's efficiency and professionalism stood as a monument to Fleming's prodigious efforts.[10]

And in full dress, the soldiers were indeed impressive, made all the more so by the simple fact that they were also a highly trained, strictly disciplined group capable of carrying out difficult missions with aplomb. In 1928, when Huey wanted to send a message to the booming, but illegal, gambling industry that he would be one governor who would not allow them to operate unfettered, he assigned Fleming the delicate task of busting up a handful of secret casinos then operating in both St. Bernard and Jefferson parishes. Fleming dispatched more than three hundred men into the

Adj. Gen. Raymond Fleming. He was certain Long was a leader destined for greatness and carried out his orders with dispatch. (Courtesy the Louisiana Collection, Howard-Tilton Memorial Library, Tulane University)

two parishes who helped him confiscate and then destroy dozens of slot machines and roulette wheels. "He gave me orders," Fleming said of Huey. "And it was to the ever-lasting credit of the National Guard that I was able to assemble hundreds of men to make the gambling raids without anybody ever knowing we were assembling."[11]

Now Fleming's men drew bayonets, battering through the thick double wooden doors of the Soule Building, across Lafayette Street from Gallier Hall, where the registrar of voters office had recently been moved to. "It's just a tea-party," one of the guardsmen was heard to say by an onlooker witnessing the scene in disbelief from Lafayette Square. Dozens of beams from the guards' flashlights pierced the building's darkness as the men prowled quickly from room to room. In minutes, Fleming exited from the busted wooden doors of the Soule Building with a package under his arms before he jumped into a dark sedan that sped out of the square. Passersby then noticed something peculiar, something never seen before: state militiamen posting machine guns in the windows of a city office building they had just broken into.[12]

It took only minutes for word of the incursion to spread through nighttime New Orleans. Soon a crowd of men, reporters from the nearby newspapers, cleanup crews on the streets, and the normal unconventional characters who called the late-night streets of New Orleans home began to gather near Gallier Hall, only to make way for a string of cars speeding up to the front of the city hall. Out of the first vehicle popped Mayor Walmsley, his octagonal glasses reflecting the beams of the soldier's flashlights.

"He can't do that," was Walmsley's first public utterance. No one had to ask who the mayor was referring to. But longtime Chief of Police George Reyer, also now on the scene, got off one of the best quotes of the night when he pointed to four machine guns mounted on shiny-top desks pointing out of the windows of the Soule Building straight toward Walmsley's Gallier Hall, toward his very office. "Well, if he can't," Reyer laconically noted, "there they are."[13]

Bewildered, Walmsley marched inside Gallier Hall, accompanied by a tense cluster of the city's finest, their backsides briefly exposed to the militia's guns. It was now nearly 2 A.M., oppressively warm without a breeze in the air. Walmsley flipped on the lights in his empty office, removed the coat to his light seersucker suit, sat at his massive desk, and pondered his options.

They were depressingly few. He had, he knew, no countervailing fire power of any real significance, certainly nothing close to the standard machine guns he could see pointed at his office windows. And even if he did, it would take hours to organize a force in response, a force that would have to be composed both of police officers and loyal citizens willing to be deputized. And those men, assembled on a moment's notice, could never be trained, disciplined, and organized the way Huey's young militia was.

He was, admittedly, captive to Huey's latest maneuver. But Walmsley also had to wonder if those troops in the building next door were also planning to seize Gallier Hall, perhaps the very office he now sat in. Was this, finally, the first military wave of a dictator's coup? Were those who wildly called Huey a Hitler now to be proven correct? Anything seemed possible.

A courier skipped up the granite steps of Gallier Hall, flying by the building's grand white portico, to deliver to Walmsley an office message. It was from Gov. O. K. Allen, but it was sent from the Roosevelt Hotel. Walmsley read the correspondence. The governor, the proclamation read in tight, small letters, had determined that for the protection of everyone's voting rights, the registrar of voters office was to be hereby placed under watch, "24 hours a day," for the foreseeable future. The City of New Orleans, the document continued, was now under "partial martial law," requiring the presence of the state militia. Nothing was said about what the troops hoped to accomplish by taking over the

Soule Building; how long they intended to stay; or why, if all they wanted to do was protect the registrar's office, the soldiers had to do it by darkness of night, forcing the building's doors and then lining the windows with machine guns.[14]

As Walmsley gazed out the floor-to-ceiling windows of Gallier Hall, he had far more questions than answers.

But this much was certain: the night before, Huey had arrived at the Roosevelt Hotel and ordered into his room the top men of his organization: his brother Earl Long, businessman and financial supporter Robert Maestri, Governor Allen, and General Fleming. Seymour Weiss, usually privy to every important decision Huey made, was out of town on business. A reporter for the *Times-Picayune,* noticing the traffic, also tried to gain entry to Huey's suite. Something important was going on. But Paul Voitier, a former prizefighter who was now one of Huey's guards, blocked any uninvited guests. "We don't want you any nearer than this," Voitier, standing sentry near Huey's suite, snapped. "If you come around that door again, I'll let you have it."[15]

No one disclosed what the meeting was about, but when reporters the next night saw copies of the partial martial law decree and noticed it had been sent from the Roosevelt Hotel rather than the governor's office, they could only surmise the nature of Huey's mysterious gathering.

By morning, Gallier Hall was plunged into panic. Dozens of national, local, and even newsreel reporters crowded in to see an exhausted Walmsley. In only days Walmsley's blanched, intent face would be on display in theaters across the country as part of the daily, dramatic, music-scored newsreels that were in the 1930s a regular part of the nation's movie-going experience. Those same newsreels would also show Huey, resplendent in a dark double-breasted silk suit as he posed in front of his handsome home on Audubon Boulevard, and a quick shot of the militiamen lurking ominously behind their machine guns at the Soule Building.[16]

Lying in wait, two guardsmen in the Soule Building draw a bead on Mayor Walmsley's Gallier Hall office. (Courtesy the Louisiana National Guard Military Library)

Walmsley took to the airwaves. Calling the militia invasion one of the "most ridiculous and absurd things that has transpired on the opera bouffe that has been staged by the Mad Hatter of Louisiana." He was outraged, Walmsley continued, and promised a valiant resistance. After all, Huey had no legal right to do what he had done, much less to go about it in the manner he did. Walmsley added that Huey was violating every legal precept governing a city's sovereignty. But when one reporter, cutting through the mayor's oratory, asked exactly what the city planned to do in response to the invasion, Walmsley was candid: "There is nothing for us to do."[17]

That day, Tuesday, July 31, the young powerful voices of dirtied newsboys filled the canyons of the city with alarming headlines: "Governor declares partial martial law; Guards force door," shouted the *Times-Picayune* vendors. The afternoon shouts from the afternoon paper, the New Orleans *Item*, summed up Walmsley's tepid response: "City declares martial law is illegal."[18]

Yet Walmsley did manage a brave front in spite of his obviously anemic position. He obtained a court injunction against the martial decree, which Huey's men promptly ignored. He was on the radio frequently to try to arouse the wrath of the public. In his harshest words yet, he denounced Huey as a despot and caustically charged that all of this was about the drubbing he gave to Huey in the January mayor's election. "Long has never been able to overcome this shock," Walmsley told his audience, which on this occasion was national, linked through a network hookup.[19]

And he scaled new rhetorical heights, comparing Huey with "Caligula, Nero, Attila, Henry the Eighth, and dozens of other madmen who have risen to almost unlimited powers." He then issued a challenge that was again reminiscent of the White League heritage he and so many of the city's elders revered: "I warn you, Huey Long, that if a life is spent in the defense of this city and its right of local self-government, you shall pay the penalties as other carpetbaggers have done before you."[20]

Finally, Walmsley himself upped the ante. Announcing he would go to any length to preserve the "peace of the community," the mayor ordered up to four hundred city police to arm themselves and report for duty immediately at Gallier Hall. Another four hundred would be put on emergency call. But there was more: the men would be supplied with shotguns and pistols. And in the next four days, Walmsley proved as good as his word as the police went on a buying spree, spending more than five thousand dollars on tear and arsenic gas bombs, as well as some two dozen submachine guns. Sentried to the side and front of Gallier Hall, Walmsley's men were on 24-hour alert and stared up at the more heavily fortified and trained militiamen, who returned their gazes in earnest.[21]

Now it was Huey's turn, and his response only heightened tensions: The original three dozen or so militiamen in the Soule Building received an additional sixty new soldiers to re-enforce them on August 3. Another five hundred were placed on active call at Jackson Barracks, the guard's New Orleans camp. But even more alarming, a *Times-Picayune* reporter noted, was the covered truck that sped up to the side of the Soule Building delivering a late-night shipment of gas masks, tear gas guns, and several hundred steel helmets, to be added to the "standard army machine guns, rifles, pistols, tear gas guns, and other munitions previously issued to the troops."[22]

Then a second proclamation signed by Governor Allen but no doubted ordered by Huey arrived. It alarmingly expanded the scope of General Fleming's authority, ordering him to investigate, under his command, "when and where red light districts are operating within the city of New Orleans," how many gambling halls were doing business, and which city employees, "if any," were getting payoffs to keep the casinos and houses of prostitution open. With this second order, Huey had cleverly now expanded the military

A cartoon typical of the negative national coverage Huey received in response to his military action in New Orleans. (Courtesy the *Dallas News*)

scope of his militia from just the voter registrar's office to the entire city of New Orleans. It was an action he was forced to take, Huey said, because the city had sunk into a "cesspool of iniquity" under Walmsley's rule.[23]

In fact, gambling and vice *was* abundant in New Orleans: the city in many ways was defined by its criminality. But such sordidness never seemed to bother Huey before. Nor had vice become, as Huey charged, a recent phenomenon, flourishing under the tolerant rule of Walmsley.

On the contrary, prostitution, drugs, and gambling in New Orleans nearly rivaled the river for the permanent role they played in the life of the city. Even before the Civil War, chroniclers of and visitors to the city remarked upon the abundance of illegal options the city offered. "Oh, the wickedness, the idolatry of this place! unspeakable the riches and splendor," Rachel Jackson, the wife of Andrew Jackson, complained by letter to a friend in 1815. For Mrs. Jackson, who late in life got religion, New Orleans was nothing more than a "Babylon-on-the-Mississippi," a view that countless others would share in the decades to come. In 1900, the widespread use of morphine and opium among both black and white prostitutes had become so commonplace that even local reporters were writing about it, noting in particular that one popular drink made up of cocaine, water, and California claret appeared to be particularly popular in black neighborhoods. "A pint of the stuff will transfer a stupid, good-natured negro into a howling maniac," the *Times-Picayune* claimed. The diffident Maj. R. Raven-Hart, meanwhile, visiting New Orleans during the Great Depression, found a plentiful supply of marijuana upon entering a local pub, ordering a drink, and telling the waiter: "A package of cigarettes, Dodo, and make it snappy." Request received, the waiter produced a small package "with a marijuana cigarette concealed among the others," the major recorded, before adding: "The total cost is fifty cents."[24]

Prostitutes by the 1930s no longer worked in the protective confines of Storyville, closed down in 1917, but were still available nonetheless. The major, evidently determined to explore every crevice of the city, said love for sale could be discovered in all varieties and colors, "from black to yellow to white." Writer Lyle Saxon noticed the same thing on his 1928 visit to the French Quarter. "Many of the ladies had their names printed on the doors," he noted. "As we went along, I read the names aloud: 'Laura' and 'Wanda' and 'Anna' and 'Bessie,' and sometimes the names are prefixed by a title, such as 'Chicago May' or 'French Marie.'" Another interloper, Harold Speakman, in his 1927 travel journal *Mostly Mississippi,* saw the Vieux Carré as the home of "Sicilians of the lowest sort, making a slum which became a rendezvous for prostitutes and their accompaniment of rakes and thugs."[25]

Of all of the city's menu of vices, however, gambling was undoubtedly the most widespread in New Orleans in the 1930s. An integral part of city life, it came in many forms: slot machines known as "chiefs" because they bore an intricately carved bronze likeness of an Indian chief's head. There were also games of roulette, craps, and lotteries, all illegal. "She, like the rest of New Orleans, is a gambler," Uptown matron Rachel Violette Campbell wrote of her black maid Sarah in the mid-1930s, "and puts her nickel 'on a number' every blessed day." Writer Elsie Martinez, remembering her childhood in the blue-collar neighborhoods near downtown New Orleans, said her block offered "bookmaking, a lottery, church bingo, and even a weekly floating poker game." The Martinez family maid, Beulah, "was an avid player of the numbers," Martinez added, oftentimes devising "exotic sounding formulas" in hopes of hitting paydirt with certain number combinations.[26]

Gambling was so extensive and entrenched by the summer of 1931 that a grand jury could confidently report that up to 1,500 people were working in some form of gaming in neighborhood joints like the Red Star Garage on Toulouse Street, the Old Spot Social Club on Julia, and the Lamb's Club on St. Charles Avenue. Most of the halls were located above or to the rear of nondescript houses and stores, mostly in French Quarter and Central City neighborhoods. A visitor, waved through by a cautious doorman, would, upon entering a typical establishment, confront a large, smoky, and busy room filled with wooden tables and chairs where women and men played blackjack, seven-and-a-half, and dice. On the walls were the daily racing charts tacked alongside lengthy sheets of paper eventually filled in by the person recording the results of horse races by phone. Inevitably, every room was anchored by a metal cage containing a cashier taking bets.[27]

Even Huey's brother Earl visited the palaces, regularly frequenting the 1-2-3 Club across from the Roosevelt Hotel, a mecca for New Orleans bookmakers owned by none other than Seymour Weiss. "In those days the guys who worked for the gambling houses would come right into the lobby of the hotel," Angelo Butera, the Roosevelt's bell captain, later recalled. "They'd be sneaking around, trying to hustle up business for their clubs."[28]

But it would not be enough for Huey to just bring in his militia with their gas bombs and machine guns to somehow stop vice in the city; more needed to be done to stomp out the scourge of sin in New Orleans, Huey declared as he announced the formation of a special committee drawn up for the sole purpose of investigating vice. The need for the committee was so urgent that it would set to work within days, and because it was also a matter of public emergency, all of the committee hearings would be conducted by none other than Huey himself.

But first important legal groundwork had to be laid. This was not going to be a kangaroo court, but a committee fully sanctioned and recognized by law, authorized to pursue a full menu of sins by the state legislature. By the second week of August the call went out: Huey wanted to convene, immediately, a special session of the legislature. Walking into the room where the members of the House Ways and Means Committee met on August 15, Huey plopped down on a long wooden table a straw hat filled with nearly thirty bills he wanted to see enacted. "I'm a taxpayer of this state and I want action," Huey ordered. In just three days time, he got what he wanted: official authorization to investigate all or any part of the city government of New Orleans, to use the state militia any way he saw fit—without interference from any court—and to overrule any decision made on any case at any time by any local district attorney, if such action was needed "for the protection of the rights and interests of the state."[29]

Life can be sweet when you are the king. Yet every move Huey now made was rewarded with scathing criticism, particularly in the press. All of the New Orleans papers were now against him; on a daily basis they reminded their readers about the tyrant they lived under. The *States,* in particular, was a hotbed of opposition and seemed capable of giving Huey the kind of treatment he usually only gave to others: referring to Huey repeatedly as the "Crawfish," sometimes even in front-page headlines, the *States* also portrayed Huey as a madman, a lobster, and even a crazed guerilla holding Lady Louisiana hostage in their daily editorial cartoons.[30]

But the national press coverage, coming at the very time that Huey was laying the groundwork for the 1936 presidential election was far more important; and in response to the militia invasion, it was just as negative. *Time* magazine declared flatly that Louisiana was now without question under a "political dictatorship," *Newsweek* called Huey a "demagogue and a menace to the nation," while the normally gentle *Christian Science Monitor* said it was now clear that "Hitlerism" was suffocating Louisiana. Meanwhile nationally syndicated columnist Westbrook Pegler, an abrasive far rightist who was usually content to verbally decimate Franklin and Eleanor Roosevelt in his daily dispatches, now went after Huey. He visited Louisiana in August and suggested that "Heil, Huey" was the only proper salutation under the "dictatorship of der Kingfish."[31]

It did not make things better that Walmsley, also in August, was the recipient of a glowing national press, particularly in the *New York Times,* which had been growing ever more negative in their coverage of Huey. On August 7 Walmsley met with controversial *Times* reporter F. Raymond Daniell to tell his side of the militia invasion story. He came out looking great, telling Daniell that Huey's invasion of the Soule Building had less to do with protecting the city's voting rolls, as Governor Allen claimed, than it did simple vindictiveness. Huey wasn't out to get him or his political organization, Walmsley claimed. "He is determined to vent his spleen on all the people of New Orleans."[32]

Two days later, Huey, obviously intent on responding to Walmsley in the same prominent forum, granted Daniell an interview. It was an all the more important interview because in Daniell Huey had one of the few sympathetic reporters of the national press, a journalist who did not every time mechanically assume that whatever Huey was up to, it was bound to be demonic.[33]

A gifted writer, Daniell saw Huey for what he was: tremendous copy. But he also saw dimensions that eluded others. Huey was trying to change things in a backward state in a backward region of the country. In this regard, he was, for Daniell, a natural. The *Times* reporter had also written about Arkansas sharecroppers fighting for better wages, coal-miner strikes in Kentucky, and the infamous Scottsboro Case in Alabama where nine black boys were charged with raping two white women. For his efforts on this latter assignment, one editorial in a local Alabama paper suggested lynching Daniell.[34]

Huey, however, was impressed not only with Daniell's reporting but his abilities as a writer. He asked for advice on books to read and even enlisted the journalist's assistance in writing his second book, the boldly titled *My First Days in the White House.* Because Daniell, too, was a Roosevelt Hotel regular, his encounters with Huey were also sometimes unconventional. Very late one night, he answered the phone in his suite one floor below Huey to hear a gruff command: "Come up here right away. There's a young lady here who wants to meet you." The phone call was from, of course, Huey, who never could sleep much at night anyway. But Daniell was more interested in his sleep and told Huey so. Minutes later Daniell heard a loud knocking at his door. Huey again, and this time he would not take no for an answer; he allowed Daniell only enough time to put on his clothes and brush his teeth and led the journalist back up to his suite to introduce him to an uncommonly attractive, very young woman named Alice Lee Grosjean, Huey's secretary (who was also rumored to be his girlfriend). Two other women were also in the room: Grosjean's mother and a female singer. Castro Carazo, the leader of the Blue Room's orchestra, was sitting at the piano that Seymour Weiss had rolled up especially for Huey's late-night use. Together the happy group was trying to make merry with Huey's campaign theme song, which went by the same title of his book, *Every Man a King.* Huey ordered Castro to hit it, and again the group broke out in song. Unsatisfied, Huey ran into the next room, only to re-emerge with a tiny guitar that he started "plunking away," Daniell recalled, "more or less in tune with the piano." This was the Huey Long Daniell remembered: "gentle, ruthless, and withal unpredictable."[35]

Gone now was the easy informality of that wet evening. Now to get to Huey's suite, Daniell was forced to maneuver his way down a crowded corridor thick with bodyguards and aides. Since the night of the invasion, everyone was tense and tired. Huey's suite reminded Daniell of some sort of mighty citadel, "impossible for a stranger to penetrate," Daniell wrote, "unless he is accompanied by a trusted follower of the Senator."[36]

Inside sat Huey in his shirtsleeves—not even the Roosevelt Hotel in 1934 had air-conditioning, although the hotel's Fountain Grill advertised that it was cooled by something called "refrigerated air." Daniell noticed as he was led into the room that there were even more guards inside, but

Huey was his usual electric self. Several times in the course of the interview, reported Daniell, he "jumped from his chair, with flailing arms and popping eyes."[37]

"What's all the fuss about?" Huey challenged, noting the criticism his military invasion had provoked. "Hasn't the governor got a right to protect a state office with the militia if he wants to? Who's going to stop him?" Curiously, as Huey was launching into this discourse on the proper use of gubernatorial powers, Governor Allen dined in the Roosevelt's main restaurant below, serenely oblivious to the decisions being made over his head above.[38]

Huey then proceeded to defend the militia's presence, arguing that at least 35,000 (on other occasions he put the figure as high as 40,000 and more) fraudulent names were on the city's voting rolls, rolls Walmsley himself tried to get hold of, he said. "We just beat them to the draw, that's all," Huey boasted.[39]

Walmsley and the Old Regulars, Huey continued, not only added false names to the registrar's list, they allowed some cronies to vote as many times as possible in the same election. "They had one man they voted as often as he could change costumes," Huey lamented. "First he came in with a mustache and cap. Then he came back with long white hair. He voted once as a woman and I can't remember all the disguises he used."[40]

Finally, Huey steered the conversation in the direction of his latest preoccupation: vice. He claimed to know of more than two dozen blocks in the city where vice was protected by the city police and upwards of $15 million a year collected by New Orleans' finest to protect busy gamblers and pimps from the consequences of the law.[41]

Upon the conclusion of the interview, Daniell left Huey, who was even more restless than usual these days. Alice Lee Grosjean was leaving Louisiana. If she had been Huey's girlfriend, she was no longer: she was heading by train this very week to Los Angeles with her mother where she would marry William Tharpe, the young secretary of the Louisiana Tax Commission. Huey now prowled the halls of the Roosevelt all night long, a habit that only seemed to have grown worse over time. "He moved all over that hotel, all through the night," recalled Charles Palmisano, the hotel's elevator operator, who carted around the sleepless Huey on his nocturnal wanderings. Sometimes Huey would meet with a group of legislators in one room of the hotel on a certain floor, then a gathering of judges or reporters in other rooms, on other floors. And on it went, throughout the night. Frequently, Palmisano, responding to a barked command from Huey, would bring over a tray of sandwiches or drinks. "But he really didn't want anything," Palmisano said, "he just wanted you to be there with him."[42]

As night gave way to day and the pink preamble of morning decorated the sky outside Huey's room, he would still be talking, frequently over the snores and groans of his guards. "He'd tell me to sit down," remembered Palmisano, who always did as he was told. "He'd offer me the very sandwich I just brought up to him or a drink or tickets to the LSU game. But he really just wanted someone to talk to."[43]

General Fleming knew the same Huey and recalled the times he was summoned to the Roosevelt Hotel simply for the company he might provide. "And I would go up there and all he wanted was to be with somebody that wasn't trying to get something out of him," Fleming commented. "I have sat with him for an hour or so in his Roosevelt suite, each of us reading a magazine or a newspaper." And that would be the extent of Fleming's visits with a man who hated to be alone.[44]

In late August, Fleming got another one of those calls from Huey at the Roosevelt Hotel. But this time there was a specific purpose for the call. On September 8 there would be a Congressional election in New Orleans, yet one more face-off between Huey's forces and the Old Regulars. But this time Huey must win. Another defeat would be ruinous.

Yet he needed to make his powers in the city felt, and to do so, he needed still more troops—hundreds more, thousands more. And they would all come bearing arms.

In fact, Huey told General Fleming, he wanted all of the state's militia, the *entire* militia, all 3,000 men, to get dressed and get to New Orleans as quickly and quietly as possible.[45]

7

"We Would Do What We Were Told"

ED GOUAZE IN THE SUMMER OF 1934 was a three-striped
sergeant serving his fifth year in the National Guard's 141st
Field Artillery Battalion housed in the city's historic Jackson
Barracks. His immediate commander was Edward P.
Benezach, Sr., a captain of the guard whose principal duty
was to execute the orders of his superior, Adj. Gen. Raymond Fleming.

All three men revered Huey Long. "We loved that man,"
Gouaze later recalled. "I don't know why. Don't ask me why.
But we really did love that man." Benezach was equally
devoted. "My father thought Huey Long was the greatest
man on earth," said Benezach's son, Edward Jr., who lived in
the family's quarters at Jackson Barracks in 1934. Edward Jr.
would come to share his father's fervor: "I think truthfully
that Huey Long had the good of the people in his heart,"
he later said. "And he saw things happening five years
ahead of anybody else. That's what made him good."[1]

General Fleming, too, by 1934, was devoted to Huey; he
was convinced after years of close exposure to him that he
was in the presence of a man somehow called to greatness,
that he possessed the "best mind of any man I ever met." It
was Fleming's task to make Huey's life easier, to turn his
ideas into things concrete and execute his orders, no matter
what those orders were, with skill and speed.[2]

The loyalty Huey engendered among the guardsmen said
as much about him as it did them. But that loyalty also gave

evidence of his power: he could, on a moment's notice, dispatch up to three thousand young trained men from every corner of the state willing to do his bidding without a moment's hesitation. In return, Huey got for his troops trucks where mostly horses worked before, new rifles and guns, even machine guns, a new administrative headquarters for Fleming in Baton Rouge—so the guard for the first time would have a bureaucratic presence in the state's capital—and new uniforms and helmets. The list was endless. But Huey's influence and popularity with his militia transcended the mere giving of gifts. With his exhortations to think big thoughts and dream even bigger dreams, Huey inspired his men and made them think of things larger than themselves; he painted for them a picture of a world where power would be, finally, in the hands of the many. To get there, they only had to follow Huey's orders.[3]

It had not always been so. In fact, during his first months as governor in 1928, Huey, who had avoided the draft in World War I and had little experience with military issues or people, didn't quite know what to make of the guard. But visiting Camp Beauregard to survey the young troops in spring training got him to thinking. "You mean I'm commander in chief of all those?" Huey asked Fleming as he pointed to the soldiers. Fleming nodded assent. "From then on he realized he had a trained force that he could use any time he wanted," Edward Benezach, Jr., said. "He thought the world of that guard."[4]

Sergeant Gouaze, twenty-two years old in 1934, was a native New Orleanian whose parents had emigrated from France. Gouaze's family fared better than most in the Depression—his father was a butcher with an eye for real estate who bought up enough property in the early 1930s to protect himself from the financial vagaries of the time. Living near City Park—a rapidly expanding upper-middle class neighborhood with large yards and graceful trees— Gouaze signed on with the guard early, in 1929. He cut the grass of Jackson Barracks' polo grounds by summer and in

Huey's guardsmen at work: members of Houma's Company C, 156th Infantry, break down their rifles. (Courtesy the Louisiana Collection, Howard-Tilton Memorial Library, Tulane University)

the winter chopped wood for the fireplaces of the antebellum officers' quarters that dotted the barracks property.

"I didn't have a lot of political opinions then," Gouaze
later recalled. But he knew enough to like Huey Long: "My
father admired Huey too. It was hard to explain. It was the
kind of thing the old Europeans would admire: someone
who was tough and hard and got things done."[5]

Young Gouaze, however, also admired Mayor Walmsley, a
man he considered above the political fray, and President
Roosevelt too. "FDR was our hero," he said. Only the Old
Regulars earned Gouaze's contempt. They looked, smelled,
and acted corrupt, thought the young solider. Surely, they
couldn't be good for the city. "They were a bunch of bums,"
Gouaze said. "They were really bums."[6]

On the first line to invade and secure the Soule Building
under Captain Benezach's command, Gouaze peeled away
much of August 1934 sleeping on a collapsible cot on the
first floor of the building when he wasn't posting guard,
keeping an eye on either the registrar's office or next-door
Gallier Hall.

It had been a duty almost unmarked by incident. Almost.
But early on the morning of August 7 a single bullet fired
through a window from the Soule Building embedded itself
in the granite exterior just above Mayor Walmsley's office.
"Instantly it flashed into my mind that the national guardsmen had opened fire on City Hall," declared police captain
Dominick Claverie, who was posted at that moment in
Walmsley's office. But it was only an accident, Sgt. Herbert
Patterson of the guard ran over to explain, a pellet inadver-
tently fired from a 12-gauge riot gun by a soldier attempting to unload his weapon. Nevertheless, three of the four
New Orleans papers spread the incident across their front
page: The *Item* blared SHOTS FIRED IN CITY 'WAR.' Not
to be outdone, the *States* responded: RIOT GUN BULLETS
GO THROUGH FLOOR, SHATTER A WINDOW. Clearly
the press was looking and hoping for more; it was a thirst
that repulsed Fleming. The reporters covering the Soule

Pistol marksmanship at Jackson Barracks, Company D, 156th Infantry. (Courtesy the Louisiana Collection, Howard-Tilton Memorial Library, Tulane University)

Building siege had one thing in mind, Fleming later complained: "trying to discredit the boys of the National
Guard."[7]

But only days later another bullet from the barrel of
another guardsmen's gun made news when a soldier
strolled into the Patio Cafe, a small, but popular diner at
749 St. Charles Avenue, some two blocks down from Gallier
Hall, and fired his weapon into the middle of a booth occupied by four fellow dining guardsmen. Maj. Gen. W. D.
Shaffer, senior ranking officer at Jackson Barracks, deemed
this particular shooting soldier a "kid who thought he was a
wild West cowboy," who "drew his gun and fired at a spot on
the wall of the cafe." Matters were only made worse when a
reporter and photographer arrived to investigate the shooting, only to be assaulted by another group of soldiers doing
what most soldiers do in a crisis—closing rank around one
of their own. "They grabbed me and began to hit me in the
face," the photographer later complained, adding that
while one soldier backed him against the cafe's wall, the
others "took turns punching my face."[8]

Meanwhile the guards also proved their loyalty to General Fleming, who tried to avoid being served a subpoena by
a local sheriff citing him for contempt of court for refusing
to disband his men at the Soule Building even though a
local judge had now ordered him to do so. When sheriff's
deputies, attempting to penetrate the Jackson Barracks
fortress where Fleming was hiding, presented the subpoena
to guardsmen at the camp's gate, the soldiers heaved the
documents out onto the street where they eventually clus-
tered in a forgotten heap.

Two days later an unfortunate man bearing a fuzzy resem-
blance to Fleming was chased by car through the streets of
New Orleans by deputies certain they finally had their man.
Dr. J. A. Estopinal, a captain in the guard's medical corps,
was driving by himself down St. Claude Avenue when suddenly a deputy from a nearby car jumped onto the running
board of the doctor's sedan. "General Fleming, I have some

papers for you from the district court," the deputy yelled. Dr. Estopinal, stopping his car, quickly thumbed through the documents before sailing them back out the window. "I don't want these," he impatiently remarked. Later realizing Estopinal was not Fleming, the frustrated deputy remarked, "He never said he *wasn't* General Fleming."[9]

Lt. Numa P. Avendano was not General Fleming either, but on August 14 he was sentenced to serve ten days in jail in lieu of Fleming because he was the next in command at the Soule Building. It was a sentence that was suspended only after the olive-skinned Avendano, who would spend most of his life as a guardsman, argued he could not be held personally responsible for failing to obey the court's order to disband his troops, because, he said in that eternal protestation of innocence, he was "only obeying orders."[10]

And there were plenty of orders to obey, but not so many that the guards did not have time to entertain themselves. Sometimes, catching the perspiring pate of Walmsley leaving Gallier Hall in his Pierce Arrow sedan, the soldiers talked about how easy it would be to pick him off. "One of the guys kept saying 'Well, if he's the one causing Huey so much trouble, why don't we just kill him?'" Benezach remembered. On other occasions the troops would size up the opposition force: Walmsley now had the Old Regular policemen guarding the front and side of Gallier Hall, with guns held close to their sides. If it did come to a battle, the soldiers agreed, the police officers would be destroyed. "They didn't dare look at us twice," laughed Gouaze. "We were young, we were crazy, and we would do what we were told. They had big fat bellies and weren't about to start a fight with us."[11]

One afternoon during the first week of the standoff, both the guardsmen and the police found something other than each other to look at: a local group of very vocal Socialists had gathered in Lafayette Square to jeer both Walmsley and Huey Long. Led in part by the confrontational, activist secretary of the New Orleans chapter, middle-aged Newcomb

College student Louise Jessen, the nearly six hundred protestors were remarkable for the neat dresses and suits they
wore in the searing summer heat, but even more so because
they presented a racially integrated front: something
unheard of in the Deep South of 1934.

They came to demonstrate, they said, their outrage in
response to a national problem only made worse in New
Orleans: mass starvation. As a result of the feud between
Huey and Walmsley, there was a less-noticed feud between
federal and state agencies over how relief funds would be
spent in Louisiana. But until the feud ended, most federal
relief efforts were suspended while New Orleanians grew
sick and weak from a lack of food. The wife of a ditchdigger
who was dying of tuberculosis took to Esplanade Avenue to
beg. An elderly black woman, years ago a slave, had not
eaten for days, sitting silently in a ramshackle house
crowded with equally hungry relatives on Howard Avenue.
In the darkness outside downtown restaurants, women and
men fed themselves from the food they found in garbage
cans at night. "Bits of meat, rice, potatoes, soggy bread, broken crackers—these they can usually find without difficulty,"
a journalist watching the unfortunates' late-night excursions
during the first week of August reported. "Rinds of can-
taloupe, pieces of watermelon, eaten but not quite to the
rind—these are delicacies." Of course, the reporter, added,
such foods could easily be sour or soiled in the summer's
soaring heat. But, at the very least, it was food.[12]

The Lafayette Square demonstrators said they had had
enough. The major political parties had failed them, they
said; Senator Long and Mayor Walmsley were a disappoint-
ment too. "Senator Long says he is the poor man's friend,
but we must judge people by their acts," Jessen yelled to a
sea of placards that demanded, among other things, milk
and bread now for the city's starving children, work for the
unemployed, union rights, and even the recognition of the
Soviet Union.[13]

Jessen was joined by organizers of the equally minuscule

Communist party of New Orleans and the pacifistic League for Industrial Democracy, which had a chapter on the Tulane University campus. Of more significance was the presence of the working men of the International Long-shoreman's Association, in the third month of a brutal strike at the Port of New Orleans. Together, the coalition of groups listened to the hot speeches on a hot day marked by clenched fists, colorful banners, and the rhetoric of alienation.

"Long says he has no money for the unemployed," Jessen went on, "but he can find money for bullets for the Guardsmen." She then turned towards the Soule Building, where the soldiers listened to her speech, and plaintively asked: "If Huey Long tells you to shoot down your brothers across the street, are you going to do it?" Silence was the response. "You don't belong there. Throw away your guns and come over here with us where you belong. If Long and Walmsley have a grievance, let them fight it out here in Lafayette Square. Are they such cowards that they must have others fight for them?"[14]

To his credit, hours later, Walmsley met with a biracial delegation from the protest meeting—perhaps the first delegation of its kind to enter the old, white Gallier Hall—but the meeting was unproductive. Walmsley told his visitors relief was now almost entirely in the hands of the federal government, but he listened politely to the group's entreaties, even enduring a personal lobby from Jessen. In fact, Walmsley had silently suffered at the hands of Jessen before. She had bitterly attacked him in the spring general election, the same race where she ran as the Socialist nominee for a seat on the city commission and finished dead last in the contest. But Jessen managed to outmaneuver Walmsley anyway. Arrested for distributing campaign handbills without a license, Jessen grandly chose to serve a ten-day sentence in the parish prison rather than pay a fine. She instantly became a sensational story for both the local and national press. Alternately reading from the Bible and the

Louise Jessen in jail. The Bible-quoting Socialist easily outmaneuvered Mayor Walmsley but was no match for a vindictive Huey Long. (Courtesy the *Times-Picayune*)

most recent issues of the *New Republic* and the *Nation*, Jessen was a public relations natural. "I admire Christ greatly and have no difficulty in agreeing with him," Jessen calmly disclosed to reporters during her prison stay as she pointed to an open Bible in her jail cell. "I think he was one of the great proletarian leaders." She lectured those who came to visit her on the Socialist solutions to the nation's problems, posed behind bars for photographers, and even sent out letters to friends signed, "Louise Jessen, Parish Prison."[15]

One of her correspondents was Norman Thomas, the famous and respected leader of the National Socialist Party, who used the power of his reputation to hopefully obtain Jessen's release. He told her in a letter that was also given to the press that he was "greatly shocked at the discrimination which puts you in jail and leaves old party politicians outside." It was finally more than Walmsley could stand. Ordering that Jessen be immediately freed, he also made certain that from now on the talkative and clever Socialist would be allowed to distribute her literature anytime and anywhere she wanted.[16]

Huey Long, however, was never so easily cowed. After Jessen's racially integrated delegation left Walmsley's Gallier Hall, they pushed on to the Roosevelt Hotel, where the plan was to present to Huey the same list of demands Walmsley had entertained. But Jessen and her friends were not even allowed inside the hotel, the Roosevelt's house detective told them at the front door. There were two black men in the Jessen party; they could only enter the Roosevelt through a side entrance. Jessen refused and led her somewhat dejected group back to Lafayette Square. But Huey was not finished with Jessen yet. Jessen's husband, Otto, also a committed Socialist, was soon mysteriously dismissed from his position as an agent for the Federal Barge Line. It was a firing that Norman Thomas, among others, was certain Huey had something to do with. The kind-hearted Thomas then fretted that by becoming involved in Jessen's case he may have only made things worse by giving Jessen even

more publicity in her attacks against Huey and earning
Huey's enmity. "With all of my heart I hope that I have not
unintentionally done more harm than good," Thomas
wrote Jessen.[17]

If Huey was briefly preoccupied with Jessen and the New
Orleans Socialists, he was not alone. In Washington, J. Edgar
Hoover ordered his agents in New Orleans to send him daily,
detailed, telegraphed reports on not only Huey's takeover of
the Soule Building but the Socialist activity in Lafayette Park.
Convinced that virtually any demonstration of dissent must
somehow be Communist-inspired, Hoover found the mixture of the armed standoff between the Huey and Walmsley
forces and the Socialist presence irresistible. "Demonstrations of this kind, in view of the tense situation, bode possi-
bilities of violence and tend to further complicate the
existing situation," Hoover quickly concluded in a memo to
President Roosevelt's acting attorney general on August 6.[18]

But the Federal Bureau of Investigation had other reasons to closely monitor events in New Orleans: Hoover well
knew that Roosevelt genuinely feared Huey's growing power
and potential. To give the White House important strategic
information on the movements of such a prominent foe
could only further endear Hoover to FDR. And that, after
all, was how Hoover clawed out an invincible turf in the frequently treacherous terrain of Washington. That at least
one top officer with the National Guard in New Orleans
began to provide Hoover inside information on Huey's military plans only made Hoover's job easier.[19]

Hoover's value was made more priceless after Roosevelt
himself admitted in a news conference on August 24 that
although he was concerned about events in New Orleans,
there was not much he could do. "In this case the legislature of the state of Louisiana has the inherit, constitutional
right to govern a municipality within that state as it sees fit,"
Roosevelt told reporters, "provided it does not violate the
right of franchise and certain rights of self-government.
That is about as far as you can go."[20]

Two weeks later, after Huey's newest shipment of troops thundered into the city, Roosevelt again expressed his reluctance to intervene, although he was shocked by the sheer number of soldiers now in New Orleans: "We are all sort of tied up," FDR candidly admitted, "and, of course, Huey Long knows it."[21]

Roosevelt was right, and Huey was quick to chortle a response: "Roosevelt knows his business. He's no damn fool." Huey added that it only made sense for the president to avoid Louisiana's internal political squabbles: after all, Huey serenely added, he had never tried to tell Roosevelt how to manage Washington. "He's running it and I haven't even bothered him in that," Huey judiciously concluded.[22]

Roosevelt's worries in response to the volume of soldiers wandering about New Orleans were well placed. On September 7 trains coming into the city were packed with troops, hundreds and hundreds of them, nearly 2,500 in all, who poured into New Orleans with rifles and ammunition belts looking for action. Hilda Phelps Hammond was among the many who went into shock. In New Orleans after a season of Huey-baiting in Washington, the Uptown reformer was visiting her crusade's French Quarter headquarters when suddenly she heard, as she later described it, "the sounds of tramping feet."[23]

"The young men of Louisiana were marching in narrow file up the banquettes of the Vieux Carre," Hammond remembered, "the youth of Louisiana clad in khaki, with helmets strapped beneath smooth chins, with rifles on their shoulders." The boys had arrived for one reason, Hammond was certain, "to protect [a] Dictatorship."[24]

On the front page of the *New York Times* for September 8, F. Raymond Daniell seemed to confirm Hammond's appraisal: "By order of the twenty-seven laws passed by the legislature in special session last month, Senator Huey P. Long became de facto dictator of this state at noon today and immediately began acting the part." Daniell went on to note that in the preceding 24 hours up to 2,500 soldiers had

—Mobile Press.

The Louisiana Heimwehr

The Mobile Press *saw Huey as both silly and sinister.* (Courtesy the *Mobile Press*)

arrived in New Orleans, bringing the total overall number now to about 3,000, all of whom were "quartered within the city tonight, awaiting the next move of the Senator in his effort to crush the political faction of Mayor T. Semmes Walmsley."[25]

But while the soldiers gave every indication of enjoying themselves in the city, many of their parents were appalled by Huey's latest move. From upstate Monroe, one group of angry mothers and fathers sent Huey a telegram promising that they would hold him personally accountable if even a "single boy is injured." Businessman Alfred D. Amant, too, was worried about his son in Baton Rouge's 156th Infantry: "This is to notify you," Amant wired Huey, "that should any harm or injury come to him as a result of this mad effort of yours, either by accident or otherwise, I will personally kill you as I would any other mad dog."[26]

It was Huey's misfortune that his military maneuvers came during a season of frightening troop action. In Wisconsin, Minnesota, and Rhode Island during the late summer of 1934, national guardsmen were called in to quell a series of violent labor strikes, the last state seeing the death of several textile-mill workers in a confrontation between the strikers and the militia. But those actions were nothing compared to the pledge of fealty exhibited by the 100,000 soldiers of the German Reichswehr in the first week of August who, in the aftermath of legendary commander Paul von Hindenberg's death, now promised to follow Adolf Hitler.[27]

The soldiers of Louisiana, for the time being, sought only a place to sleep: Jackson Barracks, with tents propped across its polo grounds, proved too small to contain their numbers. As a result, at least one hundred solders were given passes to roam the city, beginning at midnight on September 8, under order to be back at the barracks by sunrise. But before they left, a *Times-Picayune* photographer, Oscar Valeton, took a series of photos of the troops unloading machine guns from a railroad car. His camera was suddenly snatched by a corporal, who advised Valeton to "beat it, and don't let me catch you around here again." Suddenly a

group of guardsmen gathered around, prompting Valeton
to flee. "Oscar tried to tell the guardsmen that he had a
constitutional right to be there," reporter James Gillis later
observed. "But I don't think the guardsmen knew too much
about constitutional rights."[28]

Meanwhile, the young guardsmen from rural Louisiana
caroused. "In the French Quarter, the streets were full of
strolling soldiers from the country parishes," noted Daniell,
who left his room at the Roosevelt to stroll with them. The
boys sampled beer from the Quarter's many bars and waved
to startled tourists unaccustomed to the sight of armed militiamen in a place more known for bistros and galleries
fronted by balconies of delicate wrought iron.[29]

Along the decaying wharves of the Port of New Orleans
more tents were pitched for the soldiers, some of whom
complained about having to sleep on the hard boards of the
docks. "Oh, I've read about this Huey Long," remarked the
captain of the Norwegian steamship the *Sturehelm* as he
watched the boys settle in. "But I've never seen anything
like this at Stavanger fjord." Other shippers grumbled as
they pushed freight out of the way to make room for tents
and soldiers.[30]

Eventually there would be more than one thousand men
on the docks. And for the most part they had nothing to do.
They watched the catfishermen who sat along the river's
edge and they played games: "Leap frog was a favorite
sport," observed one reporter from the Associated Press.
Others dismantled and cleaned their rifles as they gazed out
on the barges loaded with hogsheads of tobacco, tractors
carrying huge bales of cotton, and the always-busy banana
ships docking. The sounds of the river, of birds and whistles
and horns blowing, of commands yelled out in Russian,
German, and Japanese, let the troops know they were far
from home indeed.[31]

When food arrived, it came by truck, and was packed in
dozens of tightly closed tins. It was an expensive undertak-
ing, but here Huey had help: his longtime friend Jimmy
Noe, a wealthy businessman, bankrolled some of the costs

for buying and distributing the three squares daily. Up to 750 hungry boys on the Toulouse Street Wharf ate eggs, grits, and bacon, washed down with barely warm coffee, while a smaller group of 250 soldiers who had slept in stuffy tents on the Robin Street Wharf gulped down plate servings of fried chicken, fresh from the Jackson Barracks' kitchen. Even Huey's family hosted a small group. "They camped right out there in our garage," Russell Long recalled of the delegation that came to stay at Huey's Audubon Boulevard mansion. "They had cots in our garages—we had two garages really—and we provided them with whatever they needed. It was a small number of people, maybe about eight or ten."[32]

The sudden infusion of so many troops into the city made many people nervous, and with good reason. For one thing, firearms were suddenly everywhere. Mayor Walmsley only added to the problem when he swore in another two hundred armed deputies and said he had several thousand more men just waiting for his call.

The soldiers wandering out on the streets, biding time at the Soule Building, in Jackson Barracks, and on the docks, all carried rifles. At the Soule Building was enough fire-power—machine guns, tear gas bombs, and riot guns—to start a small war. And to make matters worse, the New Orleans press seemed to be egging the belligerents on and hoping for some sort of a bloody armed conflict, with belli-cose stories that treated the Soule Building as a foreign war front and the state militia as an outside enemy.

Finally, it was all too much for General Fleming. What if something went wrong? Already a gun had been fired into Gallier Hall. Then there was that crazy kid who shot his rifle inside the Patio Cafe. With tempers and the temperature rising, anything might happen. The life of each young boy soldier was in his hands. "It was a pretty serious situation," Fleming said with characteristic understatement years later. "So I went out—I called up George Reyer." It was a smart call for Fleming to make.[33]

The superintendent of police, Reyer was an agreeable

man and devoted Old Regular who had risen through the bureaucracy slowly, beginning in 1917, as a beat cop and later precinct captain, before becoming, in the late 1920s, the department's chief under Walmsley.

During his tenure in office, Reyer tried to modernize his ancient department, a rich source of patronage for the Old Regulars. And he had ordered and received just in the last month alone more than five thousand dollars in new arms and equipment. But he knew that his men were no match for Huey's trained guard, and that even with Walmsley's promise to deputize up to ten thousand more men, the odds were still in Huey's favor. And besides, a war, an actual battle between both sides, would undoubtedly result in injury and probable death. And for what? A political battle between Huey P. Long and Mayor Walmsley? It didn't seem worth it. "You just can't have two people with firearms lined up against each other," Reyer declared.

On the phone, Fleming reasoned: "There are two guys here on the edge," he began. "You are one of them and I am the other." Reyer agreed, but what could he do, indeed, what could anyone do now? The whole situation was on the verge of becoming an epic disaster. "Lord, I wish you could think of something and we could do it," Reyer lamented.[34]

That was exactly what the adjutant general hoped Reyer would say: he *had* thought of something, an idea that could put an end to all of the military posturing before someone got hurt. But there was one hitch: both Mayor Walmsley and Huey P. Long would have to agree to it. And for now, Huey had other things on his mind. In two, just two, days there would be yet another election in New Orleans, one that the *Christian Science Monitor* perceptively headlined would decide the "Rise or Decline of Huey Long."[35]

The possibility of conflict, of gunfire, of an actual war pitting the boys of the country against the aging cops of the city might be great, but for now, those troops were going to stay exactly where they were.

8

The Most Spectacular Battle

IN THE CELEBRITY CARNIVAL, Huey Long had competition at summer's end. On August 20, the most famous mobster of his era, Al Capone, shot through the city shackled to his seat in the steel-reinforced car of a train taking him from one federal prison in Atlanta to another on the desperate island of Alcatraz off the California coast. New Orleans reporters, a particularly hopeful bunch, hoped to catch a glimpse of Capone's famously friendly visage, but they saw instead only a series of murky railroad cars windows barred in steel and covered with thick, wire mesh as the train sped by.[1]

Far more accessible was Cecil B. DeMille, the iron-willed Hollywood director whose "cast of thousands" movie epics were noted as much for their content as the sheer number of people they employed. Now with a cast only of dozens, DeMille affably lunched at the Roosevelt Hotel with local Rotarians, saving his lecture on the need for decency in films for dessert.[2]

But DeMille, sublime in the Roosevelt's cool oasis, was at that moment missing the turbulence of Huey Long, a far more convincing thespian than any the director herded in Hollywood, as he regally entered the city at the head of a cavalcade of scalding sedans glistening in the summer heat, sirens blaring. Along for the ride were guardsmen, lawmakers, and members of the new committee carved up by Huey to investigate gambling and vice in the sinned city.[3]

After a brief stop at Huey's Uptown mansion—where

photographer Edward Agnelly was taken into custody by the guardsmen for snapping shots of Huey's house and released only without his film—the party pushed on to the Roosevelt Hotel, where the lobby, a reporter for the New Orleans *Item* noted, was a "maelstrom of rushing bellboys, politicians, and newspaper reporters and cameramen."[4]

Huey was back in town, propelled by a fire of revenge: to right the wrong dished out to him by Mayor Walmsley and the Old Regulars in the January mayor's race and to prove to the nation that in Louisiana there was still only one Kingfish.

He would emerge triumphant, Huey thought, by revealing the sordid underbelly of Walmsley's Old Regular rule, daily conducting his vice committee investigation, to be aired over the radio, and prodding a series of witnesses to tell all they knew about how vice flourished in the city, and, just as important, how Walmsley let it happen.

Then, by night, Huey would roll up his sleeves and take to the streets to counter the powerful block-by-block precinct and ward forces of the Old Regulars. Rallies and parades were in the offing, designed to guarantee an impressive turnout for the September 11 congressional elections. The more people who voted, even the Old Regulars admitted, the more likely it was that Huey's forces would win.

There were four men Huey was backing in this election: incumbent Congressmen Paul Maloney and Joachim Fernandez, both one-time Old Regulars now in Huey's camp; appeals court judge Archie Higgins, a candidate for the Louisiana Supreme Court; and James P. O'Connor, a young contender for the same Public Service Commission that once gave rise to Huey's career.[5]

On paper, Huey's challenge seemed daunting, despite the financial and political assault he was currently conducting against the city. Huey still had, by summer's end, no viable political organization in New Orleans equal to the Old Regulars, and even with the sobering presence of his guardsmen, Huey was still haunted by the idea that the New

Huey Long, with members of the Louisiana National Guard, on his way to the September 1934 radio vice hearings in New Orleans. (Courtesy Russell B. Long Collection, Mss. 3700, Louisiana and Lower Mississippi Valley Collections, LSU Libraries, Baton Rouge, LA)

Orleans police—Old Regulars all—would intimidate enough voters at polling booths to swing the election Walmsley's way. Huey with his armed guardsmen may be demonstrating might, but the police possessed something better: memories. Monitoring each neighborhood precinct, they would know who was remaining loyal to the organization—sometimes even accompanying suspect voters into the voting booth—and who committed heresy with Huey.

But Huey held a weapon none of his opponents could equal: his captivating strength of speech and powers of persuasion, which would never be more on display than they were in September of 1934 in New Orleans. Not only were his oratorical powers superb, but his use of radio, his almost divine ability to foresee the potential of those polished wooden boxes millions of Americans gathered around in their parlors, was nearly unmatched. "Radio listeners recognized in him a remarkable broadcaster," Francis Chase, Jr., a radio historian, has written, lauding Huey's style as simple, direct, and in the "vernacular of the uneducated man."[6]

That it was. Although Huey could recite lengthy passages from the Bible or Shakespeare with the ease of a college professor, his radio addresses were inevitably folksy affairs played out for a largely rural audience. "Well, they're investigatin' me again," Huey would begin, and one could see moms and pops across the land, working farmers with the calloused hands to prove it, knowingly smiling at each other in response; or men at the village grocer slapping the knees of their britches; or thickets of black sharecroppers listening to a single radio from one small wooden cabin somewhere and chuckling. Huey's stories were nearly always lengthy, and interesting, too. They were tales of the evils of men gone bad in the big city and the country hayseeds they tried to bring down with them. These stories and the way in which Huey virtually made love to the microphone in front of him helped to transform him into a countrywide obsession by the mid-1930s. The radio, of course, was filled with popular comedy shows like Jack Benny, the songs of Bing

Crosby and church choirs, and an endless parade of faceless dance-band leaders and purveyors of pleasant patter; but listeners soon knew there was only one Huey P. Long.[7]

With the advent of national radio networks—NBC in 1927 and CBS in 1928—the potential for vast audiences of listeners for Huey beyond Louisiana's border was unlimited. And by 1934 Huey Long was unquestionably one of radio's most popular public figures.[8]

"This is Huey P. Long speaking, ladies and gentlemen. Now before I start my speech I want each one of you who are listening to go to the telephone and ring up half-dozen of your friends. Tell 'em Huey Long is on the air. Tell 'em to tune in, and stay tuned in. I'll wait till you get through phoning," Huey would oftentimes begin. Then a studio orchestra would play a few dance tunes. "The music would start," recalled James Fitzmorris, a future Louisiana politician whose boyhood in the 1930s was filled with New Orleans politics, "and, sure enough, Mother and Daddy would commence to call their friends."[9]

Huey began the radio broadcasts of his vice committee investigation on September 2, arriving in a paper-littered room on the eighteenth floor of the Canal Bank Building, one block from the Roosevelt Hotel. Accompanied by at least fifty guardsmen who crowded into the building's lobby, refusing admission to a number of visitors, including even Earl Long, Huey wore a silk coat over a bright lavender shirt and was in a bad mood: "You should have had that damn thing ready," he yelled at two technicians hurriedly tinkering with wires. "You had all night."[10]

From this room in the next weeks would emerge a portrait of New Orleans as a seedy, dangerous place where cops were on the take, public officials were either corrupt or incompetent, and sometimes both, and small-time crime bosses were allowed to operate unmolested. Dozens of people came before Huey to testify to the terrible things they had seen. Huey did not say how he had gotten the people (he called them "witnesses") to appear, or even who most

Increasingly worried about his safety, Huey, second from the right in a dark suit and straw hat, is escorted to his radio vice hearings by a thicket of bodyguards and militiamen. (Courtesy the Leon C. Trice Collection, Manuscripts Division, Howard-Tilton Memorial Library, Tulane University)

of them were—to protect his informants from probable police harassment, they were identified by their first names only. Lacking counsel, Huey's witnesses were escorted to the makeshift broadcast studio by a guardsman and then directed to sit in front of a table where Huey stared at them from behind two microphones. Then, they told their stories.[11]

And the stories were good ones, too. There was, for example, the man up from Mexico who had moved into the French Quarter nearly twenty years ago and now presided over a crumbling rooming house. Every day, the man said, he slipped to the police of the Quarter an unmarked envelope that was stuffed with dirty money from the block's prostitutes. That money, the man continued in case anyone missed the point, was the girls' insurance against arrest. In the Irish Channel, a well-known madam said she tried to work with the officers, too. She regularly paid them in cash in return for their promise to leave her business alone. If she failed to give the police money, she added indignantly, the police "stand in front of my place," making it impossible for both the girls and their customers to do business.[12]

Another witness, he said his name was Allain, rendered for the radio audience his own version of how to work with the system: everyone in the city government, he suggested, was corrupt, it was just a matter of discovering the degree of corruption. Allain, for example, regularly rounded up money from prostitutes—$5 per girl—to be used in case of their arrest. Allain would then give the money to a receptive attache of the city's night court. Money in hand, the attache would suddenly see the startling injustice of the girls' arrest and order their immediate release. "The judge," Allain helpfully continued, "knew about it."[13]

Huey's other guests claimed to have firsthand knowledge of a vast but intricate web of casino and gaming enterprises allowed to flourish in the city, they said, because Mayor Walmsley, Police Chief Reyer, and an assortment of other Old Regulars took money from them and looked the other way. One man's reading of the busy city gaming industry was even faintly anthropological: the illegal lotteries above Canal Street, he said, were white-only and operated mostly out of unmarked stores. Below Canal, the customers were primarily black, purchasing slips from any number of street vendors. While these vendors were plainly known and visible to hundreds of customers every day, somehow the police could never locate them. But, the man continued, "the street sweepers have a hard time in the morning cleaning up the numbered slips."[14]

The response to these hearings was varied, depending perhaps on the political persuasion of the radio listener. Chief Reyer, grilled for several hours by Huey, thought it was nothing more than good theater. "He made a pretty good show," Reyer said later, speaking in classic New Orleans patois. "I would have to laugh when I listened at it." Visiting Congressman Martin Dies of Texas, who would someday win headlines with his own far more ominous House Un-American Activities Committee hearings, left the Canal Bank Building in wonder: "What's going on in there seems to me to be the best politics in the world." But Harnett Kane, a New Orleans reporter who would later write a comprehensive book detailing the eventual decline of the Long regime, was outraged. The hearings, Kane charged, were nothing but a charade. Troops ushered in only the people Huey decided were going to give testimony, and everyone else could stay home. "Witnesses were hauled in by freight entrances, and hustled out again," Kane observed. Walmsley, reduced by the daily revelations, issued nightly denials—no, he did not sanction prostitution; no, he did not know of any gambling dens. Police payoffs? He knew nothing about them.[15]

But there were indications that Huey's hearings were having an effect. *New York Times* reporter Raymond Daniell, tired of sitting in the Canal Bank Building's crowded corridor, roamed outside to see if anyone was listening and found streets emptied of the normal traffic, broken up only by small clusters of people gathered in front of shop entrances where the radio hearings were aired. Similar gatherings, Daniell noticed, were taking place at "every bar, cafe, and shoe shine parlor in the downtown section."[16]

The Old Regulars, too, were listening, but it was their misfortune that they only dimly perceived what was happening. Fatted cows waiting for the slaughter, they bovinely fed on, unaware of the fate awaiting them. They had won virtually every important city election for nearly half a century now and only naturally expected to do well again. They could not see, would not be made to understand, how damaging Huey's hearings were becoming, how he was making them look like what they were: corrupt, callous insiders who had been in power for too long.

With four days to go before the election, the Old Regulars threw up a fantastic bash to make themselves feel good. More than six thousand people, most of them city workers, showed up for the huge nighttime rally on the tree-lined corner of Claiborne and Canal. It was a grand night full of fireworks, jazz bands, a flaming bonfire, and a rousing speech by Walmsley who defended himself against the charges of corruption from Huey's hearings. "There has not been a scintilla of evidence produced to show any misdoings by any city official," Walmsley protested as the boisterous audience booed every mention of Huey's name. Sailing over a sea of fedoras flew a curious figure: Huey P. Long, hung in effigy by the Old Regular captains of the Eighth Ward. A placard, pinned to his backside, labeled him "der Kaiserfish," while another message, written in Old Regular eloquence, declared: "Crayfish, get ready to crawl back to your hole because we Old Regulars are going to vote your potatoes down at the polls."[17]

Blocks away, at the river's edge, more than three thousand people cheered the Long ticket, jeered the Old Regulars, and promised Huey a historic turnout. But there was still a deadening sense of violence in the air: too many men now with too many guns. And rarely in recent years had there been an election without fights, arrests, and angry disputes at the polls. What would happen now, after nearly a month of a protracted standoff between the state militia and the city police? Adj. Gen. Raymond Fleming and Chief of Police George Reyer didn't want to know. In response the two men hammered out an agreement: because the presence of the police at the polls would make Huey's voters jumpy, the police would not be allowed near those polls on election day. But the same would hold true for the guardsmen. They must stay away from the places where people vote on election day, otherwise there was no telling what could happen. In addition, an arbitration committee would be quickly set up and composed equally of both Walmsley and Long men to settle any election-day disputes. "We will respect oneanother and not get into any battle because this could lead to quite a serious proposition," Fleming proposed to Reyer, who agreed. In return, the chief of police instantly sent out an all-stations bulletin just hours before the election: "You will not leave your stations under any circumstances Tuesday, September 11," it read in part.[18]

"That is what did it," reporter James Gillis later judged. "Without that agreement who knows what might have happened. Everyone had a gun, these guardsmen were all over the streets, and an election was just a couple of days away. It could have been a disaster."[19]

The truce was quickly advanced by a group of frantic local businessmen who had become convinced that the city was on the verge of carnage. Surprisingly it was signed by both Walmsley and Long, but probably for different reasons. The mayor gained because he would now not have to match Huey's man- and firepower, a daunting proposition that would have revealed for the entire world the weakness of the city's defenses. But even as he endorsed the truce, Walmsley could not resist a jab: "There can be no peace between the Regular organization and Huey Long until Long is in the Atlanta Penitentiary," the mayor oddly remarked.[20]

But Huey was the truce's true winner. "That agreement made all of the difference," Russell Long later contended, noting that without the intimidating presence of armed Old Regular policemen watching everyone and "helping" suspect voters, those inclined toward his father could now vote that way as well.[21]

But advantageous as the sudden truce was, it was nearly stillborn due to the dramatic arrival in the city of a dashing figure: the great Col. Guy R. Molony, up from Honduras, who had returned to New Orleans, it was said, to engineer a coup against Huey. Even in an era of forceful personalities who seemed more drawn out of fiction than fact, Molony stood out. With his powerful, square jaw, wavy dark hair, and military bearing, Molony was a man given to military confrontation and buccaneering adventure who eagerly sought and was granted the acceptance of New Orleans' social and business elite primarily because of his mercenary proclivities. In short, he was always happy to do the dirty work for those willing to pay him.

While Huey had a mortal fear of physical confrontation, Molony, by contrast, thrived on it. He had survived bullet and bayonet wounds fighting with the British in the Boer War, helped stabilize a civil insurrection in the Philippines with the U.S. Cavalry, and fought as a tailgunner in the 1910 revolution in Nicaragua. From there, Molony helped spearhead a military insurgency in Honduras the following year and was soon so adored by his sponsors that he was given command of a military school to train government soldiers in guerilla war tactics—all before his thirty-sixth birthday.[22]

But by that thirty-sixth year, one inescapable conclusion could be drawn from a study of Molony's career: he always, no matter the circumstances or the country, fought on behalf of the established order against upheaval, for those with money as opposed to those without, on behalf of the white overseers and plantation masters in opposition to their yellow and brown-skinned workers.

One of Molony's most celebrated excursions, in fact, was

on behalf of what would eventually become Samuel Zemurray's United Fruit enterprise in Honduras. A wealthy, if transplanted, New Orleanian, "Sam the Banana Man" Zemurray by 1910 had a problem: he owned 15,000 acres in Honduras ripe for building his company into a major Central American enterprise that would eventually put to work thousands of Hondurans in brutal conditions at substandard wages. But in order to get his plant off the ground, Zemurray needed the help of a friendly government to provide him with tax concessions and essential rail lines. When the incumbent president balked, Zemurray turned to Molony and another soldier of fortune named Lee Christmas for help. "Lee Christmas and Guy Molony, equipped with a machine gun, a case of rifles and three thousand pounds of ammunition, swept through Honduras in a matter of weeks," United Fruit historian Thomas P. McCain later documented. The incumbent president fell, a new president receptive to Zemurray rose, and in the next two decades, prospering from the sweat of slave labor, Zemurray's company merged with United Fruit to become a multimillion-dollar operation with financial bloodlines supplied by some of the most prestigious bankers in New Orleans. Zemurray himself, meanwhile, became yet another opponent of Huey Long after Huey had the temerity to one day suggest that U.S. troops should never be dispatched to Honduras to protect United Fruit's interests.[23]

By the early 1920s, Molony's reputation for efficient execution preceded his return to New Orleans, where he was appointed by then-Old Regular Mayor Andrew McShane to become the city's new chief of police. Molony's five-year reign as New Orleans' top cop was only naturally colored with controversy. Critics complained of his penchant for strong-arm tactics, court documents claimed he was a secret member of the Ku Klux Klan, and, in 1925, he was forced to resign his post, returning quickly to Honduras, in the wake of a scandal that saw one of the younger cops in his department framed for the burglary activities of others higher up in the police hierarchy.[24]

In spite of Molony's uneven performance as police chief, however, he remained a comfortable Old Regular, and friend to both Mayor McShane and the new young city attorney working under McShane in the early 1920s, T. Semmes Walmsley. In the years to follow, Walmsley, like countless others, became enamored of Molony's military prowess to the point where he turned to the colonel for advice on how to put down both real and imagined insurrections. In the January mayor's race, as rumors flew that even then Huey was contemplating a military invasion of the city, Walmsley sought and won Molony's assurance that the colonel would only be too happy to wage a military response of his own, should it come to that. For two weeks leading up to the balloting, Molony holed up in the elite St. Charles Hotel, waiting for the word from the mayor.[25]

Molony's connections, always lucrative in the same city he owned an impressive Uptown home in, soon produced for him a group of up to thirty-five men willing to follow Molony if he led. The colonel later denied he had established what Huey characterized as a "machine gun nest" at the St. Charles Hotel. But his daughter, Isabel Molony, would one day speculate that it would not have taken much to enlist her father's aid in offing Huey. "He wasn't a crazy person," Isabel said. "He would have had to have a plan and figure out what was expected of him. But under the right circumstances, yes, he probably would have done something."[26]

Molony left New Orleans after the January election, but now, on September 6, he floated back into the Port of New Orleans onboard the S.S. *Sixada,* where he was greeted by a herd of reporters anxious to print the reason for his sudden return to the city. "I am back in the United States on business," Molony jovially assured the press, before regaling them with his latest Central American adventures. Just hours later, however, Molony met with Walmsley at Gallier

Hall where the mayor exclaimed: "The city is being threatened by a madman." Could the colonel be counted on to protect and defend? Molony coolly replied that his services were "at the disposal of the city if they were needed."[27]

Reading the front-page accounts of Molony's arrival, Huey was suspicious, quickly issuing a subpoena for the colonel to appear before his vice committee. But when an unfortunate state deputy presented the document to the colonel at his St. Charles Hotel suite, Molony simply ripped it up. No one, the deputy learned, summoned Molony, even though his attorney in the city advised him to go to the committee of his own accord and confront Long.

When Molony finally agreed to appear before the committee, everyone knew there would be fireworks. Until now, most of those responding to Huey's summonses were cooperative, if not entirely malleable, witnesses who were almost certainly coached by Huey or his assistants on the nature of their testimony. Huey virtually admitted as much when he dismissed one witness and remarked, with the microphones still picking up his voice, "Well, I'm going to cut my testimony short," before quickly correcting himself.[28]

When Molony finally arrived at the Canal Bank Building's makeshift studio, he sat down heavily in a wooden chair facing Huey and, in response to Huey's first terse question, admitted that it was true he had ripped up the summons handed to him. "I wanted to change clothes," Molony began before adding, "I consulted a lawyer and he recommended that I come."[29]

Dryly, Huey thanked Molony for his decision to appear, but when the colonel attempted to make a response, Huey destroyed the promise of even a tenuous cordiality. "Speak up!" Huey commanded. Molony was unperturbed: "Am I talking to you gentlemen here or the radio?" he calmly responded.[30]

It was downhill from there. Huey began to pepper Molony with questions: his reign as police chief, his career as a mercenary, even his friendship with Walmsley. But

Molony was evasive and monosyllabic, although he did admit that he had already met with the mayor at Gallier Hall.

"You came back here during the last election, didn't you?" Huey then asked.

"Yes, on business."

"And this time why did you come back?" Huey pressed.

Molony, always an interrogator, never interrogated, replied: "On business and to vote."[31]

Was this man with his own flair for dramatics and stone countenance finally Huey's equal? Huey persisted, demanding to know if in January Molony had also returned to New Orleans to organize a militia at the St. Charles Hotel. Molony seemed indifferent: "We had some men there," he replied but denied they were armed.[32]

And then, an explosion from Huey: "I suppose you came back to do the same thing this time?"

Molony: "No, I didn't, but I'd be glad to try it."

Incredulous, Huey erupted: "Try and do it! Try and do it!"

Molony was even: "Just watch us."[33]

By far the most entertaining witness of the week, Molony exited the Canal Bank Building as the armed guardsmen almost by reflex parted to let him through. Outside he pushed his straw hat back on his broad forehead, unbuttoned his rumpled seersucker suit, and strutted for photographers with a faint smirk decorating his face. "Just watch us," it seemed to say.[34]

September 11 dawned warm and misty. An unsettling quiet, made drier by the election day closing of every tavern in New Orleans, blanketed the city as the wait began.

An agent for J. Edgar Hoover in New Orleans, R. Whitley, cabled to the FBI chief that he was watching the election closely and would let his boss know the results as soon as they came in. Hoover, in turn, sent a quick message to the White House telling them he was on top of things in New Orleans.[35]

Raymond Daniell left his Roosevelt Hotel suite and saw long lines of voters at every poll he visited, even as the afternoon gave way to a heavy rain. And still it was quiet; no fights, no arrests, not a single gunshot, "as peaceful as a Quaker village on a Sunday morning," Daniell noted.[36]

Colonel Molony sat well fortified at the St. Charles Hotel as Mayor Walmsley and the ward leaders of the Old Regulars gathered at the same hotel for what was certain to be their greatest victory celebration.

At the Roosevelt Hotel, Huey bounced out of bed in peach pajamas, foregoing a bath as he lunged for the telephone and received good news: the river and Central City precincts were voting heavy. Nibbling from a tray of sandwiches, Huey ambled into an adjoining studio built for him by Seymour Weiss, where every hour on the hour he urged his radio listeners to make sure they voted. Not until late afternoon did Huey clean himself and fetch wife Rose so they could vote, too. Returning to the Roosevelt he was joined by Daniell, who thought Huey looked tired, Gov. O. K. Allen, who was shaking hands with anyone who entered Huey's suite, and a crowd of politicians and reporters.

The results were slow coming in. September 11 was also Rosh Hashanah and the city's polls were kept open one hour after 7 P.M., an hour after sunset, to accommodate the roughly two thousand Jewish voters of New Orleans. But a new method of tallying votes also delayed things. With the police now prohibited from poll watching, the old way of reporting the vote precinct by precinct to neighborhood police stations was obsolete. Instead, both the Long and Walmsley precinct captains now carted wooden boxes overflowing with completed ballots to the city's new criminal courts building, where both sides listed the results on huge tally sheets.[37]

Ballot counting would be slower this way, but more fair and accurate. But new methods did not deter the captains of the Old Regulars and Huey's forces from calling into the St. Charles Hotel and Huey's suite early preliminary returns.

September 12, 1934: As Huey votes, his slate sweeps the city, reaffirming his political dominance to the chagrin of Walmsley, Roosevelt, and the Old Regulars. (Courtesy New Orleans Public Library, Louisiana Division, Huey Long Photograph Album)

For Huey, the results of only twenty of the first reporting precincts, twenty scattered precincts where he knew by heart the sort of vote he had received in past elections, were enough to give him the lay of the land. Within only minutes Huey could see his slate was sweeping the city, winning in wards the Old Regulars had dominated for decades. Even the Seventeenth Ward—taking in a large part of the notoriously anti-Long Uptown New Orleans, the home of Old Regulars president Joseph Humphrey—was going for Huey's ticket, the first time in history an Old Regular chief lost in his own neighborhood. Within the first hour after the polls were closed, Huey could see that his candidates were ahead and would remain so in eleven of the Old Regulars' seventeen wards, piling up strong margins along the riverfront and intercity precincts in a wave that only crested in the Uptown and Garden District Fourteenth and Sixteenth wards. And he didn't just win in neighborhoods where there was no work, or in the tough blocks where tough laborers— switchmen, boilermakers, sheet metal workers—lived. Huey's men won in places like the Fourteenth Precinct of the Ninth Ward, a neighborhood of craftsmen, engineers, carpenters, tailors, millwrights. Here the vote for the Long ticket exceeded 60 percent.[38]

Added to the rural parishes just outside Orleans Parish, which made up the second congressional district, the vote for Huey's slate totaled more than 141,000 to the roughly 100,000 ballots of the Old Regulars. It was a stunning victory for Huey, and a devastating defeat for Walmsley. "It's all over now," Huey yelled out as his suite was now packed with cheering, drinking visitors. The election results, Huey told his party, represented a "victory against persecution." Daniell ran to his typewriter to make his deadline for yet another front page of the *New York Times*, a front page Roosevelt, Hoover, and all of Washington would read the following morning: "Huey P. Long appeared tonight to have won the most spectacular battle of his political career," Daniell wrote. The nation's press followed Daniell's lead by ceding

-The Baltimore Sun.

The Kingfish Gives A Black Eye

One of the few favorable press portrayals of the invasion: this one, in the
Baltimore Sun, *shows a masculine Huey throttling a flaccid New
Orleans in the figure of a traditional Southern gentleman.* (Courtesy the
Baltimore Sun)

back to Huey everything he had lost in January and more. Huey was now, *Newsweek* darkly concluded, "the undisputed monarch of the sovereign state of Louisiana." Hodding Carter in the *New Republic* grudgingly admitted, "undeniably Huey Long still has a large personal following among the New Orleans masses."[39]

At the St. Charles Hotel, where Walmsley and the Old Regulars had monitored the election all day, the returns were sobering. Colonel Molony left promptly for Central America and presumably less elusive prey. Walmsley, nearly alone in this analysis, insisted that the election was not really the victory for Huey it seemed. "Huey Long has *not* taken the city of New Orleans," Walmsley declared against all evidence late in the evening. But the Old Regulars fed at the table of victory or else did not eat at all. That was how the cycle of dishing out jobs, winning elections, and dishing out more jobs worked. Without winning elections first, and then gaining access to government, the Old Regulars could quickly become irrelevant. Now in the wake of Huey's triumph, a major reappraisal among the Old Regulars was about to occur.[40]

That the Old Regulars would take stock of their suddenly depleted fortunes was only natural. They suffered, after all, one of their worst drubbings in years. But the rapidity of their conceived solution to their problems may have startled the city's political community, for practically overnight they decided that Huey P. Long was not, finally, their greatest burden. No, that burden was someone far more familiar and within proximity of the empty beer bottles, sagging streamers, and losers' posters that decorated the reception hall of the St. Charles Hotel. The burden's name was T. Semmes Walmsley and many of the Regular chieftains began to see that they could never seek peace with Huey as long as Walmsley led them.

Evidence that Walmsley had suddenly outlived his usefulness to his unsentimental sponsors was easily evident the morning after the election when Huey, somewhat more serene after his triumph, announced that the Louisiana National Guard was no longer needed to restore order in the city. The partial martial law dutifully enacted by Governor Allen was effectively over, and the troops, by the afternoon after the election, would be under order to pack their gear and catch the next train out of New Orleans. The military confrontation was, for now, at an end. But the battle against Mayor Walmsley, Huey promised, had just begun.[41]

9

The Empire of Utopia

THE MORNING AFTER HUEY'S ELECTION TRIUMPH, railroad cars lumbered into the Toulouse Street Wharf, where they were quickly loaded with machine guns, ammunition, and tents by jocular guardsmen. The commander for the Second Battalion 156th Infantry did not have much to say to the reporters there watching the scene, except to disclose that while the boys would enjoy a hearty lunch on the docks, "no plans for dinner have been made." The soldiers, packing their belongings with the same celebration they brought arriving to New Orleans, also cleared away the thick underbrush that had wrapped itself around the dock's aging piers to leave behind, in good guardsmen tradition, a cleaner camp than the one they found.[1]

At the Soule Building the soldiers lined the brick walkway that had separated them from Mayor Walmsley's office and stacked blankets, cots, uniforms, and baggage in a lorry. The ominous machine guns, for more than a month trained on Gallier Hall, were suddenly gone too, although Walmsley could still see that all of the soldiers continued to carry their sidearms as they waited to move out of the city.

By evening, more than 2,500 troops were gone, although Huey ordered left behind a small handful to guard his Audubon Boulevard home, where someone had fired a bullet through his living-room window the week before.[2]

By Greyhound bus and Southern Pacific rail, the boys

returned to their families in Houma and Shreveport, Minden and Natchitoches. The New Orleans soldiers left by truck to the Jackson Barracks.[3]

But to what were the boys returning? On the surface everything seemed as it was before. More than two hundred girls crowded into New Orleans' Heinemann Park—soon to be more widely known as Pelican Stadium—two days after the election to sing, dance, juggle, and tell jokes as they vied for the title of "Miss Louisiana 1934."[4]

Three weeks later Seymour Weiss at the Roosevelt Hotel unveiled to a celebrity-packed audience the latest renovations to his beloved Blue Room, crowned with a painted blue ceiling highlighted by sparkling stars, and headlined by a New York dance orchestra, a barrelhouse blues singer, and the tango dance team of Enrica and Novello.[5]

Sports enthusiasts, meanwhile, took heart: enough money had been finally raised by the fall of 1934 for New Orleans to host the city's first Sugar Bowl competition for the end of the year at the new Tulane University stadium. The game, which attracted an unprecedented twenty-two thousand fans, capped a triumphant season for the Tulane Green Wave and saw them beat the Temple Owls 20 to 14, sparking a citywide celebration and the first of a series of legendary Sugar Bowl face-offs.[6]

Everything seemed the same, but in reality nothing was as before. Emboldened by his New Orleans victory, Huey now swallowed Louisiana whole. In a rapid series of numbing legislative sessions beginning in November, Huey, with alacrity, buried the state in paper. There were dozens of bills now expanding his power at an alarming rate: bills giving him the power to set utility rates and property taxes everywhere in Louisiana; bills giving him control, for once and for all time, of the registrar's office; and bills moving Walmsley's largest source of patronage—the city's sewerage and water board, home to more than four thousand employees—entirely under Huey's control.[7]

The bills came fast—forty-five in the November session,

another thirty-four a month later in yet another special session. The bills came so fast that by the end of the year compliant House members were ratifying a Huey measure at the rate of one every three minutes. By Christmas, Huey had achieved a sobering record for the year: 350 new laws were passed, most enlarging Huey's power and extending his rule into virtually every section and corner of the state. No American state had ever seen anything like it before.[8]

Whether or not Huey had finally become a dictator—America's first glimpse of homegrown authoritarian rule—was no longer the talk of only Uptown New Orleans parlors. Now, as 1934 gave way to 1935, the entire nation was discussing Huey. *Time* magazine put Huey on their cover for the second time in early 1935. All the New York papers, *Newsweek,* the *Nation, Business Week,* the *Saturday Evening Post, Collier's, Scribner's Monthly,* and even the *Christian Century,*—all sought to explain how this colorful comedian from the dirt clay of central Louisiana had become such a prominent and dangerous national figure. In early 1935 the film crew for the national newsreel series the *March of Time* arrived in Louisiana for a feature profile on Huey that would be seen in thousands of theaters across the country. The result was a dark and disturbing view of a man the movie producers had undoubtedly concluded was a menace to America, a view reflected in a memo written by one of the *March of Time's* cameramen who told his New York office that there was nothing funny about Huey Long. His rule, Jack Haesler continued, "may result in civil war. Perhaps the only solution outside of his assassination."[9]

The *March of Time* film on Huey was so critical, in fact, that it was never shown in Louisiana, although what part Huey played in the film's sudden disappearance is hard to determine. He did, however, fly "into one of his rages," *Variety* later claimed, "when questioned about it."[10]

But even with an increasingly negative press, Huey's prestige and popularity across the country reached an all-time high in early 1935. One year after founding his Share Our

Wealth movement, there were now more than 27,000 local chapters with upwards of 8 million members from coast to coast. In just the month of April 1935 alone, Huey received more than 200,000 letters to his Washington office, most of them concerning the SOW clubs. When the Democratic National Committee sponsored a secret poll several months later to gauge Huey's national support, the results sent shockwaves through the White House: between 3 million and 4 million voters, the poll suggested, might vote for Huey in 1936, enough to deny President Roosevelt a second term should Huey run as a third-party candidate. Huey voters held the balance of power between the Democrats and the Republicans in any battle for the presidency, thus making Huey the biggest political challenge for FDR.[11]

But still there was work to finish up in the state, a fact Huey alluded to at the beginning of the November 1934 legislative session when he asked "How in hell do you expect Louisiana to progress under present circumstances?" He offered a unique solution: the state should simply secede from the nation, so great were her differences with the rest of the country, particularly Washington, D.C. Freed of a burdensome alliance, the happy people of Louisiana would respond in a way most native: they would copiously reproduce. "Instead of the two or three million population, we wold have maybe 45 million people right here," Huey predicted. "This state would become the Empire of Utopia."[12]

Left alone, Louisiana officials from Huey on down would also be freed of the increasingly onerous presence of the federal government, a government that, by October of 1934, had begun handing down indictments against key members of Huey's circle for tax evasion: state senator Jules Fisher and his nephew representative Joseph Fisher; Abe Shushan, a wealthy, self-made New Orleans businessman and Long supporter; and finally, on December 6, Seymour Weiss himself, whose $232,000 income over the previous five years had been reported as only $55,000 on Weiss's tax forms.[13]

There seemed no doubt that the feds were hoping that with the prosecution and hoped-for cooperation of Long's underlings they could eventually build a case against Huey himself. Treasury officials, the FBI, and even President Roosevelt were aided in this quest by an unending flood of letters, sometimes sent anonymously, other times by prominent public officials, suggesting possible places and points of fraud and malfeasance within the Long empire.[14]

But Washington reached down into Louisiana in other ways too, most infamously by suspending some $2.5 million in federal funds for a New Orleans sewerage and water board project that was expected to provide work for at least two thousand people. With Huey now in control of the city's water department, noted Harold Ickes, FDR's crafty secretary of the interior, Washington had little enthusiasm for handing out money to "build up any share the wealth program."[15]

It would have eventually had to come to this. Nearly all of the president's advisers, including the blunt, crusty, hard-drinking vice-president John Nance ("Cactus Jack") Garner, warned him that the only way to destroy Huey was to keep from him as much money as possible. To the extent that such money was federal, FDR cheerfully did all he could. But the result was a cruel trick for the people of Louisiana who, overall, stood to lose some $13 million in federal programs, programs that simply gave them the opportunity for work; work cleaning ditches or paving roads or building buildings. Now even that, in the ongoing Long-Roosevelt battle, had evaporated.

Beginning in January 1935, the city's roughly six thousand employees went on half-pay as New Orleans' coffers began to dry up. As spring gave way to summer, the situation was desperate: unable, because of its precarious financial status, to borrow the millions it needed for operating expenses, New Orleans was now seeing scheduled paydays come and go without a single city employee getting money.[16]

"Huey passed laws which I thought were pretty rough," Seymour Weiss later remembered, pointing to yet another source of the city's grief. "The laws were so rough that the mayor of New Orleans couldn't even hire his own secretary . . . it made it almost unbearable for Walmsley." Whether the cause was Roosevelt's need to weaken Huey or Huey's desire to finally destroy Walmsley, the city suffered. But Huey refused to take the next step, which would be to forcibly remove Walmsley by a two-thirds vote of the legislature. He wanted instead to see the mayor repudiated, turned out by his own people. Huey told reporters he would stop his warfare against New Orleans only if a majority of the city's voters signed a petition calling for Walmsley's ouster. It would be an exacting humiliation. "We are not going to put him out," Huey said. "It must be the people who put him out, not us."[17]

The people, however, needed a little pushing. It apparently was not enough that less than half of the city's streets were unpaved, mud obstacle courses bogging down cars and humans alike and that now, with Huey yanking New Orleans' big $700,000 street appropriation, they would likely stay that way; it wasn't enough that jobs were coming and going, and that Huey, running city departments now like the sewerage and water board, could do his own firing and some people were suddenly without work; there had to be other ways to prod New Orleanians into throwing Walmsley over, to finally arise en masse against this man Huey hated and wanted to hurt more than anyone else.

And that way was with garbage.

Hauling the city's refuse on horse-driven wagons and on the back of groaning flatbed trucks, the city's garbage collectors by the end of June 1935 were at a breaking point. Paydays came and went without money, and life was only made more unbearable by a record heat wave seeing temperatures crest above one hundred degrees. It was no surprise when the collectors decided they could take no more. They had families to feed, they said, and they were going on strike until someone gave them money.[18]

The strike was a golden opportunity for Huey. Nothing could torment city folk living in extremely close quarters more than seeing and smelling their rotting refuse go uncollected for days. It could be the final straw, the one stinking thing that would at last make New Orleanians see how expensive Walmsley had become to them. If Walmsley was not the mayor, there would be no battle between the city and the state, the city would have state money, and everyone, including the collectors, would get paid; and that stench in the streets, in front of open windows and doors, wafting across front-door stoops, where New Orleanians liked to congregate in the evening, would be finally gone.

On the morning of June 24 four dark sedans pulled up to the home of Herman Von Hoven, one of the strike's leaders, who lived in a middle-class neighborhood in Uptown New Orleans. Emerging from the cars, state senator Thomas McCormack and Dr. Joseph A. O'Hara, both New Orleans Long leaders, signaled their intention to offer Von Hoven a deal: if he kept his men out on strike, Huey would see that they eventually got paid. Just keep them on strike, O'Hara and McCormack suggested. Von Hoven made no commitment, but when O'Hara walked to a phone booth at a grocery store around the corner from Von Hoven's house, a neighbor overheard him comment: "We have told these men to ask Walmsley to resign."[19]

That, at least, was the idea, to make it seem as though the garbagemen blamed all of their troubles on Walmsley, even though the mayor had secured temporary funding through Roosevelt's Federal Emergency Relief Administration to pay them for a while. It would be a powerful protest of downtrodden city workers telling the mayor that they had now had enough.

But the plan backfired. Von Hoven and three other strike leaders not only decided to turn O'Hara down, but they appeared before the mayor in a public commission meeting to reveal their part in the plot. "I want to apologize," Von Hoven remarked, before another striker, Clarence Casey, chimed in: "We all apologize, Mr. Mayor."[20]

It was a remarkable tribute to the mayor. Despite the troubles weighing the city down, despite all of Huey's best efforts, despite the very active opposition of a far more powerful and rich state government, there was still no cry among the people of New Orleans for Walmsley's head. The city's laborers knew that while Walmsley was certainly no union activist, he was good enough by the Chamber of Commerce/Old Regulars/Uptown elite standards of doing business in New Orleans in the 1930s. They remembered that it was Walmsley who sought to end the violent 1929 streetcar-driver strike by calling for the recognition of the union shop and going on record in opposition to the very powerful New Orleans Public Service by doing so. It was Walmsley who spearheaded the construction of the Municipal Auditorium and the widening of Canal Street—projects that gave work to hundreds. And when those projects were over and the laborers needed to find work elsewhere, Walmsley was the one who set up a committee for work relief, giving jobs to some two thousand people mowing lawns and hauling trash.[21]

Even some of Huey's most devoted followers found it hard to dislike Walmsley. "He was a man with scruples," said Ed Gouaze of the National Guard who stayed behind after the invasion of New Orleans to guard Huey's house. "I think he was a good man, but he was just messed up with a bad bunch of people. It was a very difficult thing to head up a party like the Old Regulars."[22]

Just how difficult became apparent during the first week of July 1935, a week of historic upheaval in New Orleans. On July 4, hardly a day of celebration this year, Huey's supporters in the legislature introduced twenty-six bills, most of which were designed to take away from Walmsley and the Old Regulars whatever last remnants of token power they still enjoyed.[23]

All city employees would now be state employees; New Orleans would no longer have a police force to call its own; Walmsley would be denied the right to make any decisions regarding the city's finances and taxes; and even the New Orleans district attorney's office would be gutted of the right to hire and fire its own employees.[24]

At last, the Old Regulars began to cave in. On July 10, two of the most powerful members of the Choctaw Club, Joseph Skelly and R. Miles Pratt, who as members of the city commission were also two of the city's most prominent Old Regulars, announced they were deserting Walmsley and signing up with Long. The next night district attorney Eugene Stanley, for years a thorn in Huey's side, suddenly resigned, arguing that the latest legislation "strips me of every power previously possessed." And then came the avalanche: thirteen of the seventeen Old Regular ward leaders, men Walmsley had known, worked, and socialized with for all of his public career, pledged their loyalty to Long and publicly called on Walmsley to resign. In just a matter of a few days, Walmsley lost not only a voting majority on the city commission—member Fred Earhart held out as Walmsley's lone supporter—but even the good women of the Choctaw Club's women's division, the same women who praised Walmsley in a lavish public banquet in song and rhyme, now sang a different tune.[25]

In a pilgrimage of contrition, the fleeing Old Regulars fled to Huey's suite at the Roosevelt Hotel. They were a particularly anxious bunch: Ulic Burke, the first ward commissioner who once challenged Huey to a duel by leaving behind his pistol cartridge at the Roosevelt Hotel; Stanley Behrman, the son of the late Mayor Behrman; Capt. William Bisso, owner of a local tugboat company who always wore a pink rosebud in his lapel and a sparkling diamond horseshoe stickpin in his tie; and the legendary Third Ward boss and liquor dealer James Comiskey, among others.[26]

"You gentlemen know I don't need you," Huey growled to his most recent, if unwilling, converts. "You know I don't need your help in the city and I certainly don't need your help in the country. I don't need you through amalgamation or annexation."[27]

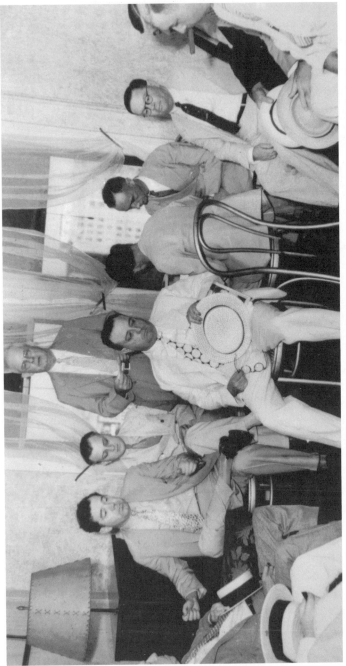

The abdication of the Old Regulars. Ulic Burke (standing), Stanley Behrman (seated in the center), and the leaders of more than a dozen of the Regulars' ward organizations contemplate their depleted fortunes as they surrender to Huey Long at the Roosevelt Hotel. (Courtesy the Leon C. Trice Collection, Manuscripts Division, Howard-Tilton Memorial Library, Tulane University)

What Huey did need, he went on, was to have the Old Regulars circulate "block to block" a recall petition against Walmsley. He wanted the names of real voters on it, the registered voters of New Orleans, documented proof that the people of New Orleans wanted to be rid of Walmsley. And he wanted the signed petitions delivered to his room at the Roosevelt the next day. That said, Huey abruptly left. It had been a hot July and Huey liked to cool down in the afternoon with what he called a "hot weather highball." He went to the Blue Room below and left the Old Regulars behind.[28]

But the Old Regulars were muddled, unable to decide among themselves not only if they should do what Huey asked them, but if they could. It would not be easy to get the names of more than half of the city's registered voters in just one day. Some would say it was impossible.

Then there was the question of Walmsley's popularity. While people in the city were unquestionably tired of the ongoing battle between the mayor and Huey there was no indication that voters disliked Walmsley, at least not to the degree that Huey did. On the contrary, in the moment of his greatest political despair, Walmsley was not without friends. "Read out of the party all the scalawags and renegades who deserted and sold their souls for less than a sack of potatoes," New Orleanian J. K. Riggs advised the mayor on July 18, as he promised the support of "a citizen who cannot boast of controlling a large number of votes but who can and does admire your honesty and courage." Rev. Edwin Rombouts, pastor of St. Francis Xavier Church, also condemned the Regulars: "The more so-called friends have gone back on you, the more I appreciate and admire your stand."[29]

Other writers offered drastic solutions: "Let the Knights of the Klan ride again and get rid of him [Long] and his kind that way," suggested Louis B. Davis on July 23, identifying himself as a "lifetime Old Regular" disenchanted with his party.[30]

Walmsley's prominence as Huey's greatest foe in

Louisiana also returned dividends as well. Members of the recently formed anti-Long Square Deal Association pledged to meet with the dozens of Roosevelt for President clubs around the state to build a new party and give support to Walmsley in his battle, even though any new political organization would be hard-pressed to equal the patronage powers of the Old Regulars and Huey's forces.[31]

Walmsley's support was also faintly quixotic as evidenced by the late-night activities of one Arthur J. Romaguera, the mayor's former chauffeur, who broke into the Old Regulars' Choctaw Club on the evening of July 19 and ran off with a huge color drawing of President Roosevelt that had decorated the club's walls. By aligning themselves with Huey Long, Romaguera reasoned, the Old Regulars "have no right to this picture."[32]

Romaguera, under threat of arrest, sheepishly returned the FDR portrait a week later; that same day Huey, declaring it would be a "terrible loss," invited him to "break into my office and get my whole bunch of Roosevelt pictures."[33]

But the only support that really mattered came from the Old Regular trenches: the more numerous precinct captains who did the unthinkable and rebelled against their own ward leaders as they condemned the truce with Huey and swore continued allegiance to Walmsley. It was a particularly courageous display of rebellion given the dearth of paychecks and the Old Regulars' well-known habit of punishing opponents or turncoats through economic retribution.

While the pro-Walmsley precinct captains were all from wards 11, 12, 14, 16, and 17—the Garden District and Uptown base the mayor had always called his own—their refusal to participate in any anti-Walmsley initiative made the success of a petition to recall the mayor unlikely. Even worse, the captains in the large Fourteenth Ward, home to Tulane University and the Silk Stocking reformers, were now in open revolt against Bisso, their longtime ward leader who lived in a spacious mansion just outside Audubon Park. Because he had betrayed Walmsley, they said, Bisso should step down.[34]

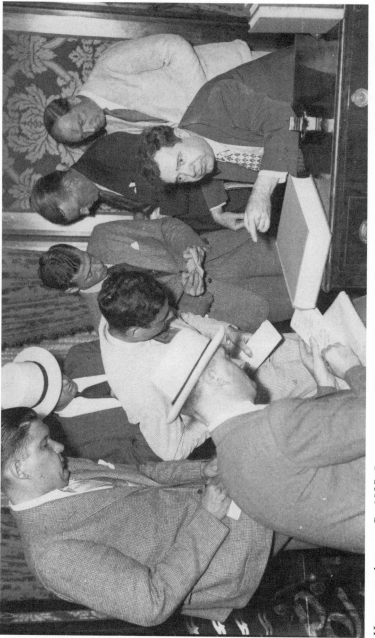

Huey meets the press. By 1935, Long was one of the most important figures in the nation; "use of his first name is universal," noted one journalist. Huey was also the head of a grass roots movement with more than 8 million members and the recipient of up to 30,000 letters a day. (Photo used by permission of Photofest)

The pro-Walmsley precinct captains stalled things long enough for the clock to run out on Huey's latest legislative session. Leaving for Washington, where he was now putting into place the structure needed to run for president in 1936, Huey promised he would be back soon for yet another legislative session. But before departing, Huey warned New Orleanians that their delays in finally ridding themselves of Walmsley had only made things worse. "It is not possible for me, or anyone else, to do very much for New Orleans, or the city government, or the employees of the city, unless Semmes Walmsley gets out of the mayor's office," Huey said in a final radio speech in New Orleans before he left.[35]

Two weeks later Walmsley received yet another letter of support, this one from a woman who identified herself only as Mrs. John Singer of North Villere Street in the city's tough Ninth Ward, just blocks from the river's edge. It was a mark of the times that she felt she knew both Walmsley and Huey personally, and that they, in return, cared about her. "I am an old woman with white hair," Mrs. Singer wrote, "but I have a heart of a mother who is grieved to see two of her sons angry with each other." The old woman then added that she had been praying, hoping that peace would come to the city, a peace made rich by the love of forgiveness she was certain right now existed within both Walmsley and Huey. "I am praying," she said, "that He who is the ruler of all hearts may touch both your hearts and you two will be friends again."[36]

There is no record of a response from Walmsley.

10

A Spirit Never Rests

THE OTHERWISE QUIET SUMMER AIR—oppressive heat in New Orleans has always had a deadening effect—was shattered on the afternoon of July 17, 1935, when at least a dozen armed state policemen smashed down the door to Oscar Whilden's French Quarter apartment.

The New Orleans leader of the Square Deal Association, a vehemently anti-Long group that frequently talked of using physical force against Huey, Whilden was also a long-time horse and cattle breeder who only a week before had urged Mayor Walmsley to buck up in his battle against Huey and promised the "unanimous physical support of the Square Deal Association," if it was so needed.[1]

Now Whilden's maid stood to the side as the officers ransacked his third-floor St. Louis Street apartment, pried open an armoir, and confiscated a pistol found in a suitcase. No home is safe, Whilden declared in the raid's aftermath, noting that Louisiana was now a police state where anyone opposed to Huey is "open to the same sort of thing."[2]

It was that kind of season. Only the night before the troopers broke into his apartment, Whilden had attended an organizing meeting of a new Square Deal chapter in the Old Regular stronghold of the Eighth Ward, where a fellow Square Dealer, W. Davis Hass, ominously proclaimed: "We had expected to avoid bloodshed, but the way things seem now, bloodshed is inevitable."[3]

Four days later Whilden, too, was breathing fire. Speaking

during a meeting of the last remaining anti-Long leaders in the city at the downtown DeSoto Hotel—Walmsley was in prominent attendance—Whilden's mind was on the next election battle pitting Huey against his foes. "I am out to murder, kill, bulldoze, steal, or anything else to win this election," Whilden declared, before Walmsley excused himself, claiming he had left his coat in an adjoining room. "I thought Huey Long had gotten your coat and pants both," another Square Dealer cracked as Walmsley departed.[4]

The DoSoto Hotel meeting was soon to become a gathering of historic, legendary importance. It was not simply because of the men who attended—Walmsley, Congressmen John Sandlin and Jared Y. Sanders, Jr., and others—nor the passionate rhetoric on fiery display. The DeSoto gathering would soon be the talk of the country because Huey Long claimed that the men there openly discussed killing him, and for proof he had the typed transcript from a dictograph planted by two of his men in an adjoining room.

The transcript, if authentic, was a fascinating document reflecting the views and frustrations of men who felt that they had run out of options battling Huey. The only option left was to murder him. "I haven't the slightest doubt that Roosevelt would pardon anyone who killed Long," an unidentified voice on the transcript said, before adding: "The best way would be to just hang around Washington and kill him right in the Senate."[5]

Such thoughts were not confined to the DeSoto Hotel meeting. "Everyone was talking about killing him all of the time," recalled Kathleen Gibbons, Mayor Walmsley's niece. "Huey Long was just hated."[6]

"I think after a certain period of time the people who were opposed to Huey just became so desperate by his cleverness that they began to talk more and more in terms of killing him," said Cecil Morgan, the one-time anti-Long legislator.[7]

People sending letters to Walmsley were equally vociferous. "If there was ever a time to kill Huey Long, the time is *now,*" penned Leroy Stafford Boyd, a Tulane University graduate now living in Virginia on July 21. "Long will be far more dangerous in 1936 if he is not killed off *now*."[8]

Others noted a growing resentment in the air. Perry Young, the editor of the New Orleans magazine *Garden* and a Mardi Gras insider who would one day publish a famously anti-Semitic history of the carnival, told Walmsley on August 20 that he had been interviewing the city's street sweepers concerning the fight between the mayor and Huey, and found they were all, to a man, "violent in their talk against Long."[9]

The hot rhetoric blended sickly with the hot weather: on August 9 the temperature peaked just below 100 degrees as a crew of black women collapsed after stitching quilts all day for a Federal Emergency Relief Administration program in a French Quarter factory with no ventilation. It was not a good time for most workers: most city employees were now getting only half-time pay for full-time work. Others got no money at all. Walter Escarra, an employee in the city's license tax department, decided to take matters into his own hands. With a wife and three children to support and a notice from the New Orleans Public Service disconnecting his electricity, Escarra sent a letter to Commissioner of Finance A. Miles Pratt, now one of the most powerful Old Regulars in the city since his break with Walmsley. The letter read, in part, "You had better get me my money. You know it is due." If Pratt failed to deliver, Escarra continued, he might find it prudent to "put in an order for a casket." The following day Escarra was arrested and charged with threatening to kill a public official. Pratt explained that he had tried to be cooperative with Escarra in the past, but there simply wasn't all that much money to go around. That same week, Ulic Burke, another Old Regular now dancing in Huey's harem, accepted a salary increase of more than a thousand dollars as the attorney for the city's Board of Health.[10]

The last week of August was the cruelest: nearly one

thousand families fell off the city's relief rolls due to Huey's refusal to contribute any state money—as every state did— to any federal, and hence, Roosevelt, program.[11]

Walmsley was aghast, charging over the radio on August 23 that the "blood of many a child and mother who has died of starvation, want, and hunger," would now be on Huey's hands.[12]

But on September 6 the news got even worse: up to twelve thousand relief workers would also fall victim in the battle between Long and Roosevelt, a cut made crueler by an earlier 25 percent FERA reduction in June. On the morning of September 6 up to two hundred workers gathered for a protest parade set to travel down the middle of Canal Street. But a banner declaring "Down with Long," was left behind by the marchers who said they were not motivated by politics, they only wanted to work.[13]

By then Huey was back in Louisiana by way of Pennsylvania where he attended the annual meeting of more than two thousand members of the extremely extended Long family clan, and Oklahoma, where on a dusty Labor Day he spoke to more than six thousand people about his Share Our Wealth program. When reporters asked, Huey confirmed—yes, he was running for president.[14]

A surprise announcement followed Huey's return: the legislature would be called into session yet again for a brief five-day session to take up and undoubtedly pass another twenty-one measures, most of which were bills that would gut New Orleans' authority while enhancing Huey's. Two bills were particularly notable: one took yet more state money out of New Orleans with Huey reminding reporters that because Walmsley was still sitting in City Hall, New Orleans must still be made to suffer. Another measure made it an offense, punishable by up to one year in jail and a one thousand-dollar fine, for any federal official to come to Louisiana to dispense money or jobs—an obvious, blatant stab at Roosevelt's relief efforts in the state.[15]

In New Orleans, Walmsley noted with alarm, the latter

measure would mandate the immediate elimination of at
least thirty thousand federal jobs in the metropolitan area,
most of them for laborers in public works projects—if federal people could not come into Louisiana to oversee their
own programs, then there would be no programs at all. But
no one listened. In the old days Walmsley could help design
the Old Regular strategy for Long's legislative sessions. As
mayor and the most visible Old Regular in the city, Walmsley could sound off on certain issues and arouse public
opinion, all to the satisfaction of the Regulars. But he was
an Old Regular no more. He was no longer invited to the
Choctaw Club, and even if he went it would be a futile visit:
the vast majority of Old Regulars in the New Orleans legislative delegation were now solidly voting with Huey.[16]

At the Roosevelt Hotel, Seymour Weiss had a busy summer. Workmen were putting the final touches on the construction of a new restaurant to be called the Dome Rome
while also installing the hotel's first air-conditioning system.
But now with Huey back in town, Weiss spent some time
with his old friend. The two men played golf at Audubon
Park. "We played 18 holes," Weiss later recalled. "That
meant all day. We'd play and talk politics for 30 minutes. Or
walking down the fair-way we would stop in the middle and
talk politics."[17]

By Saturday, September 7, Huey was driven to Baton
Rouge to follow the success of his measures that were being
introduced in the House that night. But it was not until the
following evening, Sunday, September 8, that Huey got
involved in his legislation, as he strode about the House
floor during the protracted reading of the nearly two dozen
bills he wanted to see passed. There were at least two hundred spectators crowding the galleries and railings off the
lower floor of the House of Representatives.

It had been another boiler, a hot day common with the
sight of sweat-soaked seersucker. The distant hymns of Sunday evening church service mingled easily with the songs of
dance orchestras dominating the night's radio fare. Inside

the capitol lawmakers and their assistants noisily went about
the task of convening the special session. Diminutive Allen
Ellender, whom Huey thought had a limited future in politics because he was too short, surveyed the floor from the
Speaker's chair. From above, sat Robert Heilman, an
entranced young professor of English at Louisiana State
University who, watching Huey enter the chamber, later rec-
ollected, "It was my one experience of seeing a single political leader in command."[18]

Huey, for once, seemed serene, amiably chatting with lawmakers as the gallery audience bird-dogged his every move.

Finally he sat, briefly, next to Ellender before agreeing to
an interview with reporter Chick Frampton, who was looking for a colorful Huey quote on the drowning deaths of
hundreds of Civilian Conservation Corps workers in the
Florida Keys several days before. Already Ernest Hemingway,
a Roosevelt-hater, had privately charged FDR with murder in
the affair; now Huey would make the indictment public.[19]

Quickly lifting himself out of the swivel chair beside
Ellender, Huey departed the chamber, swiftly followed by a
small knot of bodyguards on his way to the governor's
office, where he had promised to meet with Frampton.

Down from Huey in the marble corridor a slender young
man, wearing wire-rimmed glasses and a white linen suit,
slipped out from behind a column with a Panama hat in
one hand and a pistol in the other. The gun went off, firing
at least one bullet into Huey, who, slumping, began to run.
His assailant was a physician, a family man, and by all
accounts apolitical. But instantly Dr. Carl Weiss—no relation
to Seymour—was also dead as Huey's bodyguards shot him
so many times, at least fifty, that part of his youthful face was
blown away while his white suit turned red.[20]

Nursing a swollen foot injured in polo that afternoon,
Adj. Gen. Raymond Fleming was relaxing in his Jackson
Barracks quarters just minutes later when he received a
frantic call. "Huey's been shot, Huey's been shot," Governor
Allen was yelling. "Come up quick."[21]

Fleming immediately put the state guard on alert and headed for Baton Rouge. "I can tell you we were all very surprised," recalled Edward P. Benezach, Jr., who was also at Jackson Barracks with his father, the same man frequently assigned to guard Huey. "There had been all kinds of talk about people shooting at Long or killing him, but I never for the life of me thought it would come to that."[22]

The two-lane Airline Highway between New Orleans and Baton Rouge that night was singed with speeding cars: Russell Long, driving up with his mother, brother, and sister in the family DeSoto, ran into a section of broken road; two New Orleans surgeons, summoned by Dr. Arthur Vidrine in Baton Rouge to help remove the bullet that had entered Huey's abdomen and pierced his kidney, swerved their car onto the side of the uneven highway to avoid a collision with an oncoming car when they got stuck; Seymour Weiss and Robert Maestri drove so fast in Weiss's new custom-built Cadillac that they burned out the car's engine.[23]

The doctors and the nurses in attendance that night at Our Lady of the Lake Hospital were hampered in their efforts by the presence of Huey's guards and political cronies. "What a scene! Here was a man maybe dying, and the room was full of politicians," recalled Fred Dent, a politician.[24]

Huey lived through the operation, but during the next day drifted between darkness and light. A team of physicians nearly twenty hours after Huey's shooting came to an alarming conclusion: Huey was dying from the hemorrhaging of his injured kidney, but he was too weak to endure a second operation.[25]

By Tuesday morning, September 10, before sunrise, Huey Long died. "What was the last thing Huey said?" a reporter asked a shaken Seymour Weiss in the hallway outside Huey's room. "I can't remember," Weiss replied before Governor Allen interrupted, "Yes, yes, the last thing he said when he was still conscious was 'I wonder what will happen to my poor university boys.'" It could have been true. Only three days before, Huey, whose pride in LSU knew no bounds, unexpectedly promised the university's president, James Monroe Smith, at least three hundred thousand dollars in state financing to pay for the tuition and lodging of nearly one thousand impoverished students.[26]

The news of Huey's death caught everyone by surprise. The radio networks broke into their regular programming with bulletin flashes. In Hyde Park, New York, Rev. Charles Coughlin—an equally troubling voice of dissent—was visiting President Roosevelt and called Huey's shooting, after glimpsing a giant black newspaper headline, *Huey Long Dead,* "the most regrettable thing in modern history." Roosevelt, finally rid of the onus of Huey, kept his private thoughts private.[27]

In Washington, J. Edgar Hoover received the news by teletype from the FBI's New Orleans office. But when an agent questioned whether or not the FBI should do anything, Hoover revealed his disregard for Huey in a blunt handwritten note: "No investigation, as no Federal law violated."[28]

In Nevada, the poet and LSU professor Robert Penn Warren was returning to Louisiana after a summer out west when a gas station attendant, seeing Warren's Louisiana license plate, told him of Huey's shooting. "And all across the continent I made a habit of stopping at the smallest places, not at big filling stations," Warren later remarked. "Well, people would gather immediately around a Louisiana license and talk about Long, and I got the impression from these conversations that his power was much more diffused than I had supposed."[29]

In Jackson, Mississippi, Mary Morrison, soon to move to New Orleans where she would become an anti-Old Regular reformer, was sharing a boardinghouse with several other young women of her age. Normally upon hearing shouts from the outside news vendor, one of the women would run out and purchase a paper that the rest would all share and read. "But when that boy started yelling 'Huey Long has been shot,' well, we practically killed ourselves getting down the stairs for each one of us to get a paper," Morrison later recalled. "There was that much interest in it. And we were young then. There were other things that should have had more priorities than something about a man we didn't know and what was happening in Louisiana, but that was the way it was."[30]

In New Orleans, Mayor Walmsley issued a brief statement that he read over the radio: "I'm sorry the Senator has died," Walmsley began, adding, "I have consistently opposed violence as the proper means for correcting conditions in Louisiana, and naturally, I sincerely regret this occurrence." Upon hearing the mayor's remarks, his niece, Kathleen Gibbons, reflected: "I think this was the only time he was a hypocrite."[31]

An estimated 250,000 people, people from the shotgun row houses of New Orleans to the swampy bottom of Acadiana and the clay earth of the state's north, traveled so many sun-baked miles to see Huey off. They came by train, car, mule, and some even by foot. Vehicles waiting to cross the Mississippi River by ferry were backed up for eight miles.[32]

Many of the people brought with them sad little offerings, wildflowers plucked from the side of the road, homemade wreaths and candles.

General Fleming dispatched a detail of two officers and twelve men from New Orleans for funeral duty and ordered Sergeant Gouaze to stand guard at Huey's casket, where Gouaze saw Huey lying in state, outfitted in a tuxedo bought for him by Seymour Weiss. "The line started at two in the morning and ran all across that big park outside the capitol," said Gouaze, who noted two vivid responses among the mourners: "Some would come up, kneel down, and cry and cry and cry. Others would come up just to make sure he was dead."[33]

The sun beat bright and unbearably on the capitol crowd on the day of Huey's burial. Both black and white mourners mingled easily, oblivious to the segregationist standards of the day. "Black folk had as much to gain from Huey as poor white folks did," Avery Alexander, who would someday emerge as a major civil rights force in Louisiana, later remarked. "Huey was shaking up the established order, and to that end we cheered him on, 'Go ahead on, Huey,' we said."[34]

More than two hundred people, as the heat and passions rose, passed out. *New York Times* reporter Raymond Daniell noted that the "cement walks and bare earth about the grave itself were hidden by flowers of every description, including tiny bunches of daisies gathered from the fields by admirers too humble to contribute more elaborate belongings." Above him, Daniell saw "negroes perched in live oak trees festooned with Spanish moss," while the roofs of buildings a quarter of a mile away, climbing up the soft hills that surround the capitol grounds, were burdened with hundreds of onlookers.[35]

Finally the great bronze doors fronting the state capitol swung open as Huey's coffin, carried by a struggling Governor Allen, Seymour Weiss, and Robert Maestri, among others, emerged, on its way to its final resting place: a grave dug in the middle of the capitol's 1,200-foot sunken garden the night before by workmen who lined it in concrete reenforced by steel.[36]

A Huey Long follower, Gerald L. K. Smith, who would gradually emerge as one of America's most vicious anti-Semites, gave a stunning funeral oration: "This place marks not the resting place of Huey," Smith said. It marked only the resting place for his body. "His spirit," Smith went on, his magnificent voice reaching the outer limits of the grieving crowd, "shall never rest as long as hungry bodies cry for food, as long as human frames stand naked, as long as homeless wretches haunt this land of plenty."[37]

Seymour Weiss broke off a handful of orchids from the wreath of flowers covering Huey's casket and handed one each to Huey's family, one for wife Rose and one for each of the children.

Then Huey Long was lowered into the earth.

***

For Mayor Walmsley, Huey Long's sudden departure solved nothing.

The symbols of his power continued to exist—when the soil stained with the blood of Jeanne d'Arc was presented by the visiting leaders of Orleans, France, to New Orleans' most prominent leader, it was Walmsley who accepted the grisly gift. When New York's colorful Mayor Fiorella La Guardia bounded into New Orleans for Mardi Gras, Walmsley was his happy host. In fact, as he had for each of the previous six years, Walmsley again presided over carnival, again inviting an orphaned girl to present to King Rex the keys to the city from the mayor's grand reviewing stand at Gallier Hall.[38]

Walmsley still sat as head of the city commission, still enjoyed his airy palace office, and was still greeted or griped about as "the Mayor." But in reality, Walmsley's power had begun to seep away, usurped by the Old Regulars who nearly ritualistically now overruled Walmsley's major decisions in the city commission. Meanwhile the resolve of Huey's heirs to carry on their fallen leader's enmity towards the mayor continued to deprive the city of its funds, making an impossible situation for Walmsley even more so.[39]

The enthusiasms of Huey's men—many of whom were sadly duller than the Kingfish they sought to emulate—were never more evident than on the morning of December 16, 1935, at the official unveiling of the new, nearly two-mile-long, twin-span Huey P. Long Bridge that crossed the Mississippi River. Almost from its inception the bridge, which finally connected both banks of the city, had been a headache for Walmsley. Conceived during his temporary alliance with Huey, the bridge as a works project was subject to the constant scrutiny of the federal Reconstruction Finance Corporation—which provided most of its funding, even as it paid the roughly 1,500 men who labored on the project at levels below the standard union rate.[40]

As construction began, local veterans thought they should be given first consideration for the jobs that would go with the project; then union laborers, skilled craftsmen who had been out of work for months, pleaded their case; meanwhile project engineers tried to sort of some kind of working schedule that would allow the installation of the bridges' massive pilings before the river rose; and everyone, day after day, asked to get more money. It fell to Walmsley to somehow see the project through to completion. And as he had in the past, the mayor sided with the workers in their quest for more money, writing to RFC chairman Jesse Jones—a crusty contrarian in the Roosevelt Administration—on July 17, 1933: "It is my opinion that labor has not been treated fairly and that they are entitled to increased wages." Three months later Walmsley told President Roosevelt that some sort of action from Washington must be taken soon as the workers' families "need the money badly." He added: "The situation here is getting desperate."[41]

But even though Walmsley was able to secure higher wages for the bridges' construction crew, and perhaps more than anyone else in the state deserved credit for spearheading the bridge through to completion, that fact was lost during the official dedication of the bridge. Taking a prominent place among a host of state and national dignitaries, Walmsley was greeted with a thunderous response when his time to speak came: jeers, orchestrated by the same man who had conspired to lengthen the city's garbage strike the summer before—Dr. Joseph O'Hara, head of Huey's New Orleans organization.[42]

"My friends I would appreciate it if you will not make so much noise and allow Mayor Walmsley to speak," Huey's heir, Gov. O. K. Allen, beseeched, removing his hat. But neither his admonitions nor the frantic gestures of the radio announcer who warned that the ceremony could only be allotted so much time, nor even the noted response of Mrs. Huey Long—Rose—who steadfastly applauded the mayor, would silence the detractors. For more than fifteen deafening minutes they booed Walmsley and he stood there and endured it; hundreds of Huey's men who looked at the mayor and saw in him the living nemesis of the now-dead man they had loved. Finally Julia Walmsley, the mayor's durable wife, emerged from the audience and proceeded to the speaker's stand, where she stood arm in arm with her husband and resolutely stared the crowd into silence. "That evening at the dinner to celebrate the occasion," the RFC's Jones later recorded, "the hostile groups occupied tables at opposite ends of the room."[43]

Despite the visible exhibition of continued Long support, Walmsley, Uptown reformers, and the still-vituperative Square Deal Association perceived a possible return to state power with the January 1936 Democratic primary elections that would elect a new governor as well as two U.S. Senators, one of whom would fill out the remaining two years of Huey's term.

But the power and appeal of Huey as a bloodied martyr was not to be underestimated. Running in opposition to the candidates pledged to carrying on Huey's dream—including Governor Allen who was now running for Huey's old Senate seat, and Richard Leche, a relatively obscure parish court judge running for governor with a modified version of Longism—Walmsley and friends forgot that they were actually battling Huey Long yet one more time.

Posters for Allen and Leche curiously bore Huey's face and name; no speech was given without hallowed and frequent references to Huey, and even his voice, booming and bombastic, was heard again on radio as it broadcast in the last week of the campaign three 15-minute recordings Huey made before his death. The Old Regulars, now entirely aligned with the Long faction, pledged the efficacy of "ballots, not bullets," as they slammed Walmsley one final time: "His blundering, stupid leadership," all of the Choctaw Club's ward leaders declared in an open letter, have combined to "make him a man in whom no trust or faith can be placed." It did not matter to the Old Regulars that Walmsley himself was not a candidate in this race, the election provided only the most recent opportunity for the Regulars to display their disdain for the mayor.[44]

On January 21 all of the Long candidates prevailed, creating the kind of election sweep that Huey could only dream of. Allen, Leche, and Allen Ellender—running for the second U.S. Senate seat—won a combined statewide vote of more than 67 percent; they beat the anti-Long candidates, the same candidates Walmsley had endorsed, by two to one. To make matters worse, all eight of Louisiana's congressional seats were won by Long men, while both state chambers were flooded in pro-Long fervor, which created a comfortable margin for Leche to implement virtually any kind of Long program.[45]

Events after this election sped to a blur. Allen, weary after his service under Huey in the most tumultuous years of both men's lives, and frequently complaining of exhaustion, was seized by a coughing spell on the morning of January 25 and died of a cerebral hemorrhage two hours later. A massive funeral on the same capitol grounds where Huey was buried only four months before reminded those who followed of all that had been lost.[46]

One week later, Fred Earhart, the last Old Regular member of the city commission to still support Walmsley, decreed that support pointless and joined the opposition. Walmsley, by March 11, finally agreed to go, but only if the legislature would return to New Orleans all it had taken from the city under Huey. Failing that, Walmsley promised, he would prove as obdurate in the future as he had been in the past—he would stay in Gallier Hall. In a meeting between the new Governor Leche, Seymour Weiss, and Robert Maestri in faraway Hot Springs, Arkansas, Walmsley's conditions were met. Enabling legislation for New Orleans would be approved in return for the mayor's promised abdication.[47]

Maestri, improbably, was selected to become Walmsley's successor, a feat that would be accomplished without an election. The Old Regulars instantly and enthusiastically signed on.[48]

On June 30, said legislation passed, Walmsley, impeccable in a white linen suit, gathered his family and friends in Gallier Hall for an extraordinary ceremony. "It is not my purpose here to launch forth into a long, drawn-out recital of any record of achievement during the last six years," Walmsley said, as he began to do just that in a speech broadcast across the city for forty-five minutes. He never once mentioned the name of Huey Long.[49]

There was champagne on ice, telegrams of tribute from New York's La Guardia and other mayors across the country, and even the loud applause of the Old Regulars who had done so much to undo him.[50]

And then T. Semmes Walmsley walked out of the pristine Gallier Hall as the city's mayor for the last time.

"I'll say this in justice to him," Seymour Weiss later said of Walmsley: "rather than see the city absolutely bankrupt, he graciously resigned."[51]

Weiss, like O. K. Allen, was tired. The passion's fires of life with Huey had singed him too. But, unlike Walmsley, who was also near collapse, Weiss had nothing to resign from. "If I had to do it all over again," Weiss reflected much later, "I would have never gone into politics." At the moment of Walmsley's historic farewell, Weiss floated in his political apogee—the boy from Bunkie had come far indeed, helping to throw all of Louisiana's delegate votes at the 1936 Democratic National Convention in Philadelphia to Roosevelt in return for a promise from Washington to drop the federal prosecution of the remaining leaders of the Long machine. Other Longites—Maestri, Congressman Paul Maloney, and Earl Long, now the state's new lieutenant governor—convinced FDR's men to return to Louisiana its share of the New Deal money revoked during the war against Huey.[52]

But many figures in the Long organization were prosecuted and imprisoned nonetheless, eventually including,

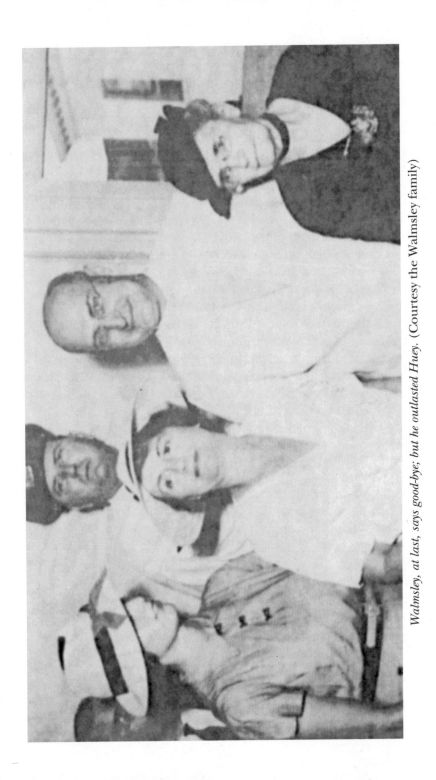

Walmsley, at last, says good-bye; but he outlasted Huey. (Courtesy the Walmsley family)

most famously, Governor Leche and LSU president James Monroe Smith. A second indictment at last did Weiss in. It would take four long years, but by the end of 1940, Weiss ran out of options. Lining up the many people who worked for him at the Roosevelt Hotel, men and women who respected and admired him, Weiss promised them they would not lose their jobs and that the hotel would remain open for business. He, however, was on his way to federal prison. "I feel like hell about it," one of the hotel's garage-men said. "It was something to see," recalled Joe Scaffidi, a room service waiter. "Here he was one of the richest and most powerful men in the city, and he was going to prison. I'll never get over it."[53]

Weiss would, however, rise again. Upon release from prison in the spring of 1942, Weiss became a prominent civic leader and lent his name and hotel to hundreds of charity events and only occasionally spoke out on issues of the day. In the early 1960s, as Louisiana reacted to the Southern civil rights movement by reaffirming many of its most stringent segregation laws, Weiss spoke out for integra-tion by arguing that to do anything else was very bad for business. By the mid-1960s, Weiss was one of the richest men in New Orleans. He lived alone in a seven-room suite on the tenth floor of the Roosevelt, where his meals were sent up by a French chef and the nights were sometimes punctuated by anonymous callers wanting to know if he was the Seymour Weiss who had gone to prison. By the time of his death in 1969, Weiss left an estate valued at more than $15 million. So successfully had he remade his image in the eyes of the city fathers that the obituaries from the New Orleans' two dailies gave only scant attention to Weiss's years with Huey, the same years that would come to fasci-nate dozens of historians and reporters writing about the Long era. "The thing I regret most," he told an interviewer in the 1960s, "is that the papers and the public generally referred to me as a political boss, a Long henchman, never as a hotelman, which is what I really am." Upon his wife

Faye's death in 1960, Weiss devoted all of his attention and affection to the Roosevelt Hotel, calling it "the only child I have . . . I love everything about it."[54]

Other figures in the Long era never returned to their former political prominence. Col. Guy Molony, no longer needed to spearhead an anti-Long putsch, returned to Honduras to oversee a profitable rice mill. He made a splash in the New Orleans papers only one more time, when he told the city's press that he was keeping an eye on possible Nazi activity in his Central American home during World War II. In the late 1950s, sitting down to type out himself his years as a Central American soldier of fortune, Molony attempted to put on paper his remarkable life. But he gave up after a few colorfully written pages and declared, "I cannot tell you for the life of me why I write all of this trash. I am not going to try and write any book and I cannot think of anyone who would be interested in it, even amongst my own family." His global wanderings, he wrote, stemmed from the fact that he had been "born lazy" and avoided work by traveling. But he lived until 1972, traveling between New Orleans and Honduras where, he claimed, he had managed to "accumulate quite a respectable bit of dough." He died on a cold February, a much weaker, frail man than he had been in his prime. He was eighty-eight years old.[55]

The Socialist Louise Jessen, a thorn in the side of both Long and Walmsley, served out one last jail sentence in New Orleans for leading a protest against the local showing of a militaristic movie called *Red Salute* before moving to Hawaii with her husband, Otto. She left at an opportune time: local patriotic groups in New Orleans, beginning in 1936, announced a policy of blacklisting union activists, Tulane University campus peace demonstrators, and members of the city's Socialist and Communist chapters. Many lives would be destroyed before it was over. In Hawaii, for more than a dozen years, Jessen promoted agricultural solutions to the island's economic problems, taught English at a day school, and nurtured a view of a utopian society to her final days. In the spring of 1952, after a long illness, Louise Jessen swallowed a handful of barbiturates and died. She was sixty-five years old. A handwritten note, quoting from Tennyson's "Crossing the Bar," expressed her desire to move on.[56]

The redoubtable Old Regulars, too, eventually disappeared into the night. All that they did and stood for was soon made obsolete by the advances of progress and time. Civil service reform protected the city jobs the Regulars once so cunningly gave and took away, while electric voting machines deprived them of the chance to doctor votes. As new political organizations in New Orleans emerged reflecting the ethnic, racial, and ideological moorings of the people they served, the Regulars were gradually reduced to an insignificant group of older white men, eventually incapable of winning all but the smallest vote as they prodded on with memories of a glory now faded. Even the club they once so magnificently reigned in was gone, the victim of urban progress, as the aging members of the ever-smaller group retreated into semi-regular meetings held in local bars and restaurants.[57]

For Walmsley, the years after Gallier Hall were frustrating ones, tinged with the bitter aftertaste of an undeserved isolation. He was only forty-seven years old when he was forced to leave City Hall, and his public career was behind him. He yearned, however, to return to office, and twice attempted to do so, only to be thwarted by voters who had moved on to other candidates and causes. "Why he wanted to go back to that type of life, none of us could ever figure out," Walmsley's niece, Kathleen Gibbons, later pondered. "But he did want to come back."[58]

At the end of 1937, Walmsley's name reappeared in the papers, but in an unwelcome way: driving home to New Orleans from a hunting trip to Texas, Walmsley struck and killed a black man, he said, who suddenly walked onto the middle of the road. "He was detained on his return," the *New Orleans Item* indelicately noted, "stopping in Crowley to

Sitting in his law office, surrounded by souvenirs from the Old Regulars who betrayed him, Walmsley contemplates what might have been two months after his historic resignation. (Courtesy the Walmsley family)

attend to the particulars of the Negro's death."[59]

Although well known for his fast driving, Walmsley was soon cleared by a coroner's jury who deemed the accident "unavoidable."[60]

Walmsley still had a law practice and the social entry that his name and rank in the Boston and a handful of carnival clubs provided him. The friendships he forged as mayor endured, too, giving Walmsley the title of inspector general and deputy director to Fiorello La Guardia when the New York mayor was tapped to head the new office of Civilian Defense. In early 1942, Walmsley called upon White House connections forged long ago to ask to be returned to active military service. Request fulfilled, Walmsley happily reported for duty on March 6 at Randolph Field in San Antonio, Texas, the so-called "West Point of the Air." He was fifty-three years old.[61]

Three months later, playing softball in the Texas summer heat, Walmsley collapsed and died shortly afterwards of a heart attack. Last rites with the flourish of full military honor were held at the old Walmsley family manor on Prytania Street in the Garden District of New Orleans, where the visiting crowd that came to see his flag-draped coffin in the house's double parlor overflowed to the sidewalk and rain outside.[62]

Other New Orleans mayors, in succeeding years, would have their chroniclers and tributes, but Walmsley's life and career has been largely abandoned by historians. His name today decorates only an Uptown street. A handsome oil painting of his face peers out in the corridor of Gallier Hall, but his is the only portrait without an identifying name. In the few books in which he has earned a mention, Walmsley is primarily remembered for his fights with Huey Long, and then usually because of the damning moniker Huey gave him—"Turkey Head." He is, in all other ways, forgotten.[63]

Huey Long, however, has lived well beyond his time, spiriting the most important political battles in the state for the next half-century to come.[64]

Near the capitol he built, over the state he transformed, Huey Long, more than half a century later, reigns. (Courtesy Louisiana Office of Tourism)

In his intelligent study of Louisiana's political science, Allen P. Sindler in 1956 noted that the state once divided by racial, religious, ethnic, and geographic predilection, had become, in Huey's wake, governed by two distinct and seeming implacable forces: the Long and anti-Long factions. Their battles, deciding dozens of elections at the state, parish, and municipal levels, would wage on for at least the next two generations.[65]

Meanwhile Huey's blood and flesh would predominate, seeing a Long family member in some political office for nearly all of the middle of the twentieth century: Earl as governor three separate times between 1939 and 1960; Russell in the U.S. Senate from 1948 to 1987; and a knot of cousins and widows serving in both Washington and Baton Rouge.[66]

But perhaps Huey's most tangible legacy comes with the essential things he made: the government programs that eventually transformed Louisiana from one of the most ruthlessly irresponsible caretakers of its people in the nation to one of the most beneficient; the thousands and thousands of miles of paved roads transporting Louisiana from its antebellum moorings to a nascent modern age; the Charity Hospital system, with its anchor and architecturally handsome New Orleans base, providing the necessity of health care for those who are frequently the most sick; and the visually satisfying, sleek state capitol, suggestive of Fritz Lang's futuristic society. These are the tangibles that Long's leadership wrought.[67]

It is no surprise then that the emotional and aesthetic highlight of any visit to Baton Rouge, decades after Long's death, remains the bronze likeness of him erected in 1948 and lit in a sort of celestial glow from the very capitol Long created. Here, finally, Huey Long stands as his own eternal tribute.

Notes

CHAPTER 1

1. Rosemary James, "The Majority Leader—A Short Biography of a Controversial Man," *New Orleans Magazine* 5, no. 7 (July 1971): 42; Mary Louise Christovich et al., *New Orleans Architecture, Volume II: The American Sector* (Gretna: Pelican Publishing Company, 1972), 61.

2. T. Harry Williams, *Huey Long* (New York: Vintage Books, 1981), 434-35; Al Rose and Edmond Souchon, *New Orleans Jazz—A Family Album* (Baton Rouge: Louisiana State University Press, 1984), 81.

3. A. J. Leibling, *The Earl of Louisiana* (Baton Rouge: Louisiana State University Press, 1990), 8.

4. *Soards City Directory, 1935* (New Orleans: Soards Publishing Company, 1935), 138, 1076, 1222, 1257; *The WPA Guide to New Orleans* (New York: Pantheon Books, 1983), 290; Augusto Miceli, *The Pickwick Club of New Orleans* (New Orleans: The Pickwick Press, 1964), 266; Photos 1979.325.5011, 1979.325.5022, 1979.325.4953, 1979.325.4958, and 1979.325.5003, The Charles Frank Collection, The Historic New Orleans Collection, New Orleans, La.

5. Leonard V. Huber, *Landmarks of New Orleans* (New Orleans: Louisiana Landmarks Society, 1984), 38; Rose and Souchon, *New Orleans Jazz*, 226; Robert Mann, *Legacy to Power—Senator Russell Long of Louisiana* (New York: Paragon House, 1992), 39.

6. James Gillis, interview by author, tape recording, New Orleans, La., 25 March 1995.

7. Cecil Morgan, interview by author, tape recording, New Orleans, La., 10 April 1995.

8. Paul A. Greenburg, "Fabled Hotel Poised to Enter New Century," *Preservation in Print* 20, no. 11 (November 1993): 6; Jeff Redford, "Can an Old Hotel Change Its Sheets?" *New Orleans Magazine* 9 (September 1975): 37-44; Public Relations Department, the Fairmont Hotel, New Orleans, Louisiana; *WPA Guide to New Orleans,* liv.

9. *WPA Guide to New Orleans,* liv; "Blue Room Opens at the Roosevelt," *Times-Picayune,* 3 October 1934, p. 16, col. 3; Mel Washburn, "Blue Room Reopened," *New Orleans Item,* 2 October 1934, p. 22, col. 6.

10. Joe Scaffidi, interview by author, tape recording, New Orleans, La., 11 April 1995; Williams, *Huey Long,* 435-36.

11. Greenburg, "Fabled Hotel Poised," 6; *WPA Guide to New Orleans,* lx; Russell Long, interview by author, tape recording, New Orleans, La., 13 April 1995.

12. Tom Voelker, "Local Color—The Hands That Kneaded the Longs," *New Orleans Magazine* 10, no. 7 (July 1976): 116.

13. Eleanor Early, *New Orleans Holiday* (New York: Rhinehart and Company, 1947), 23-26.

14. Long, interview; Williams, *Huey Long,* 838.

15. Williams, *Huey Long,* 430-32; William Ivy Hair, *The Kingfish and His Realm* (Baton Rouge: Louisiana State University Press, 1991), 192-93; Glen Jeansonne, *Messiah of the Masses* (New York: Harper Collins Publishers, 1993), 83; "J. Y. and Huey Mix in Fistic Combat," *Times-Picayune,* 16 November 1927, p. 1, col. 6.; "Long Flees in Fight with J. Y. Sanders," *New Orleans Item,* 16 November 1927, p. 1, col. 3.

16. Gillis, interview.

17. *WPA Guide to New Orleans,* lxi, 108, 313; Redford, "Can an Old Hotel Change," 37-44; Angelo Butera, interview by author, tape recording, New Orleans, La., 13 April 1995.

18. "Seymour Weiss, a Key Advisor in Huey Long Regime, Is Dead," *New York Times,* 19 September 1969, p. 47, col. 3; "Business, Civic Leader Is Dead," *Times-Picayune,* 18 September 1969, p. 1, col. 5; David Zinman, "Seymour Weiss Is Man Who Climbed Back from Disaster," *Baton Rouge Morning Advocate,* 5 August 1963, p. 3A, col. 1.

19. Zinman, "Seymour Weiss Is Man Who Climbed Back from Disaster," p. 3A, col. 1; Williams, *Huey Long,* 374-75.

20. "Seymour Weiss, a Key Advisor in Huey Long Regime, Is Dead," p. 47, col. 3; By the time of Weiss's death in 1969, his estate had an estimated worth of nearly $10 million and included holdings in more than 80 major corporations including Dow Chemical, Texaco, and Holiday Inn. As late as 1996, the descendents of Seymour Weiss were still sifting through what they hoped would be their share of his massive estate (Weiss Succession, Number 498-163 folder, Civil District Court of New Orleans, La.).

21. Ed Reed, *Requiem for a Kingfish* (Baton Rouge: Award Publishers, 1986), 131. Reed says Weiss was "suave to the point of oiliness." Hodding Carter, a highly partisan anti-Long journalist, refers to Weiss as "an oily former shoe clerk" (*The Aspirin Age, 1919-41* [New York: Touchstone Books, 1976], 340). Seymour Weiss, interview by T. Harry Williams, 3 July 1957, the Interview Collection, the Louisiana Lower Mississippi Valley Collections, Hill Memorial Library, Louisiana State University, Baton Rouge, La.

22. Butera, interview; Scaffidi, interview.

23. Weiss, interview.

24. Williams, *Huey Long,* 826, 876; Hair, *Kingfish and His Realm,* 169; John Salvaggio, *New Orleans' Charity Hospital—A Story of Physicians, Politics, and Poverty* (Baton Rouge: Louisiana State University Press, 1992), see pages 332-33 for Salvaggio's amusing interview with longtime New Orleans sculptor Enrique Alfarez and his use of ducks in his work to symbolize Long's paycheck deductions; Only Huey and Weiss knew the exact amount of money in the deduct box, and as both men were secretive, no one else was ever sure. Before his death in 1935, Huey moved the deduct box out of the Roosevelt Hotel, and even Weiss was not sure where it ultimately ended up. What happened to the deduct box, a longtime employee with the patronage-rich New Orleans Sewerage and Water Board later related, became a favorite Old Regular guessing game (Williams, *Huey Long,* 862, 876; Louis Reidl, interview by author, tape recording, New Orleans, La., 5 January 1993).

25. Weiss, interview; Senate Special Committee on Campaign Expenditures, *Hearings Before the Special Committee on Investigation of Campaign Expenditures,* 72nd Cong., 2nd sess., 5 October 1932 and 6 October 1932, 462-93 and 73rd Cong., 1st sess., 3 February 1933 and 17 February 1933, 1047-60; "Long Bids Defiance to Senate Inquiry," *New York Times,* 8 February 1933, p. 2, col. 6; "Paid Long Money, Kept No Record," *New York Times,* 10 February 1933, p. 2,

216 HUEY LONG INVADES NEW ORLEANS

col. 6; "Committee Defied by Weiss on Use of Funds in Campaign," *Times-Picayune,* 8 February 1933, p. 1, col. 8; "Offer by Witness to 'Get Out of City' Charged by Donner," *Times-Picayune,* 10 February 1933, p. 1, col. 8; "Vote Investigations Recess to Report Results to Senate," *Times-Picayune,* 18 February 1933, p. 1, col. 8.

26. "Committee Defied by Weiss," p. 1, col. 8; "Offer by Witness to 'Get Out of City' Charged by Donner," p. 1, col. 8; "Vote Investigations Recess to Report Results to Senate," p. 1, col. 8.

27. Weiss, interview.

28. Ibid.

29. Raymond Fleming, interview by T. Harry Williams, 25 June 1957, the Interview Collection, the Louisiana Lower Mississippi Valley Collections, Hill Memorial Library, Louisiana State University, Baton Rouge, La.; "Militia Mobilized in New Orleans," *New York Times,* 1 August 1934, p. 9, col. 1; "Long's Guardsmen Seize Poll Lists in New Orleans," *Christian Science Monitor,* 31 July 1934, p. 1, col. 5; "Militia Seizes Registration Office Under Allen's Order," *Times-Picayune,* 31 July 1934, p. 1, col. 8.

30. "Militia Seizes Registration Office," p. 1, col. 8; Jeansonne, *Messiah of the Masses,* 49; Nicholas Lemann, "The Not So Great Dictator," *New York Review of Books* 39, no. 10 (28 May 1992): 17-22; Robert S. McElvaine, *The Great Depression, America, 1929-1941* (New York: Times Books, 1993), 246-49.31. Williams, *Huey Long,* 723; Edward Gouaze, interview by author, tape recording, New Orleans, La., 22 January 1996; Edward P. Benezach, Jr., interview by author, tape recording, New Orleans, La., 19 January 1996.

CHAPTER 2

1. F. Raymond Daniell, "Long Keeps Rule Over Voter Rolls," *New York Times,* 8 August 1934, p. 12, col. 2.

2. At the time of Walmsley's birth, his family lived at 1236 Fourth Street in the Garden District, moving to the grander Prytania property when Walmsley was about six years old. *Soards City Directory, 1897* (New Orleans: Soards Publishing, 1897), 884. *Soards City Directory, 1898* (New Orleans: Soards Publishing, 1898), 836; *WPA Guide to New Orleans,* 352; Daniell, "Long Keeps Rule," p. 12, col. 2; "Major Walmsley, Foe of Huey Long," *New York Times,* 18 June

1942, p. 12, col. 3; "Walmsley Dies," *Times-Picayune*, 18 June 1942, p. 1, col. 4; "Rites Set for Walmsley Friday," *New Orleans States*, 18 June 1942, p. 1, col. 2.

3. "Walmsley Dies," p. 1, col. 4; Walker Percy, *The Moviegoer* (New York: Ballantine Books, 1988), 25.

4. Hodding Carter, ed., *The Past as Prelude—New Orleans 1718-1968* (New Orleans: Tulane University Press, 1968), 324; "Major Walmsley, Foe of Huey Long," p. 12, col. 3; "Walmsley Dies," p. 1, col. 4; "Rites Set for Walmsley Friday," p. 1, col. 2.

5. Williams, *Huey Long*, 185; Pamela Tyler, "Silk Stockings and Ballot Boxes: Women of the Upper Class and New Orleans Politics: 1930-1955" (Ph.D. diss., Tulane University, 1989), 3, 5-6; Kathleen Gibbons, interview by author, tape recording, New Orleans, La., 7 May 1996.

6. Carter, *Past as Prelude*, 324; "Major Walmsley, Foe of Huey Long," p. 12, col. 3; "Walmsley Dies," p. 1, col. 4; "Rites Set for Walmsley Friday," p. 1, col. 2; *Eastern Louisiana—A History* (Louisville, Kentucky: The Historical Record Association, circa 1938), 628-30; W. K. Patrick, *Club Men of Louisiana in Caricature* (Aurora, New York: Patrick Publishing, 1917), 94; James M. Thompson, *Louisiana Today* (New Orleans: Louisiana Society, 1939), 147; Walmsley family scrapbook in possession of Kathleen Gibbons and T. Semmes Favrot; Gibbons, interview.

7. "Rites Set for Walmsley Friday," p. 1, col. 2.

8. "Rites Set for Walmsley Friday," p. 1, col. 2.

9. *Mayors of New Orleans* (New Orleans: Works Project Administration, 1940), 238; "Labor—New Orleans, et al," *Time* 14, no. 3 (15 July 1929): 13; "Labor—Blood in New Orleans," *Time* 14, no. 9 (26 August 1929): 10; Adam Fairclough, "The Public Utilities Industry in New Orleans: A Study in Capital, Labor and Government, 1894-1929," *Louisiana History* 22 (winter 1981): 63-65; Bernard A. Cook and James R. Watson, *Louisiana Labor—From Slavery to "Right to Work"* (New York: University Press of America, 1985), 180-89.

10. Cook and Watson, *Louisiana Labor*, 180-89; "Walmsley Asks Police Ban on Radicals," *Times-Picayune*, 5 March 1931, p. 1 col. 1.

11. "City Employees to Receive Pay Today in Cash," *Times-Picayune*, 14 June 1930, p. 1, col. 1; "Mayor Promises Paving, Better Police, Traffic Safety, and New City Hall," *Times-Picayune*, 6 May 1930, p. 1, col. 6; Howard K. Smith, *Events Leading Up To My Death—The Life of*

a Twentieth Century Reporter (New York: St. Martin's Press, 1996), 23; Howard K. Smith, interview by author, tape recording, New Orleans, La., 17 June 1996.

12. *Thirty-five Years of Progress in New Orleans* (New Orleans: Hyatt Press, circa 1934), 69-71; James Fitzmorris, *Frankly Fitz!* (Gretna: Pelican Publishing Company, 1992), 113; James Fitzmorris, interview by author, tape recording, New Orleans, La., 11 November 1994.

13. Robert Maloney, interview by author, tape recording, New Orleans, La., 7 September 1994.

14. Ibid.

15. Williams, *Huey Long,* 189.

16. Iris Kelso, "When the Caucus Ruled the World," *New Orleans Magazine* 5, no. 5 (May 1971): 20.

17. Robert Maloney, interview.

18. George M. Reynolds, *Machine Politics in New Orleans, 1897-1926* (New York: Columbia University Press, 1936), 109.

19. Harnett T. Kane, *Louisiana Hayride: The American Rehearsal for Dictatorship, 1928-1940* (Gretna: Pelican Publishing Company, 1986), 32-33; Tyler, "Silk Stockings and Ballot Boxes," 21.

20. Edward F. Haas, *DeLesseps S. Morrison and the Image of Reform— New Orleans Politics, 1946-1961* (Baton Rouge: Louisiana State University Press, 1986), 8.

21. "Walmsley, Council Ticket and Stanley Win Nominations," *Times-Picayune,* 5 February 1930, p. 1, col. 6; "Walmsley Given Night Serenade by Legion Band," *Times-Picayune,* 6 February 1930, p. 3, col. 3.

22. "Mayor Promises Paving," p. 1, col. 6.

23. "Mayor Promises Paving," p. 1, col. 6. In the summer of 1934, Walmsley drove nearly 1,000 miles in less than 24 hours, an admirable feat given the substandard condition of the mostly two-laned roadways of the 1930s ("Mayor Offers to Resign," *Times-Picayune,* 31 July 1934, p. 3, col. 3).

24. Douglas L. Smith, *The New Deal in the Urban South* (Baton Rouge: Louisiana State University Press, 1988), 21-22; "Mayor Walmsley Attends Lunch with De Priest," *Times-Picayune,* 28 February 1930, p. 1, col, 2; "Mayor Explains Attendance at Thompson Lunch," *Times-Picayune,* 2 March 1930, p. 1, col. 2.

25. "All City Employees Given Warning to Take Item-Tribune," *Times-Picayune,* 25 October 1931, p. 1, col. 1; "Police and Firemen Seek Subscriptions for Item-Tribune," *Times-Picayune,* 13 December 1931, p. 1, col. 1.

26. Paul Maloney, interview by T. Harry Williams, 26 June 1957, the Interview Collection, the Louisiana Lower Mississippi Valley Collections, Hill Memorial Library, Louisiana State University, Baton Rouge, La.

27. Williams, *Huey Long,* 276; Hair, *Kingfish and His Realm,* 159-60; Jeansonne, *Messiah of the Masses,* 56-57.

28. Allen P. Sindler, *Huey Long's Louisiana: State Politics, 1920-1952* (Baltimore: Johns Hopkins University Press, 1956), 45-46.

29. Williams, *Huey Long,* 22-24; Hair, *Kingfish and His Realm,* 15-19; Sindler, *Huey Long's Louisiana,* 26.

30. Neal R. Peirce and Jerry Hagstrom, *The Book of America—Inside Fifty States Today* (New York: Warner Books, 1984), 495.

31. Sindler, *Huey Long's Louisiana,* 26.

32. C. Vann Woodward, *Origins of the New South, 1877-1913* (Baton Rouge: Louisiana State University Press, 1971), 235-63; Stefan Lorant, *The Presidency* (New York: Macmillan Company, 1952), 425-99. For the Populist influence in Louisiana, see William Ivy Hair, *Bourbonism and Agrarian Protest, Louisiana Politics, 1877-1900* (Baton Rouge: Louisiana State University Press, 1971), 200-204, 214-15.

33. Williams, *Huey Long,* 26; Alan Brinkley, *Voices of Protest—Huey Long, Father Coughlin and the Great Depression* (New York: Vintage Books, 1983), 18; Jeansonne, *Messiah of the Masses,* 27-31; Hair, *Kingfish and His Realm,* 86-100, 102-3, 107, 115-18.

34. "Long Arrives for Dinner of 1,000 Friends," *New Orleans Item,* 15 February 1928, p. 5, col. 1.

35. Robert Webb Williams, "Martin Behrman: Mayor and Political Boss of New Orleans, 1904-1926" (master's thesis, Tulane University, 1952), 9.

36. Williams, *Huey Long,* 355-83; Hair, *Kingfish and His Realm,* 174, 178-88, 207; Brinkley, *Voices of Protest,* 29; Jeansonne, *Messiah of the Masses,* 73-83.

37. "Mayor and Long Admit Parley Was Held, But Deny 'Merger,'" *Times-Picayune,* 10 March 1931, p. 1, col 1.

38. Williams, *Huey Long*, 460-80; Jeansonne, *Messiah of the Masses*, 90-91; Sindler, *Huey Long's Louisiana*, 70-73; Michael L. Kurtz and Morgan D. Peoples, *Earl K. Long—The Sage of Uncle Earl and Louisiana Politics* (Baton Rouge: Louisiana State University Press, 1990), 46.

CHAPTER 3

1. Frank Driggs and Harris Lewine, *Black Beauty, White Heat—A Pictorial History of Classic Jazz* (New York: Morrow and Company, 1982), 20.

2. Rose and Souchon, *New Orleans Jazz*, 216; *WPA Guide to New Orleans*, lxi.

3. Kurtz and Peoples, *Earl K. Long—The Saga of Uncle Earl and Louisiana Politics*, 35; Louis Prima, Number 202-140, Division E, Docket 5, Civil District Court of New Orleans; Lyle Saxon, "Have a Good Time While You Can," *Century Magazine* 117, no. 1 (November 1928): 85-94.

4. James K. Feibleman, "Literary New Orleans Between World Wars," *Southern Review* 1 (1965): 702; Richard Kennedy, *Literary New Orleans* (Baton Rouge: Louisiana State University Press, 1990), xiv. For an insightful survey of the city's influence in literature, see Violet Harrington Bryan's *The Myth of New Orleans in Literature* (Knoxville: University of Tennessee, 1993).

5. *Louisiana Almanac 1984-85* (Gretna: Pelican Publishing Company, 1984), 142; A. F. Perkins, *Who's Who in Colored Louisiana* (Baton Rouge: Douglas Loan Company, 1930), 19; Rachel Violette Campbell, "At Home in New Orleans," *Commonweal* 22, no. 8 (June 1935): 209-11; James Lincoln Collier, *Louis Armstrong—An American Genius* (New York: Oxford University Press, 1983), 13.

6. Adam Fairclough, *Race and Democracy—The Civil Rights Struggle in Louisiana, 1915-1972* (Athens: The University of Georgia Press, 1995), 23; Paul Oliver, *Songsters and Saints—Vocal Traditions on Race Records* (Cambridge: Cambridge University Press, 1984), 275; William Ivy Hair, *Carnival of Fury—Robert Charles and the New Orleans Race Riot of 1900* (Baton Rouge: Louisiana State University Press, 1976), 69-93; Pierce F. Lewis, *Contemporary Metropolitan America—Nineteenth Century Ports* (Cambridge: Ballinger Publishing, 1976), 146-47.

7. Daniel Rosenberg, *New Orleans Dockworkers—Race, Labor, and Unionism* (New York: State University of New York Press, 1988), 174; Smith, *New Deal in the Urban South*, 31-33; Cook and Watson, *Louisiana Labor—From Slavery to "Right to Work,"* 199-216.

8. Fairclough, "Public Utilities Industry in New Orleans," 63-65; *Streetcar Stories*, WYES-TV documentary, 60 min., New Orleans, 1995; Charles Gerald Carpenter, "The New Orleans Street Railway Strike of 1929-1930" (master's thesis, Tulane University, 1970).

9. Joy L. Jackson, *Where the River Runs Deep* (Baton Rouge: Louisiana State University Press, 1993), 152; Smith, *New Deal in the Urban South*, 11.

10. Salvaggio, *New Orleans' Charity Hospital*, 122-23.

11. Smith, interview.

12. Avery Alexander, interview by author, tape recording, New Orleans, La., 20 June 1996.

13. Louise S. Jessen, "The Student and Politics," *The Newcomb Lagniappe* 27 (January 1935): 12-14; "Council Begins Canvassing Bond Vote," *New Orleans States*, 4 April 1934, p. 1, col. 1; Floyd Newlin, interview by author, tape recording, New Orleans, La., 21 April 1997.

14. Cook and Watson, *Louisiana Labor*, 199-200; Roman Heleniak, "Local Reaction to the Great Depression in New Orleans, 1929-1933," *Louisiana History* 10 (spring 1969): 294-97; Gibbons, interview; "Mayor Will Seek $250,000 to Meet Jobless Problem," *Times-Picayune*, 12 July 1931, p. 10, col. 1.

15. Gillis, interview.

16. *Fiscal and Administrative Survey of New Orleans* (New York: National Industrial Conference Board, 1933), 26-28; see also the semiannual *Statistical Report of the Attorney General* (New Orleans: Attorney General's Office, 1931, 1932, 1933, 1934, and 1935).

17. *Fiscal and Administrative Survey of New Orleans*, 216-18.

18. Lewis, *Contemporary Metropolitan America*, 160-63; "Shotgun House Month," *Preservation in Print* 24 (March 1997): 19-22.

19. Brinkley, *Voices of Protest*, 71.

20. Meigs O. Frost, "Banquet Seals Pledge for State Peace and Progress," *New Orleans States*, 18 September 1930, p. 2, col. 1; "Governor Declares Himself for Program of Progress at Testimonial Banquet," *Times-Picayune*, 18 September 1930, p. 2, col. 1; "Prosperity Is Pledged by Long," *New Orleans Item*, 18 September

1930, p. 10, col. 3; Huey Long, *Every Man a King* (Chicago: Quadrangle Books, 1964), 229-30.

21. Hair, *Kingfish and His Realm,* 207; "Louisiana Takes Long to Its Breast," *New York Times,* 5 October 1930, p. 6, col. 3; Long, *Every Man a King,* 229-30.

22. Frost, "Banquet Seals Pledge," p. 2, col. 1; "Governor Declares Himself for Program of Progress," p. 2, col. 1; "Prosperity Is Pledged by Long," p. 10, col. 3.

23. "Edmund G. Burke Boasted by Long and Old Regulars," *Times-Picayune,* 9 March 1931, p. 1, col. 1; "Governor Backed by Old Regulars for Ewing's Post," *Times-Picayune,* 3 July 1931, p. 1, col. 1; "Choctaw Forces to Support Allen in Governor's Race," *Times-Picayune,* 24 July 1931, p. 1, col. 1.

24. "Choctaw Forces to Support Allen," p. 1, col. 1.

25. Webster Smith, *The Kingfish: A Biography of Huey P. Long* (New York: G. P. Putnam's Sons, 1933), 229; "'Merger' Unites Political Gangs, Williams Warns," *Times-Picayune,* 9 March 1931, p. 1, col. 1.

26. Williams, *Huey Long,* 482; George N. Coad, "Truce in Politics Hailed in Louisiana," *New York Times,* 12 July 1931, sec. 3, p. 5, col. 6.

27. Williams, *Huey Long,* 539; "Delegation That Accompanied Senator Long to Washington," *Times-Picayune,* 27 January 1932, p. 3, col. 3; Sindler, *Huey Long's Louisiana,* 78; Hair, *Kingfish and His Realm,* 225.

28. Hair, *Kingfish and His Realm,* 226; Williams, *Huey Long,* 552; "Allen, Walmsley, Fournet in Group on Special Car," *New Orleans Item-Tribune,* 24 January 1932, p. 1, col. 7; "Long to Take Seat in Senate," *Times-Picayune,* 24 January 1932, p. 1, col. 1.

29. Hair, *Kingfish and His Realm,* 234; "Mrs. Long Thrills Over Oath; Not Sure of Residency Yet," *New Orleans Item,* 27 January 1932, p. 2, col. 4; "Delegation That Accompanied Senator Long to Washington," p. 3, col. 3.

30. James MacGregor Burns, *Roosevelt—The Lion and the Fox* (New York: Harcourt and Brace, 1956), 135-42; Martha Swain, *Pat Harrison—The New Deal Years* (Jackson: University Press of Mississippi, 1978), 27-30; Hair, *Kingfish and His Realm,* 242-45; Williams, *Huey Long,* 571-82.

31. "Huey Long's Feuds Menace Roosevelt," *New York Times,* 27 June 1932, p. 11, col. 3; "Credentials Fight May Sway Result," *New*

York Times, 28 June 1932, p. 1, col. 6; "Walsh Defeats Shouse for Chairman; Long's Delegation Recognized," *Times-Picayune,* 29 June 1932, p. 1, col. 6.

32. James E. Crown, "Close Vote in Louisiana Contest Is Forecast," *New Orleans States,* 28 June 1932, p. 1, col. 5; Williams, *Huey Long,* 579; "Delegate Contests Cause Tense Hour," *New York Times,* 29 June 1932, p. 14, col. 1.

33. "Delegate Contests Cause Tense Hour," p. 14, col. 1.

34. Williams, *Huey Long,* 603; Hair, *Kingfish and His Realm,* 252; "200 Sign Up with League," *New Orleans Item,* 2 November 1932, p. 1, col. 6; "Walmsley Hits G.O.P. in East," *New Orleans Item,* 1 November 1932, p. 2, col. 1; "Allen Predicts Big Victory for Gov. Roosevelt," *New Orleans Item,* 1 November 1932, p. 1, col. 6;

35. Hilda Phelps Hammond, *Let Freedom Ring* (New York: Farrar & Rhinehart, 1936), 63; Jeansonne, *Messiah of the Masses,* 131; Thomas Martin, *Dynasty—The Longs of Louisiana* (New York: G. P. Putnam's Sons, 1960), 81-85; Sindler, *Huey Long's Louisiana,* 75.

36. For more on Hammond and her crusade against Long, see Pamela Tyler's *Silk Stockings and Ballot Boxes, Women and Politics in New Orleans, 1920-1963* (Athens: University of Georgia Press, 1996), 32-77; Doris Kearns, *Lyndon Johnson and the American Dream* (New York: Harper & Row, 1976), 92. In the 1960s both the president and vice-president of the United States were admirers of Huey Long. In his memoirs, Hubert H. Humphrey said he thought Long was a demagogue, but that he also "had guts. And commitment." Humphrey, who attended LSU in the late 1930s, adds that Huey Long tried to change things in Louisiana for the better, "and the people knew it" (Humphrey, *The Education of a Public Man—My Life and Politics* [Minneapolis: The University of Minnesota Press, 1991], 40-41).

37. Swain, *Pat Harrison,* 127-29; Merle Miller, *Plain Speaking—An Oral Biography of Harry S. Truman* (New York: Berkley Publishing, 1974), 170-71.

38. For more on the Share Our Wealth movement, see Alan Brinkley, "Huey Long, the Share Our Wealth Movement, and the Limits of Depression Dissidence," *Louisiana History* 22 (spring 1981): 117-34; Arthur M. Schlesinger, Jr., *The Age of Roosevelt—The Politics of Upheaval* (Boston: Houghton Mifflin, 1960), 62-65; Edwin Amenta, Kathleen Dunlevy, and Mary Bernstein, "Stolen

Thunder? Huey Long's 'Share the Wealth,' Political Mediation, and the Second New Deal," *American Sociological Review* 59 (October 1994); 678-702; Henry M. Christmas, ed., *Kingfish to America: Share Our Wealth* (New York: Schocken Books, 1985).

39. Brinkley, "Huey Long, the Share Our Wealth Movement, and the Limits of Depression Dissidence," 117-34.

40. Williams, *Huey Long*, 638-40; Jeansonne, *Messiah of the Masses*, 148-49; "Petitioners Call Long a 'Traitor,'" *New York Times*, 15 April 1933, p. 9, col. 1; "Louisiana Revolt Harries Huey Long," *New York Times*, 8 October 1933, p. 26, col. 1; William E. Leuchtenberg, "FDR and the Kingfish," *American Heritage Magazine* 36 (October-November 1985): 56-63; Schlesinger, *Age of Roosevelt*, 55-56.

41. Circular B38, William B. Wisdom Collection, Special Collections, Howard-Tilton Memorial Library, Tulane University, New Orleans, La.; "Long Breaks with Group," *New York Times*, 14 September 1933, p. 4, col. 5.

42. "Long's Ultimatum to Old Regulars Spurned by Caucus," *Times-Picayune*, 20 December 1933, p. 1, col. 8; "Long Denounces, Breaks with Mayor," *New Orleans States*, 21 December 1933, p. 1, col. 8.

43. "Long's Ultimatum to Old Regulars Spurned by Caucus," p. 1, col. 8.

44. "'War On'; Long Men Arrested, Senator Offers No Ticket," *Times-Picayune*, 21 December 1933, p. 1, col. 7.

45. "Long Denounces, Breaks with Mayor," p. 1, col. 8. "Mayor Says Long Agreed to Aid Him," *New Orleans States*, 22 December 1933, p. 1, col. 8.

46. Weiss, interview.

47. "'War On'; Long Men Arrested, Senator Offers No Ticket," p. 1, col. 7.; "Mayor Says Long Agreed to Aid Him," p. 1, col. 8.

48. "'War to the Knife,' Mayor Pledges Crusade," *New Orleans Item*, 3 January 1934, p. 4, col. 1.

49. The actual vote for Roosevelt in New Orleans was 81,536 to President Hoover's 4,939 ("Unofficial Figures for City," *Times-Picayune*, 9 November 1932, p. 10, col. 4); "Ladies and Gentlemen: The President," *New Orleans Item-Tribune*, special FDR tribute edition, 4 March 1934, pp. 1-16; the Cooke quotation is from the

1994 three-part PBS *American Experience* series, *FDR*, part one, "The Center of the Universe."

50. "Huey Long Gets a Black Eye in Row at Long Island Party," *New York Times*, 29 August 1933, p. 1, col. 3; Williams, *Huey Long*, 648-54; Hair, *Kingfish and His Realm*, 258-59; Leuchtenberg, "FDR and the Kingfish," 56-63; "A Senator's Black Eye," *Times* (London), 22 September 1933, p. 11, col. 6.

51. Jeansonne, *Messiah of the Masses*, 136; Mason Dixon, "Senator Long Faces Revolt in Louisiana," *New York Times*, 5 November 1933, sec. 8, p. 2, col. 8.

CHAPTER 4

1. Hermann B. Deutsch, "Factions Dig into Campaign," *New Orleans Item-Tribune*, 7 January 1934, p. 1, col. 2. For general information on the 1934 mayoralty race, see the Albert L. Lieutaud Collection, Huey Long, 1934-1935, Box 1, Folder 25, Special Collections, Howard-Tilton Memorial Library, Tulane University, New Orleans, La.

2. Deutsch, "Factions Dig into Campaign," p. 1, col. 2; "Boom Ahead for Alcohol Plants Here," *New Orleans Tribune*, 30 December 1933, p. 1, col. 6; Edward Behr, *Prohibition—Thirteen Years That Changed America* (New York: Arcade Publishing, 1996), 235-36.

3. Mel Washburn, "The Spotlight," *New Orleans Tribune*, 2 January 1934, p. 4, col. 1; *Statistical Report of the Attorney General*, January 1 to June 30, 1933 (New Orleans: Attorney General's Office, 1933), 50; and January 1 to June 30, 1934 (New Orleans: Attorney General's Office, 1934), 42.

4. Washburn, "The Spotlight," p. 4, col. 1; Mel Washburn, "The Spotlight," *New Orleans Tribune*, 3 January 1934, p. 9, col. 2; Mel Washburn, "The Spotlight," *New Orleans Tribune*, 4 January 1934, p. 14, col. 4; "Mayans Turned Over New Leaf in Gala New Year's Festivity," *Hullabaloo* 5 January 1934, p. 4, col. 3; Mel Washburn, "The Spotlight," *New Orleans Tribune*, 28 December 1933, p. 4, col. 4; "Prominent Society Visitors Bid City Adieu,"*New Orleans Item*, 3 January 1934, p. 8, col. 1.

5. "Boom Ahead for Alcohol Plants Here," p. 1, col. 6; "N.Y. Night Life Big; Jersey Off," *Variety* 29, no. 26 (26 June 1934): 48; Lewis A.

Erenberg, "From New York to Middletown: Repeal and the Legitimization of Nightlife in the Great Depression," *American Quarterly* 38 (winter 1986): 761-78.

6. "Emancipation Celebration Here with 2 Parades and 4 Anniversary Programs," *Louisiana Weekly*, 6 January 1934, p. 1, col. 7; "Negroes Fete Emancipation Anniversary," *New Orleans Tribune*, 2 January 1934, p. 2, col. 1; "Crowds at Fete," *New Orleans Item*, 8 January 1934, p. 7, col. 1; "Home Anniversary Sunday," *Jewish Ledger*, 5 January 1934, p. 9, col. 3. Of the three major candidates who would run in the 1934 mayor's race, only Walmsley actively solicited the city's Jewish vote with ads in the *Ledger* on January 19 and 26, 1934. For a rough breakdown on the number of Jews living in New Orleans in the 1930s see *The WPA Guide to New Orleans*, 43-44, and "Genesis and Exodus," *Times-Picayune*, 25 May 1997, p. E-1, col. 1.

7. "City's Debutantes to Ride in Flower Carnival on Horseback," *New Orleans Item-Tribune*, 7 January 1934, p. 14, col. 6; "Marcus Show Unique of Kind," *New Orleans Item*, 9 January 1934, p. 14, col. 5.

8. Movie advertisement for *Eskimo*, *New Orleans Item*, 10 January 1934, p. 7, col. 2; Mel Washburn, "The Spotlight," *New Orleans Tribune*, 5 January 1934, p. 7, col. 2.

9. Advertisement for George's Tavern, *New Orleans Item*, 7 January 1934, p. 13, col. 2; "Franklin D., Huey and Fu Vie at Show," *New Orleans Item*, 7 January 1934, p. 12, col. 4.

10. "Long on Way Home to Aid in Campaign," *New Orleans Tribune*, 10 January 1934, p. 1, col. 3; Weiss, interview.

11. Weiss, interview.

12. "'War to the Knife,'" p. 4, col. 1; "Mayor Predicts 'Elimination' of Long Influence," *Times-Picayune*, 31 December 1933, p. 2, col. 1; "Long Chief Issue in City Election, Says Walmsley at Opening Rally," *Times-Picayune*, 9 January 1934, p. 1, col. 1; "Long Man Beaten, Waives New Vote," *New York Times*, 25 January 1934, p. 2, col. 4.

13. "Long Condemned by Old Regular Leaders' Caucus," *Times-Picayune*, 3 January 1934, p. 1, col. 7; "Regulars Confident," *New Orleans Item-Tribune*, 16 January 1934, p. 14, col. 1.

14. "Long Chief Issue in City Election," p. 1, col. 1; William Ivy Hair, *Kingfish and His Realm*, 265; Hermann B. Deutsch, "The

Kingdom of the Kingfish," *New Orleans Item*, 3 September 1939, p. 7, col. 1. This newspaper series ran irregularly in the *Item* from July 19 to September 20, 1939 and is available in its entirety at the Louisiana Collection of the Howard-Tilton Memorial Library, Tulane University, New Orleans, La.; Weiss, interview; George Reyer, interview by T. Harry Williams, 15 July 1957, the Interview Collection, the Louisiana Lower Mississippi Valley Collections, Hill Memorial Library, Louisiana State University, Baton Rouge, La.; "40,000 Unlawful Registrations in Rolls, Says Long," *Times-Picayune*, 26 January 1934, p. 1, col. 7.

15. "Long Chief Issue in City Election," p. 1, col. 1.

16. "Long Real Issue, Says Walmsley," *New Orleans States*, 7 January 1934, p. 5, col. 4; Deutsch, "Kingdom of the Kingfish," p. 7, col. 1.

17. "Walmsley, Long Fight Won't Last, Asserts Gamble," *New Orleans States*, 24 December 1933, p. 1, col. 3.

18. J. C. Williams (the New Orleans Athletic Club's official historian), interview by author, tape recording, New Orleans, La., 26 October 1995.

19. Hair, *Kingfish and His Realm*, 200-210; Williams, *Huey Long*, 436-37; J. C. Williams, interview; "Huey P. Long Was Member of the Club," *The Punch* 12, no. 11 (October 1936): 7. The athletic club's membership was at the very least diverse, including, beyond Walmsley and Long, musician Louis Prima, businessman and close Long associate Robert Maestri, newspaper columnist and historian Charles ("Pie") DuFour, Congressman Robert Maloney, and Rabbi Louis Binstock of the Uptown Temple Sinai, who was also very active in the same leftist and Socialist circles shared by Newcomb student and Socialist organizer Louise Jessen ("What Our Members Are Doing," *The Punch* 12, no. 10 [January 1936]: 11).

20. "Long Sent Luck Charm for Klorer," *New Orleans Item-Tribune*, 14 January 1934, p. 10, col. 8.

21. "Klorer's 1st Speech," *New Orleans Item*, 3 January 1934, p. 7, col. 1; "Walmsley Seen As Leader in City Primary," *New Orleans Item-Tribune*, 14 January 1934, p. 1, col. 8; Deutsch, "Kingdom of the Kingfish," p. 7, col. 1.

22. "Long Makes First Speech in Klorer's Behalf," *Times-Picayune*, 14 January 1934, p. 1, col. 7. McCarthy Park, bounded by Burgundy, Pauline, and Alvar streets, was a favorite Ninth Ward gathering place until the late 1940s when the city gave it to the

schoolboard for the construction of Nicholls Senior High School (John Maher, interview by author, tape recording, New Orleans, La., 29 December 1995).

23. "Long Makes First Speech," p. 1, col. 7; "Walmsley Seen As Leader in City Primary," p. 1, col. 8. Circulars related to the Long-Klorer campaign can be found in the William B. Wisdom Collection in the Special Collections of the Howard-Tilton Memorial Library; see in particular circulars number 17, 29, 30, and 31. Delivered by the thousands to the doorsteps of voters, the tracts were both weighty and humorous. Typical of the material is Long's lengthy and intelligent discussion of graft and electricity rates on 20 January 1934, circular 31, which begins: "To his honor (if he has any) Turkeyhead Sulphur Walmsley (High Mayor of the City of New Orleans)."

24. Hair, *Kingfish and His Realm*, 265; "Long Denounces Mayor for Night Raid and Arrests," *Times-Picayune*, 17 January 1934, p. 1, col. 5.

25. "Long Continues to Assail Mayor Despite Threats," *Times-Picayune*, 18 January 1934, p. 1, col. 6.

26. "Long Continues to Assail Mayor," p. 1, col. 6. Deutsch, "Kingdom of the Kingfish," p. 7, col. 1; Forest Davis, *Huey Long: A Candid Biography* (New York: Dodge Publishing Company, 1935), 209; "Long Seeks Votes by Radio Crooning," *New York Times*, 23 January 1934, p. 21, col. 2; Louis Alfarez, *The New Orleans Bicycle Book* (New Orleans: Little Nemo Press, 1984), 19-21; "Genesis and Exodus," p. E-1, col. 1.; Williams, *Huey Long*, 673-74.

27. "Long Sees a Racket," *New Orleans Item-Tribune*, 21 January 1934, p. 11, col. 6.

28. "Barnes, Others Free," *New Orleans Item*, 16 January 1934, p. 1, col. 8; "Court Foils Clown Move by Long," *New Orleans States*, 17 January 1934, p. 1, col. 8; "Long Sees a Racket," p. 11, col. 6; "Police Arrest C. S. Barnes, 10 Others in Midnight Raid," *Times-Picayune*, 16 January 1934, p. 1, col. 8; "High Court Denies Barnes' Petition, Rolls Under Guard," *Times-Picayune*, 17 January 1934, p. 1, col. 8; "Walmsley Warns Long to Be Good on Election Day," *Baton Rouge Morning Advocate*, 17 January 1934, p. 1, col. 6. For information on Barnes and how he viewed his job, see the transcription of his testimony, Senate Special Committee on Campaign Expeditures, *Hearings before the Special Committee on*

Investigation of Campaign Expenditures, 73rd Cong., 1st sess., 17 February 1933, 1108-15.

29. "Barnes, Others Free," p. 1, col. 8; "Long Continues to Assail Mayor," p. 1, col. 6; Deutsch, "Kingdom of the Kingfish," p. 7, col. 1. One of Neu's favorite songs was the Bing Crosby hit of that same year, "June in January," which the prisoner sang in a rich baritone the night before he was hung (F. Edward Hebert, *The Last of the Titans—The Life and Times of Congressman F. Edward Hebert of Louisiana* [Lafayette: The Center for Louisiana Studies. 1976], 90-93).

30. Gillis, interview.

31. "Court Orders Registration Fully Probed," *New Orleans Item,* 15 January 1934, p. 1, col. 1; "Barnes, Others Free," p. 1, col. 8.

32. "Barnes, Others Free," p. 1, col. 8.

33. Joe Cangiamilla, interview by author, tape recording, New Orleans, La., 15 September 1995; Gillis, interview.

34. Gillis, interview.

35. "Long Denounces Mayor for Night Raid and Arrests," p. 1, col. 5. Six days before the Long-Klorer rally, the Old Regulars rented out the same Loyola auditorium to pay tribute to the mayor while denouncing the registrar of voters episode (William B. Wisdom Collection, broadside number 4, Special Collections, Howard-Tilton Memorial Library, Tulane University, New Orleans, La.).

36. Williams, *Huey Long,* 689-92; Smith, *The New Deal in the Urban South,* 65-66; Alan Brinkley, "The New Deal and Southern Politics," *The New Deal and the South* (Jackson: University Press of Mississippi, 1984), 101, 110-111; Hair, *Kingfish and His Realm,* 287-88; "Foes Vituperation Proved of Great Value to Walmsley," *New Orleans Item,* 26 January 1934, p. 1, col. 3.

37. "Walmsley Leads, With Klorer Second and Williams Third," *Times-Picayune,* 24 January 1934, p. 1, col. 8; "No Second Primary; Walmsley Pledged to Eliminate Long," *Times-Picayune,* 25 January 1934, p. 1, col. 8; "Long Man Beaten, Waives New Vote," p. 2, col. 4.

38. "No Second Primary," p. 1, col. 8;

39. "Report to Senate Absolves Overton," *New York Times,* 17 January 1934, p. 2, col. 4.

40. "Many to Serve for Candidates," *Hullabaloo,* 5 January 1934, p.

1, col. 5; Lindy Boggs, *Washington Through a Purple Veil—Memoirs of a Southern Woman* (New York: Harcourt, Brace & Company, 1994), 49-50; Lindy Boggs, interview by author, tape recording, New Orleans, La., 16 March 1992.

41. Weiss, interview; Long, interview; "40,000 Unlawful Registrations in Rolls," p. 1, col. 7.

42. Long, interview; "Long Keeps Rule Over Voter Rolls," *New York Times*, 8 August 1934, p. 12, col. 2.

43. "Long to Oust Barnes As His Machine Crumbles," *New Orleans States*, 27 January 1934, p. 1, col. 5; "C. S. Barnes, Former Vote Registrar, Dies," *New Orleans States*, 25 April 1939, p. 1, col. 5; "Funeral Service Is Conducted for Charles S. Barnes," *Times-Picayune*, 26 April 1939, p. 2, col. 4.

CHAPTER 5

1. "Long Hoping He Doesn't Meet Mayor," *New Orleans Item*, 1 February 1934, p. 1, col. 1; "Washington Is Laughing at Crawfish," *New Orleans States*, 3 February 1934, p. 1, col. 5; Kane, *Louisiana Hayride*, 105; Hair, *Kingfish and His Realm*, 266. The Mayflower was also the permanent residence of nearly two dozen members of Congress and the place where, according to legend, President Roosevelt wrote his inspirational "the only thing we have to fear is fear itself" first inaugural speech in 1933 (Judith Cohen, T*he Mayflower Hotel—Grand Dame of Washington, D.C.* [New York: Balance Books, 1987], 42, 78-79).

2. Harnett T. Kane, "Walmsley Rites Friday; Career Is Recalled," *New Orleans Item*, 18 June 1942, p. 1, col. 4; "Long Hoping He Doesn't Meet Mayor," p. 1, col. 1; Kane, *Louisiana Hayride*, 105; "Guards Keep Long Out of Mayor's Path," *New Orleans States*, 2 February 1934, p. 1, col. 4; "Walmsley Vows to 'Beat Up' Long at Sight If Two Meet at Capital," *Times-Picayune*, 1 February 1934, p. 1, col. 1.

3. "Washington Is Laughing at Crawfish," p. 1, col. 5; "Walmsley Vows to 'Beat Up' Long at Sight If Two Meet at Capital," p. 1, col. 1; Williams, *Huey Long*, 471; "Long Denies He Struck Reporter," *Times-Picayune*, 3 February 1934, p. 12, col. 1; "Walmsley Ready to Leave Capital," *Times-Picayune*, 4 February 1934, p. 1, col. 6.

4. "Washington Is Laughing at Crawfish," p. 1, col. 5.

5. "Huey Is Saved by the Bell," *New Orleans Item,* 4 February 1934, p. 1, col. 3; "Mayor Home, Seeks 10 Million for Works," *New Orleans Item,* 5 February 1934, p. 1, col. 8.

6. "Senate Body Delays Long Ouster Case," *New Orleans Item,* 14 February 1934, p. 1, col. 4; Lanius Williams to Cecil Morgan, 27 January 1934, 1934 file, Cecil P. Morgan Papers, Special Collections, Howard-Tilton Memorial Library, Tulane University, New Orleans, La.; Burt Henry to Morgan, 30 January 1934, 1934 file, Cecil P. Morgan Papers.

7. Cecil Morgan, interview. Although Morgan's subsequent career was full and distinguished, including his service as a state judge and his tenure as dean of the school of law at Tulane University in the 1960s and 1970s, he repeatedly revisited the Long years, most notably in his interviews with historian Williams in the late 1950s, in an oral interview seminar sponsored by Louisiana State University at Shreveport in 1970, and in Ken Burns' 1985 documentary *Huey Long.* As late as 1995 Morgan told the author that Long was "one of the most intelligent, visionary leaders" to have risen to power in Louisiana, but that Huey's "obsessive thirst for power" contaminated all of the good he did. Long, Morgan finally concluded, was a man capable of only excesses: excessive good or excessive evil. "That's what made him so dangerous," Morgan added. See also Morgan's review of Williams' *Huey Long* in the April 1971 issue of the *Tulane Law Review,* 676-82; and a brief biographical sketch of Morgan in the *First Constitution of the State of Louisiana* (New Orleans: Historic New Orleans Collection, 1975), xiv.

8. Mason Dixon, "Huey Long's Star Is Seen As Setting," *New York Times,* 4 February 1934, sec. 8, p. 2, col. 7; Hammond, *Let Freedom Ring,* 218; Tyler, S*ilk Stockings and Ballot Boxes,* 32-77; Hair, *Kingfish and His Realm,* 283.

9. Hair, *Kingfish and His Realm,* 283; Long, interview; Williams, *Huey Long,* 784; Tyler, *Silk Stockings,* 72. Tyler makes the point that even though Williams in his biography of Long lists Hammond as a member of the fire-breathing Square Dealers, "no published source indicates that Hilda Phelps Hammond joined this body." Even so, it is clear that she and the Square Dealers by the spring of 1934 were becoming increasingly rancorous in a shared obsession: the final destruction of Huey Long.

10. Ann Waldron, Hodding Carter—The Reconstruction of a Racist (Chapel Hill: The University of North Carolina Press, 1993), 50-59; Hodding Carter, "Kingfish to Crawfish," The New Republic 77 (24 January 1934): 302-5; "Hodding Carter Jr. Dies at 65; Outspoken Mississippi Editor," New York Times, 5 April 1972, p. 48, col. 3; "Hodding Carter Taken by Death," Times-Picayune, 5 April 1972, p. 1, col. 5; John T. Kneebone, Southern Liberal Journalists and the Issue of Race, 1920-1944 (Chapel Hill: The University of North Carolina Press, 1985), 108-10.

11. Carter, "Kingfish to Crawfish," 302-5.

12. Brinkley, Voices of Protest, 67-68; Carter, "Kingfish to Crawfish," 302-5; Dixon, "Huey Long's Star Is Seen As Setting," sec. 8, p. 2, col. 7; "Huey Long's Political Defeat in His Own State," Literary Digest 117, no. 5 (3 February 1934): 7.

13. Waldron, Reconstruction of a Racist, 55; Hair, Kingfish and His Realm, 282; "Long's Bills Go to Senate After Rapid Passage in House," Times-Picayune, 17 August 1934, p. 1, col. 7.

14. Gillis, interview.

15. Salvaggio, New Orleans' Charity Hospital, 111, 327.

16. Waldron, Reconstruction of a Racist, 52.

17. "Long CWA Charge Hit," New Orleans Item, 27 February 1934, p. 10, col. 1; Walmsley's attention to detail and his penchant for always doing the right thing was in evidence during Mardi Gras when he invited Helen Sonnier, a 15-year-old orphan, to present the keys of the city to Rex. It was, in fact, Sonnier's second invitation: the year before rain forced the cancellation of Fat Tuesday parades, prompting Walmsley to promise the girl he would call her back for the next Mardi Gras. True to his word, Walmsley sat with Sonnier a year later in the grand reviewing stand in front of Gallier Hall. "I never thought he'd have the time to invite me," said a grateful Sonnier ("Orphan to Give 'Rex' City Key; Mayor Pledges to Girl," New Orleans Item, 12 February 1934, p. 1, col. 5).

18. Hair, Kingfish and His Realm, 277; Williams, Huey Long, 714.

19. "Burgess Supports Anti-Long Plan for New House Leaders," Times-Picayune, 14 May 1934, p. 1, col. 8; "Speakership Fight Delayed," New Orleans States, 14 May 1934, p. 1, col. 7.

20. "Speakership Fight Delayed," p. 1, col. 7; George N. Coad, "Long's Foes Gather to End His Reign," New York Times, 13 May

1934, sec. 7, p. 7, col. 7; "Long Sets Up Base to Fight State Foes," *New York Times,* 15 May 1934, p. 13, col. 13; "Burgess Supports Anti-Long Plan for New House Leaders," p. 1, col. 8; Hermann Deutsch, "Much Heralded Row Again Fails to Come Off As Crowds Watch," *New Orleans Tribune,* 22 May 1934, p. 1, col. 8; Hermann B. Deutsch, "Allen Forces Caucus on Auto Fees; Child Labor Bill to Senate," *New Orleans Tribune,* 24 May 1934, p. 1, col. 8; Long, interview; Cecil Morgan to Bell Wiley, 9 May 1970, Cecil P. Morgan Papers.

21. See Alfred Steinberg's *The Bosses* ([New York: MacMillan Company, 1972], 1-9) for a discussion of political bosses in general. The author contends that "at no time in American history have local bosses been collectively more powerful and more debilitating to democratic principles than during the 1920s and [19]30s." See also William S. Shannon's "The Political Machine: The Age of the Bosses," *American Heritage Magazine* 20, no. 4 (June 1969): 26-31. I contend that up to 1934, Long's machine was little different from that of perhaps the century's most notable political boss, Chicago Mayor Richard J. Daley. See in particular Mike Royko's *Boss—Richard J. Daley of Chicago* (New York: Signet Classics, 1971), 65-78. For a general reference on other machines of Long's era, particularly in the South, see V. O. Key's *Southern Politics* (New York: Knopf, 1950), 62-69, 108-13, 196-98, and 273-74.

22. Jeansonne, *Messiah of the Masses,* 137; Brinkley, *Voices of Protest,* 68-70; Hair, *Kingfish and His Realm,* 105-6; C. E. Frampton, "Walmsley Charges 'Insiders' of Administration Made Huge Profits Buying Up Road Bonds," *New Orleans Tribune,* 11 June 1934, p. 1, col. 6; George N. Coad, "Opponents of Long Chafe at Defeat," *New York Times,* 22 July 1934, p. 6, col. 1.

23. Frampton, "Walmsley Charges 'Insiders' of Administration," p. 1, col. 6.; "Long Pushes Bill for Tax on Press," *New York Times,* 4 July 1934, p. 10, col. 1; "Newspaper Ads Taxed," *New York Times,* 10 July 1934, p. 24, col. 1. For an in-depth discussion on the newspaper tax and its chilling effect on the Fourth Estate, see Richard C. Cortner's *The Kingfish and the Constitution—Huey Long, the First Amendment, and the Emergence of Modern Press Freedom in America* (Westport: Greewood Press, 1996).

24. George Vandervoort, "Legislative Inquiry into Affairs of New Orleans Asked by Weber," Times-Picayune, 29 May 1934, p. 1, col.

4; "Hearing on Primary Fraud Bill Balked by Long-Allen Men," Times-Picayune, 30 May 1934, p. 1, col. 8; "Seven City Bills Voted by Committee," New Orleans Tribune, 30 May 1934, p. 1, col. 1.

25. Vandervoort, "Legislative Inquiry into Affairs of New Orleans," p. 1, col. 4; Hermann B. Deutsch, "Appropriations Bill Up for Battle in Legislature Today," *New Orleans Tribune*, 20 June 1934, p. 1, col. 8; "Seven City Bills Voted by Committee," p. 1, col. 1.

26. Vandervoort, "Legislative Inquiry into Affairs of New Orleans," p. 1, col. 4.

27. Coad, "Opponents of Long Chafe at Defeat," p. 6, col. 1.

28. Hammond, *Let Freedom Ring*, 20. For an overview on the political and historical symbolism of the White League see James H. Gillis, "Monument Should Stand," *Times-Picayune*, 9 February 1981, p. 13, col. 1; and "The Battle of Liberty Place—A Matter of Historical Perception," by Judith Schaefer, an address given to the Louisiana Historical Society in New Orleans, La., on October 13, 1992.

29. "Constabulary Bill Killed As City Maps Fight," *New Orleans Item-Tribune*, 3 June 1934, p. 1, col. 7.

30. "Mass Meeting Demands Economics; Statewide Rally Called at Capital; Five Mayors to Fight Tax Bill," *New Orleans Tribune*, 7 June 1934, p. 1, col. 7; Hermann B. Deutsch, "Budget Plan Blocked As State 'Revolts,'" *New Orleans Item*, 7 June 1934, p. l, col. 6; "New Taxes Hit at Rally; Legislature Pledges Economy," *Times-Picayune*, 7 June 1934, p. 1, col. 7; "Mass Meeting Roars Warning on Tax Grab," *New Orleans States*, 7 June 1934, p. 1, col. 4.

31. "Mass Meeting Demands Economics," p. 1, col. 7.

32. "Louisianians Threaten Force to Gain Rights," *New Orleans Tribune*, 13 June 1934, p. 1, col. 7.

33. George Vandervoort, "Mass Meeting Threatens Use of Force 'If Necessary,'" *Times-Picayune*, 13 June 1934, p. 1, col. 7; "Trip Called 'Drunk,' Women Indignant," *New Orleans Item*, 13 June 1934, p. 1, col. 6;

34. "Trip Called 'Drunk,'" p. 1, col. 6; "Louisianians Threaten Force to Gain Rights," p. 1, col. 7.

35. "Louisianians Threaten Force to Gain Rights," p. 1, col. 7. Deutsch once claimed that Long asked him to help write his autobiographical *Every Man a King* in the fall of 1932, but that Huey dropped the idea after meeting with Deutsch and being corrected

by the New Orleans journalist for mispronouncing the name of a character from *Les Miserables.* "What the hell difference does it make how you pronounce it?" Long retorted, never talking to Deutsch about being his coauthor again (Deutsch, review of *Huey Long,* by Hugh Davis Graham, *Louisiana History* 11, no. 4 [fall 1970], 376-77).

36. "Trip Called 'Drunk,' Women Indignant," p. 1, col. 6; "Louisianians Threaten Force to Gain Rights," p. 1, col. 7.

37. "Louisianians Threaten Force to Gain Rights," p. 1, col. 7.

38. Deutsch, "Budget Plan Blocked As State 'Revolts,'" p. l, col. 6.

39. Hermann B. Deutsch, "Appropriations Wildly Changed in Legislative Rush," *New Orleans Tribune,* 28 June 1934, p. 1, col. 8.

40. Williams, *Huey Long,* 718-22; Jeansonne, *Messiah of the Masses,* 137-38; *Official Journal of the Proceedings of the House of Representatives, Seventh Regular Session of the Legislature* (Baton Rouge: Ramieres-Jones Printing, 1934), 907. To see the general lopsided Long majorities, see pages 1748-1968. For the Senate, Long's overwhelming vote success is recorded in the *Official Journal of the Senate, Seventh Regular Session of the Legislature* (Baton Rouge: Ramieres-Jones Printing, 1934), 1564-1757. Perhaps Long's greatest strides in the 1934 regular session came with the number of Old Regular lawmakers he won to his side. Of the roughly twenty members of the New Orleans metropolitan area who once voted in a bloc against Huey, by the early summer of 1934 at least six were now regularly supporting Long, a number that would increase to nearly half of the Old Regular delegation by the end of the year (*Official Journal of the Proceedings of the House of Representatives,* 900-908, 1437, and 1606-1609).

41. Hermann B. Deutsch, "Both Tugwell Bills Passed; Taking $700,000 from City; Liquor Control Approved," *New Orleans Tribune,* 27 June 1934, p. 1, col. 6.

42. Frank C. Allen, "Economy Measures Killed; Shreveport Menaced," *Times-Picayune,* 29 June 1934, p. 1, col. 7.

43. "40,000 Unlawful Registrations in Rolls, Says Long," *Times-Picayune,* 26 January 1934, p. 1, col. 7.

CHAPTER 6

1. Harold B. McSween, "Huey Long at His Centenary," *Virginia*

Quarterly Review 69, no. 3 (summer 1993): 509-20; Ken Burns, *Huey Long*, 88 min. (RKB/Florentine Films, 1985).

2. David C. Smith, *H. G. Wells, Desperately Mortal—A Biography* (New Haven: Yale University Press, 1986), 133; H. G. Wells, "New America," *Collier's* 50, no. 5 (25 May 1935); 7-8; James Thurber, "Talk of the Town," *The New Yorker* 8, no. 35 (2 September 1933).

3. Edward Burns, ed., *The Letters of Gertrude Stein and Carl Van Vechten, 1913-1940,* vol. 1 (1913-1940) (New York: Columbia University Press, 1986), 390, 401; Charles Modlin, ed., *Sherwood Anderson's Love Letters to Eleanor Copenhauer Anderson* (Athens: University of Georgia Press, 1987), 297; Howard Manford, *The Letters of Sherwood Anderson* (New York: Little, Brown & Company, 1953), 310-11.

4. Joan Givner, *Katherine Anne Porter: A Life* (New York: Simon & Schuster, 1982), 355-56; Townsend Ludington, ed., *The Fourteenth Chronicle—Letters and Diaries of John Dos Possos* (Boston: Gambit Publishers, 1973), 413.

5. James T. Jones, "A Middle Class Utopia: Lewis' *It Can't Happen Here,*" *Sinclair Lewis at 100—Papers Presented at a Centennial Conference* (St. Cloud: St. Cloud University, 1985), 217; James Lundquist, *Sinclair Lewis* (New York: Frederick Ungar Publishers, 1973), 110-13; Mark Schorer, *Sinclair Lewis—An American Life* (New York: McGraw-Hill, 1961), 608.

6. Sinclair Lewis, *It Can't Happen Here* (New York: Doubleday, 1935), 82, 88, 89; Williams, *Huey Long,* 48-50, 437-39, 430-32.

7. Lewis, *It Can't Happen Here,* 35, 37, 86; Burns, *Huey Long.*

8. Lewis, *It Can't Happen Here,* 111, 220, 268.

9. The exact number of guardsmen to enter the Soule Building is uncertain. A *Times-Picayune* report, filed on the scene, estimated that "approximately two score of armed Guardsmen," were there, while the *Christian Science Monitor's* local correspondent put the number at "more than a score." In his dispatch to FBI Director J. Edgar Hoover, New Orleans agent R. Whitley said he saw "15 or 20 National Guardsmen in uniform," while Long scholars Williams and Jeansonne use the largest figure, both claiming that fifty men came in and took control of the registrar's office. The only certain statistic is that many more men were on call at nearby Jackson Barracks. The official report filed before the Office of the Chief of the National Guard Bureau says simply that 167 enlisted men were called in response to guarding the Soule Building, but

most of those men did not see any action ("Militia Seizes Registration Office Under Allen's Order," *Times-Picayune*, 31 July 1934, p. 1, col. 8; "Mayor Orders 400 Police to Report for Service Today," *Times-Picayune*, 1 August 1934, p. 1, col. 8; "Long's Guardsmen Seize Poll Lists in New Orleans," *Christian Science Monitor*, 31 July 1934, p. 1, col. 5; R. Whitley to Hoover, 8 August 1934, serial number 62-32509-01, a copy of the FBI papers on the invasion of the Soule Building in the author's possession; Williams, *Huey Long*, 723; Jeansonne, *Messiah of the Masses*, 139; *Annual Report of the Chief of the National Guard, Congressional Record, Proceedings and Debates of the Second Session of the Seventy-Fourth Congress* [Washington: Government Printing Office, 1936], 80, pt. 2:2069-77); *Legal Issues Concerning the Role of the National Guard in Civil Disorders* (Greenwood, North Carolina: National Association of Attorneys General, 1973), 56, 109.

10. Evans Casso, *Louisiana Legacy—A History of the State National Guard* (Gretna: Pelican Publishing Company, 1976), 136; Fleming, interview; "Orleans National Guard Is Praised," *New Orleans States*, 23 April 1934, p. 18, col. 1.

11. Fleming, interview.

12. Williams, *Huey Long*, 342-43; "Long's Guardsmen Seize Poll Lists," p. 1, col. 5; "Militia Seizes Registration Office Under Allen's Order," p. 1, col. 8; "Mayor Orders 400 Police to Report," p. 1, col. 8; "Comedie Louisianaise," *Time* 24, no. 6 (13 August 1934): 13; "Louisiana: Kingfish's Troops and Mayor's Police Draw Beads at Each Other Over Gun-Sights," *Newsweek* 4, no. 6 (11 August 1934): 7.

13. "Militia Seizes Registration Office Under Allen's Order," p. 1, col. 8; "Mayor Orders 400 Police to Report," p. 1, col. 8; see also Reyer, interview. Walmsley, within the first three days of the military invasion of the registrar's office, said Long could do as he pleased with the office as it was a state agency controlled by Huey. But the rest of the offices in the Soule Building were city agencies: the New Orleans welfare department was on the building's second floor, and the city electrical inspector's office was on the third (*Soards City Directory, 1933* [New Orleans: Soards Publishing 1933], 978).

14. "Militia Seizes Registration Office Under Allen's Order," p. 1, col. 8; "Mayor Orders 400 Police to Report," p. 1, col. 8; "Militia Mobilized in New Orleans," p. 9, col. 1; "Four Machine Guns

Guard Registrar of Voters Office," *New Orleans Tribune,* 1 August 1934, p. 9, col. 1; "Guard Ordered to Probe Vice," *New Orleans Tribune,* 2 August 1934, p. 1, col. 5; *Historical, Military Data on Louisiana Militia, July-April 30, 1922-1936* (New Orleans: Works Project Administration Project OP 665, 1940), 170-71.

15. "Militia Seizes Registration Office Under Allen's Order," p. 1, col. 8; "Rush to Join Force As 500 More Police Are Sworn In, Armed," *New Orleans States,* 1 August 1934, p. 1, col. 7.

16. Burns, *Huey Long.* If the national newsreels—a potent source of image-making in the 1930s—were not particularly pro-Walmsley, they were nevertheless decidedly anti-Long. A *March of Time* program that would be shot in early 1935 portrayed Long in such a dark, critical manner that Huey later pushed through the state legislature a bill regulating newsreels in Louisiana (Raymond Fielding, *The American Newsreel, 1911-1967* [Norman: The University Press of Oklahoma, 1972], 285; Fielding, *The March of Time, 1935-1951* [New York: Oxford University Press, 1978], 12, 46-53).

17. "Militia Seizes Registration Office Under Allen's Order," p. 1, col. 8; "Mayor Orders 400 Police to Report," p. 1, col. 8; "Special Policement Held Ready, Troops Await New Orders," *Times-Picayune,* 2 August 1934, p. 1, col. 8; "Rush to Join Force As 500 More Police Are Sworn In, Armed," p. 1, col. 7; "Long Moves to Grab All Assessors," *New Orleans States,* 2 August 1934, p. 1, col. 8; "New Orleans Tense As Police Await a Move by Troops," *New York Times,* 2 August 1934, p. 1, col. 4.

18. "Court Bars Troops' Use; Deputies Fail to Serve Fleming," *Times-Picayune,* 3 August 1934, p. 1, col. 8; "Troops Stay Despite Court Order," *New Orleans States,* 3 August 1934, p. 1, col. 7.

19. "Comedie Louisianaise," 13.

20. "Comedie Louisianaise," 13.

21. "Court Bars Troops' Use," p. 1, col. 8.

22. "Court Bars Troops' Use," p. 1, col. 8.

23. Fleming, interview; Kane, *Louisiana Hayride,* 108-9; Williams, *Huey Long,* 727-30.

24. Robert V. Remini, *Andrew Jackson and the Course of American Empire, 1767-1821* (New York: Harper & Row, 1977), 316-17; William Ivy Hair, *Carnival of Fury* (Baton Rouge: Louisiana State University Press, 1976), 76; Major R. Raven-Hart, *Down the Mississippi* (Boston: Houghton-Mifflin, 1938), 214. In Donald Marquis'

vivid *In Search of Buddy Bolden—First Man of Jazz* (New York: De Capo Press, 1978), the author pieces together the cultural and oftentimes criminal life of the central city neighborhoods of Rampart and Perdido in the first decade of the twentieth century and discovers through police records and the annual city directories a black Storyville inhabited by "professional criminals," although most criminal activity in the area was confined to "pickpockets, senak thieves, pimps, and gamblers" (46-56).

25. Raven-Hart, *Down the Mississippi*, 215; Saxon, "Have a Good Time While You Can," 85-94; Harold Speakman, *Mostly Mississippi* (New York: Dodd, Mead, and Company, 1927), 354.

26. John Davis, *Mafia Kingfish—Carlos Marcello and the Assassination of John F. Kennedy* (New York: McGraw-Hill, 1989), 34-35; Campbell, "At Home in New Orleans," 209-11; Ned Brady, "The Louisiana Lottery," *New Orleans Magazine* 5, no. 8 (August 1971): 52; "Gambling—Then and Now," *New Orleans Magazine* 9, no. 7 (July 1975): 27; Elsie Martinez and Margaret LeCorgne, *Uptown/Downtown—Growing Up in New Orleans* (Lafayette: The Center for Louisiana Studies, 1986), 24-25.

27. "Open, Protected Gambling Flourishes in City, Says Grand Jurors," *Times-Picayune*, 5 August 1931, p. 1, col. 5.

28. Kurtz and Peoples, *Earl K. Long*, 29, 158; Butera, interview.

29. "Legislature to Seek to Destroy Old Regulars," *Baton Rouge Morning Advocate*, 15 August 1934, p. 1, col. 7; "Bills Are Pushed Through House As Scheduled," *Baton Rouge Morning Advocate*, 17 August 1934, p. 1, col. 7; "Arms Added, Row Gains in New Orleans," *Baton Rouge Morning Advocate*, 17 August 1934, p. 1, col. 5; "Session Closes Amid Wild Disorder," *Baton Rouge Morning Advocate*, 18 August 1934, p. 1, col. 7; "Louisiana: Blustering, Cajoling, and Threatening, Huey Long Seizes Dictatorial Powers Amid Rumblings of Insurrection," *Newsweek* 4, no. 8 (25 August 1934): 7; "Heil, Huey!" *Time* 24, no. 9 (27 August 1934): 14; F. Raymond Daniell, "Long Speeds for 'Purifying' War," *New York Times*, 16 August 1934, p. 1, col. 5; Hair, *Kingfish and His Realm*, 280-81.

30. "Special Policemen Held Ready," p. 1, col. 8; "Long Steam-Roller in Senate Crushes Foes in Spite of Bills," *New Orleans States*, 17 August 1934, p. 1, col. 17.

31. "Comedie Louisianaise," 13; "Heil, Huey!" 14; "Louisiana: Blustering, Cajoling, and Threatening," 7; "Louisiana Is Told That

It Is Headed Toward 'Hitlerism,'" *Christian Science Monitor,* 16 August 1934, p. 4, col. 6. Although Hilda Phelps Hammond praised Pegler for "giving a splendid picture of the situation" in Louisiana, he was hardly an unbiased observer. On the contrary, Pegler was enormously partisan, and oftentimes recklessly vindictive. In the 1930s his nationally syndicated column was marked by a series of vituperative attacks on not only FDR and the New Deal, but also Eleanor Roosevelt, a favorite Pegler target. By the early 1950s, Pegler not only defended the excesses of Sen. Joseph R. McCarthy but began to produce a series of anti-Semitic articles that frequently appeared in *American Opinion,* a magazine produced by the John Birch Society. Westbrook Pegler, "Pegler Finds Jovially Cynical Legislature Creating Dictator," *New Orleans Item,* 17 August 1934, p. 1, col. 3; Westbrook Pegler, "It's Heil Huey to Louisiana! Just Putsch-Over for Der-Kingfish," *New Orleans Item,* 18 August 1934, p. 1. col. 6; Hammond, *Let Freedom Ring,* 219-20; George Wolfskill and John A Hudson, *All But the People—Franklin D. Roosevelt and His Critics, 1933-1939* (London: MacMillan, 1969), 174; Joseph P. Lash, *Eleanor: The Years Alone* (New York: New American Library, 1972), 32, 136, 149-50, 168, 183, 225, 230-31. For a well-rounded survey of Pegler's career, see Oliver Pilat, *Pegler—Angry Man of the Press* (Westport: Greenwood Press, 1963).

32. F. Raymond Daniell, "Long Keeps Rule Over Voter Rolls," *New York Times,* 8 August 1934, p. 12, col. 2.

33. F. Raymond Daniell, "Huey Long Defends New Orleans 'War,'" *New York Times,* 10 August 1934, p. 14, col. 1. Because of his reporting on Long, Daniell "was considered to be one of the best reporters on the national scene" by the mid-1930s the *New York Times* noted upon Daniell's death in 1969. See also, Harrison E. Salisbury, *A Journey for Our Times—A Memoir* (New York: Harper and Row, 1983), 126-34; and Daniell's *We Saw It Happen* (New York: Simon & Schuster, 1938), 90-95.

34. "Raymond Daniell Is Dead at 68; A Times Reporter for 39 Years," *New York Times,* 13 April 1969, p. 11, col. 1.

35. Daniell, *We Saw It Happen,* 93-94; Williams, *Huey Long,* 558, 845; Kane, *Louisiana Hayride,* 138, 152.

36. Daniell, "Huey Long Defends New Orleans 'War,'" p. 14, col. 1

37. Ibid.

38. Ibid.

39. Ibid.

40. Ibid.

41. Ibid.

42. "Fortier Takes Post to Sift City Affairs," *New Orleans Item*, 22 August 1934, p. 1, col. 7; Charles Palmisano, interview by author, tape recording, New Orleans, La., 15 April 1990.

43. Palmisano, interview.

44. Fleming, interview.

45. *Historical, Military Data on Louisiana Militia*, 170-71; *Special Orders, Adjutant General's Office, New Orleans*, 31 August 1934, in the Military Library at Jackson Barracks, New Orleans, La.

CHAPTER 7

1. Gouaze, interview; Benezach, interview.

2. Fleming, interview.

3. Ibid.; William A. Blackwell, interview by author, tape recording, New Orleans, La., 22 January 1996; General Clip File, 1930s, in the Military Library at Jackson Barracks, New Orleans, La.

4. Fleming, interview; Benezach, interview.

5. Gouaze, interview.

6. Ibid.

7. "Injunction Plea Against Guard to Be Argued Today," *Times-Picayune*, 7 August 1934, p. 1, col. 7; "Contempt Charged to Fleming; Writs Left at Barracks," *Times-Picayune*, 8 August 1934, p. 1, col. 8; "SHOTS IN CITY 'WAR,'" *New Orleans Item*, 7 August 1934, p. 1, col. 1; "Plan Coup to Oust Troops," *New Orleans Item*, 8 August 1934, p. 1, col. 1; "TROOPS FIRE TWO SHOTS," *New Orleans States*, 7 August 1934, p. 1, col. 1; "General Fleming Is Closely Guarded at Jackson Barracks," *New Orleans States*, 8 August 1934, p. 1, col. 1; "Fleming Writ Served on Militia Corporal at Jackon Barracks," *New Orleans Tribune*, 8 August 1934, p. 1, col. 1.

8. "Guardsman Fires Shot in Crowded Cafe," *New Orleans Tribune*, 15 August 1934, p. 1, col. 4.

9. "Senator Indicates 'Martial' Activity Will Be Continued," *Times-Picayune*, 10 August 1934, p. 1, col. 8; "Doctor Mistaken for Gen. Fleming Is Served by Deputy," *New Orleans States*, 10 August 1934,

p. 1, col. 4; "Deputies Flouted in Attempt to Serve Guard Chief," *New Orleans Tribune*, 10 August 1934, p. 1, col. 8.

10. "Civil Sheriff Can't Go into Barracks," *New Orleans Item*, 14 August 1934, p. 1, col. 6; "Joe Messina Sticks Close to Long Despite Denials He Serves As Bodyguard," *Times-Picayune*, 14 August 1934, p. 1, col. 5.

11. Benezach, interview; Gouaze, interview.

12. "Unemployables Told They Get No More Food," *New Orleans Item*, 2 August 1934, p. 1, col. 4; "15,000 Lacking Next Meal," *New Orleans Item*, 6 August 1934, p. 1, col. 3; "Aged Mammies, Starving, Don't Care What Happens Now," *New Orleans Item*, 8 August 1934, p. 1, col. 5; "Unfed Dig in Garbage Cans to Keep Alive," *New Orleans Item*, 9 August 1934, p. 1, col. 6; "Courage Dims Tragedy for This Family," *New Orleans Item*, 10 August 1934, p. 1, col. 6; "Food Arriving for Starving," *New Orleans Item*, 12 August 1934, p. 1, col. 4.

13. "Jobless Gather in Square, Voice Call for Relief," *Times-Picayune*, 7 August 1934, p. 7, col. 1; "Mass Meeting Demands End of Martial Law," *New Orleans Tribune*, 7 August 1934, p. 1, col. 7; "Plea of Jobless for Relief Eases New Orleans War," *Christian Science Monitor*, 7 August 1934, p. 1, col. 4; Alexander Kendrick, "Huey Long's Revolution," *Nation* 39, no. 3607 (22 August 1934): 207-9.

14. "Jobless Gather in Square," p. 7, col. 1; "Mass Meeting Demands End of Martial Law," p. 1, col. 7.

15. "Mass Meeting Demands End of Martial Law," p. 1, col. 7; "Jobless Gather in Square, Voice Call for Relief," p. 7, col. 1; "Woman Socialist Chooses Prison Over $2.50 Fine," *Times-Picayune*, 29 March 1934, p. 1, col. 4; "Socialist in Trial Delays Defies Police," *New Orleans Item*, 28 March 1934, p. 1, col. 3; "Mrs. Jessen Reads Bible," *New Orleans Item*, 29 March 1934, p. 1, col. 6; "Send Wire to Mayor," *New Orleans Item*, 30 March 1934, p. 9, col. 4.

16. W. A. Swanberg, *Norman Thomas: The Last Idealist* (New York: Scribner and Sons, 1976), 162, 500; "Walmsley Frees Mrs. Jessen," *New Orleans Item*, 31 March 1934, p. 1, col. 4; "Mrs. Jessen Asks Repeal of Act on Bill Distribution," *Times-Picayune*, 30 March 1934, p. 9, col. 5; "Frees Woman Socialist," *New York Times*, 1 April 1934, p. 29, col. 8.

17. "Mass Meeting Demands End of Martial Law," p. 1, col. 7; Swanberg, *Norman Thomas*, 162, 500.

18. R. Whitley to Hoover, 6 August 1934, serial number 62-32501-6; Hoover to Harold M. Stephens, 6 August 1934, serial number 62-32501-6.

19. Hoover to Stephens, 6 August 1934, serial number 62-32569-5; Hoover to Stephens, 17 August 1934, serial number 62-32569-17. See also Jay Robert Nash, *Citizen Hoover* (Chicago: Nelson-Hall, 1972), 140-45; Hank Messick, *John Edgar Hoover* (New York: McKay Company, 1972), 56-61; Anthony Summers, *Official and Confidential—The Secret Life of J. Edgar Hoover* (New York: G. P. Putnam's Sons, 1993), 102-7, 109-13, 142-46, 148-53; Athan G. Theoharis and John Stuart Cox, *The Boss—J. Edgar Hoover and the Great American Inquisition* (Philadelphia: Temple University Press, 1988), 150-54—Each author argues that FDR, while wary of Hoover, nonetheless significantly contributed to the expansion of Hoover's powers, principally by permitting the FBI to increase its domestic surveillance operations not only against suspected spies, but political foes of the White House. Hoover's surveillance of Long was only the beginning of a long line of "favors" he performed for a series of presidents ending with Richard M. Nixon in the early 1970s.

20. *Complete Presidential Press Conferences of Franklin D. Roosevelt, Volume 3-4, 1934* (New York: Da Capo Press, 1972), 4:22-23, 24 August 1934.

21. *Complete Presidential Press Conferences of Franklin D. Roosevelt, Volume 3-4, 1934* (New York: Da Capo Press, 1972), 4:57-58, 7 September 1934.

22. "Louisiana: Factions Seethe and Boil: Dictator Goes Camping," *Newsweek* 4, no. 9 (1 September 1934): 8; Jeansonne, *Messiah of the Masses,* 139.

23. "2,500 National Guardsmen Occupy New Orleans with Mobilization Unexplained," *Times-Picayune,* 8 September 1934, p. 1, col. 4; "All State Militia on Way to New Orleans for Duty; Allen Asks Clergy Help," *New Orleans Tribune,* 7 September 1934, p. 1, col. 6; Hammond, *Let Freedom Ring,* 218-20.

24. Hammond, *Let Freedom Ring,* 218-20.

25. F. Raymond Daniell, "2,000 Troops Move into New Orleans; Long Is 'Dictator,'" *New York Times,* 8 September 1934, p. 1, col. 3.

26. Daniell, "2,000 Troops Move into New Orleans" p. 1, col. 3; "All State Militia on Way to New Orleans for Duty," p. 1, col. 6; "Parents of Soldiers Warn Long and Allen," New Orleans States, 7

September 1934, p. 1, col. 7; Williams, Huey Long, 731-32; Hair, Kingfish and His Realm, 281-82.

27. "Labor: Troops in Minneapolis; Peace Near on Western Front," *Newsweek* 4, no. 5 (4 August 1934): 9; *Annual Report of the Chief of the National Guard, Congressional Record, Proceedings and Debates of the Second Session of the Seventy-Fourth Congress* (Washington: Government Printing Office, 1936), 80, pt. 2:2069-80; "Long's Guns Move to Vote Registry, Police Face Them," *New York Times,* 3 August 1934, p. 1, col. 5; "Foes of Long Map Contempt Action to Remove Troops," *New York Times,* 4 August 1934, p. 1, col. 3; "Defies Long to Try Seizing City Hall," *New York Times,* 5 August 1934, p. 1, col. 4; F. Raymond Daniell, "All Quiet at Front in Louisiana 'War,'" *New York Times,* 6 August 1934, p. 2, col. 6.

28. "More Troops Rush to City, Transform Docks into Camps," *New Orleans States,* 7 September 1934, p. 1, col. 7; Gillis, interview.

29. Daniell, "2,000 Troops Move into New Orleans," p. 1, col. 3.

30. "All State Militia on Way to New Orleans for Duty," p. 1, col. 6; "2,500 National Guardsmen Occupy New Orleans with Mobilization Unexplained," p. 1, col. 4; "Agreement Signed to Insure Peaceful Primary in City," *Times-Picayune,* 9 September 1934, p. 1, col. 8; "U.S. and State Courts Overrule Dictatorship Assumed by Huey Long," *Baton Rouge Morning Advocate,* 8 September 1934, p. 1, col. 6; "Armed Men to Be Kept from Polls," *Baton Rouge Morning Advocate,* 9 September 1934, p. 1, col. 7.

31. "All State Militia on Way to New Orleans for Duty," p. 1, col. 6; "2,500 National Guardsmen Occupy New Orleans with Mobilization Unexplained," p. 1, col. 4.

32. Hebert, *Last of the Titans,* 122; "U.S. Court Takes Hand in Poll; Long Loses in High Tribunal, Militiamen Quartered in Docks," *New Orleans Tribune,* 9 September 1934, p. 1, col. 7; "Deat Takes Justice Overton; Regulars Find 500 Mistakes, Protest to Allen Against Guards," *New Orleans Tribune,* 9 September 1934, p. 1, col. 7; "More Troops Rush to City, Transform Docks into Camps," p. 1, col. 7; "Entire National Guard of Louisiana Called to Arms," *Times-Picayune,* 7 September 1934, p. 1, col. 7; "National Guard Moving on New Orleans," *Baton Rouge Morning Advocate,* 7 September 1934, p. 1, col. 7; "U.S. and State Courts Overrule Dictatorship Assumed by Huey Long," p. 1, col. 6; "Armed Men to Be Kept from Polls," p. 1, col. 7; Long, interview.

33. Fleming, interview; Reyer, interview.

34. Fleming, interview; Reyer, interview.

35. "Louisiana Primary to Decide Rise of Decline of Huey Long," *Christian Science Monitor,* 11 September 1934, p. 2, col. 7.

CHAPTER 8

1. "Capone Passes Through City on Prison Train," *New Orleans Tribune,* 20 August 1934, p. 1, col. 1; Robert F. Schoenberg, *Mr. Capone* (New York: Morrow, 1992), 335.

2. "Cecil DeMille to Speak Here," *New Orleans Item-Tribune,* 26 August 1934, p. 2, col. 6; "DeMille and His Retinue Arrive," *New Orleans Item,* 1 September 1934, p. 2, col. 2.

3. "Probers Roar Into Town with Great Show of Arms; But Nobody Knows Just Why," *New Orleans Tribune,* 1 September 1934, p. 1, col 7.

4. "City Probe Opens Today; Press, Public Reported Barred," *Times-Picayune,* 1 September 1934, p. 1, col. 7; "Probers Roar Into Town with Great Show of Arms," p. 1, col 7.

5. "Fernandez Rites Today," *Times-Picayune,* 10 August 1978, p. 12, col. 2; "Ex-lawmaker 'Bathtub Joe' Dies at 80," *New Orleans States-Item,* 10 August 1978, p. 14, col. 1; Robert Maloney, interview; "Boggs Praises Maloney," *Times-Picayune,* 4 April 1967, sec. 3, p. 2, col. 4; "Paul Hebert Maloney," *Biographical Directory of the American Congress* (Washington: Government Printing Office, 1971), 1332; Paul Maloney, interview; Williams, *Huey Long,* 722-23.

6. Francis Chase, Jr., *Sound and Fury—An Informal History of Broadcasting* (New York: Harper & Brothers, 1942), 80-89; Hadley Cantril and Gordon Allport, *The Psychology of Radio* (New York: Harper and Brothers, 1935), 7-9. See also Ernest Bormann's study on the effectiveness of Long's radio addresses, "A Rhetorical Analysis of the National Radio Broadcasts of Senator Huey P. Long" (Ph.D. diss., State University of Iowa, 1935); "This young man—he is only forty-three—would be exactly nowhere if it weren't for radio," journalist George Kent exclaimed in an early 1935 article for the industry publication *Radio Stars* ("Radio Bows to Huey Long," *Radio Stars* 12, no. 6: 14), in the William B. Wisdom Collection, Special Collections, Howard-Tilton Memorial Library.

7. Cantril and Allport, *Psychology of Radio*, 7-9; Hugh Mercer Blain, ed., *Favorite Huey Long Stories* (Baton Rouge: Otto Claitor, 1937), 11-15.

8. Cantril and Allport, *Psychology of Radio*, 7-8; Williams, *Huey Long,* 629-30; Brinkley, *Voices of Protest*, 62, 71, 169.

9. Fitzmorris, *Frankly Fitz!*, 80.

10. Hermann B. Deutsch, "Kingdom of the Kingfish," *New Orleans Item*, 4 September 1939, p. 3, col. 1; Hermann B. Deutsch, "Kingdom of the Kingfish," *New Orleans Item*, 6 September 1939, p. 11, col. 1. This newspaper series ran irregularly in the *Item* from July 19 to September 20, 1939 and is available in its entirety at the Louisiana Collection of the Howard-Tilton Memorial Library, Tulane University, New Orleans, La.; "Long Bars Press, Public at Hearing Testimony on Vice Heard by Probers," *New Orleans States,* 1 September 1934, p. 1, col. 7; "Long Blocks Fair Election Offer," *New Orleans States*, 2 September 1934, p. 1, co. 8; "Long's Probers, Under Guard, Hear Charges of Vice, Graft," *Times-Picayune*, 2 September 1934, p. 1, col. 8; "Louisiana: Long Holds and Open Hearing Behind Closed Doors," *Newsweek* 4, no. 10 (8 September 1934): 9; Williams, *Huey Long*, 727-30.

11. "More Witnesses Before Probers," *New Orleans States*, 8 September 1934, p. 9, col. 1; "More Witnesses Heard by Group of Investigators," *Times-Picayune*, 8 September 1934, p. 1, col. 3; "Long Committee Resumes Hearing on City Affairs," *Times-Picayune*, 9 September 1934, p. 1, col. 5; "Long Keeps Up His Threat of Impeachment," *New Orleans Tribune*, 8 September 1934, p. 1, col. 7; "U.S. and State Courts Overrule Dictatorship Assumed by Huey Long," p. 1, col. 6.

12. "More Witnesses Before Probers," p. 9, col. 1; "More Witnesses Heard by Group of Investigators," p. 1, col. 3; "Long Committee Resumes Hearing on City Affairs," p. 1, col. 5; "Long Keeps Up His Threat of Impeachment," p. 1, col. 7; "U.S. and State Courts Overrule Dictatorship Assumed by Huey Long," p. 1, col. 6.

13. "More Witnesses Before Probers," p. 9, col. 1; "More Witnesses Heard by Group of Investigators," p. 1, col. 3; "Long Committee Resumes Hearing on City Affairs," p. 1, col. 5; "Long Keeps Up His Threat of Impeachment," p. 1, col. 7; "U.S. and State Courts Overrule Dictatorship Assumed by Huey Long," p. 1, col. 6.

14. Reyer, interview; "More Witnesses Before Probers," p. 9, col. 1; Kane, *Louisiana Hayride*, 108.

15. "More Witnesses Heard by Group of Investigators," p. 1, col. 3; "More Witnesses Before Probers," p. 9, col. 1.

16. "Long Committee Resumes Hearing on City Affairs," p. 1, col. 5; "Probers Quit Until Monday," *New Orleans Item*, 9 September 1934, p. 1, col. 4; F. Raymond Daniell, "Long and Mayor Declare a Truce," *New York Times*, 9 September 1934, p. 33, col. 1.

17. "People's Rights Election Issue, Voters Are Told," *Times-Picayune*, 9 September 1934, p. 1, col. 6.

18. Fleming, interview; Reyer, interview; "Election Peace Pact Signed," *New Orleans Item*, 9 September 1934, p. 1, col. 7; "City Flocks to Polls," *New Orleans Item*, 11 September 1934, p. 1, col. 7; Daniell, "Long and Mayor Declare a Truce," p. 33, col. 1; "U.S. Court Takes Hand in Poll," p. 1, col. 6. Curiously, Long, by agreeing to the truce, made real a dream long harbored by the Uptown Silk Stocking reformers who had frequently complained about the intimidating presence of the Old Regular policemen on election day (see Tyler, *Silk Stockings and Ballot Boxes*, 13); League of Women Voters Collection, Box One, Folder 41, Special Collections, Howard-Tilton Memorial Library, Tulane University, New Orleans, La.; for Long's announcement of the truce, see circulars 50, 56, and 64 of the William B. Wisdom Collection, Special Collections, Howard-Tilton Memorial Library, Tulane University.

19. Gillis, interview.

20. Williams, *Huey Long*, 732-33; Fleming, interview; "Probers Quit Until Monday," p. 1, col. 4.

21. Long, interview.

22. "Moloney Final Rites Arranged," *Times-Picayune*, 15 February 1972, p. 8, col. 2; "Soldier of Fortune Guy Molony Dies," *New Orleans States-Item*, 14 February 1972, p. 4, col. 6; "Guy Ross Molony, Police Chief, Soldier," *Washington Post*, 16 February 1972, p. D3, col. 2; Hermann B. Deutsch, "Guy Molony's Off Again; But This Time on Peaceful Pursuits," *New Orleans Item*, 13 August 1941, p. 3, col. 5. See also Guy Molony's unpublished memoirs, "General Data" and "Names and People I Remember," Guy R. Molony Papers, Special Collections, Howard-Tilton Memorial Library, Tulane University, New Orleans, La.; Isabel C. Molony, interview by author, tape recording, New Orleans, La., 19 September 1996.

23. Thomas P. McCann, *An American Company—The Tragedy of United Fruit* (New York: Crown Publishers, 1976), 14-32; Williams,

Huey Long, 466, 468; for more on Zemurray, see "Samuel Zemurray, 84, Is Dead; Headed United Fruit Company," *New York Times,* 2 December 1961, p. 23, col. 2. Although Deutsch somehow managed to maintain a journalistic balance in his reporting on Long, Walmsley, and the Old Regulars, he clearly admired Molony, as can be most vividly seen in his account of Molony and Lee Christmas's Latin American adventures in *The Incredible Yanqui—The Career of Lee Christmas* (London: Longmans, Green, and Company, 1931), see in particular pages 83-91. In his own unpublished memoirs, Molony offers contradictory testimony on how much money he made as a mercenary, first claiming "I can truthfully say that I never earned the money I would have been paid for digging ditches . . ." but two pages later he remarks: "I have managed to accumulate quite a respectable amount of dough for my family and staff . . ." (Molony Papers).

24. John V. Biamonte, Jr., *Spirit of Vengeance—Nativism and Louisiana Justice, 1921-1924* (Baton Rouge: Louisiana State University, 1986), 16-17; "Police Frameup Cases Passed in Court," *New Orleans States,* 1 May 1925, p. 1, col. 8. Of his years as the city's top cop, Molony would later write disarmingly: "Was superintendent of Police New Orleans 1921-1925, and not a very good one" (Molony Papers); "Let's face it, he was no politician," his daughter Isabel later put it (Molony, interview).

25. "Orleans' Trouble Dodger Is Home—He's Guy Molony," *New Orleans Item,* 11 January 1934, p. 1, col. 3. Walmsley actually came in as the New Orleans city attorney on 5 May 1925, four days after Molony quit as chief of police, but between 1921 and 1925 Walmsley, in New Orleans, served as assistant attorney general in charge of criminal law, a position that would have brought him into regular contact with Molony (*Eastern Louisiana—A History,* 629); "Rites Set for Walmsley Friday," p. 1, col. 2; "Police Frameup Cases Passed in Court," p. 1, col. 8.

26. "Fighting Colonel Molony Back in New Orleans for a Visit," *New Orleans Item,* 6 September 1934, p. 1, col. 4; "Col. Molony Not Hired, Says Mayor," *New Orleans Item,* 7 September 1934, p. 5, col. 7; "Witnesses Tell City Probers of Being Molested," *Times-Picayune,* 7 September 1934, p. 1, col. 6; "Court 'Racket' Charged by Quiz Witness," *New Orleans Tribune,* 6 September 1934, p. 1, col. 6; "Molony Tifts with Long at City Probe," *New Orleans Tribune,* 7 September 1934, p. 1, col. 7; Williams, *Huey Long,* 731; Molony, interview.

27. "Molony Tifts with Long at City Probe," p. 1, col. 7; "Witnesses Tell City Probers of Being Molested," p. 1, col. 6.

28. "Molony Tifts with Long at City Probe," p. 1, col. 7; "Witnesses Tell City Probers of Being Molested," p. 1, col. 6.

29. "Molony Tifts with Long at City Probe," p. 1, col. 7; "Witnesses Tell City Probers of Being Molested," p. 1, col. 6. Like Walmsley, Molony thought Long was his social inferior, as evidenced by this exchange during the vice committee hearings: when Huey asked Molony what he thought of the truce to keep the police and guardsmen away from the polls, Molony said he was for it. "I'm glad you agree with me," Huey continued. "It's the only thing we do agree on," Molony replied. Said Huey: "It's the only thing we do agree on, but if we were to work together more often, I think we would find many things we agree on." Molony: "I doubt it" ("Court 'Racket' Charged by Quiz Witness," p. 1, col. 6).

30. "Molony Tifts with Long at City Probe," p. 1, col. 7; "Witnesses Tell City Probers of Being Molested," p. 1, col. 6.

31. "Molony Tifts with Long at City Probe," p. 1, col. 7; "Witnesses Tell City Probers of Being Molested," p. 1, col. 6.

32. "Molony Tifts with Long at City Probe," p. 1, col. 7; "Witnesses Tell City Probers of Being Molested," p. 1, col. 6.

33. "Molony Tifts with Long at City Probe," p. 1, col. 7; "Witnesses Tell City Probers of Being Molested," p. 1, col. 6.

34. "Molony Tifts with Long at City Probe," p. 1, col. 7; "Witnesses Tell City Probers of Being Molested," p. 1, col. 6.

35. J. Edgar Hoover to R. Whitley, 10 September 1934, serial number 62-32509-50; Hoover to Marvin H. McIntyre, assistant secretary to the president, 11 September 1934, serial number 62-32507-50.

36. "Louisiana Gives Long a Big Margin in Primary Vote," *New York Times,* 12 September 1934, p. 1, col. 3.

37. "Louisiana Gives Long a Big Margin," p. 1, col. 3; "Long's Candidates Win in Democratic Primary for Various Positions," Baton Rouge Morning Advocate, 12 September 1934, p. 1, col. 7; "National Guardsmen Held in N.O. for Nearly Week Are Sent Back to Homes," Baton Rouge Morning Advocate, 13 September 1934, p. 1, col. 3; "O'Connor, Higgins, Maloney, and Fernandez Victorious," Times-Picayune, 12 September 1934, p. 1, col. 8; "Long's Candidates Victorious in Primary," New Orleans Tribune,

12 September 1934, p. 1, col. 7; "Returns from State Show Six Districts Held by Anti-Longs," New Orleans States, 12 September 1934, p. 1, col. 2.

38. The Long ticket's best showing came in the same low income precincts and wards Huey swept in his successful 1930 U.S. Senate race, places previously dismissed as Old Regular strongholds. In Ward 5, Precinct 4; Ward 9, Precinct 14, 18, and 19; Ward 12, Precinct 1; and Ward 13, Precinct 1—all places Long won more than 60 percent of the vote in 1930, his candidates in the fall of 1934 won by at least two-to-one margins. The correlation between this vote and the economics of the neighborhoods they represent is rather startling; Gayle Catherine Singer, "Huey P. Long and New Orleans in the Senatorial Election of 1930" (master's thesis, St. Mary's Dominican College, 1970), 137-42; see also *Official Precinct Registrar, 9th Ward, 1931-1934,* Louisiana Division, New Orleans Public Library. The final tally gave all of the Long candidates handsome wins: Paul Moloney's 35,615 to Gus Blanchard's 25,254 in the Second Congressional District, J. O. Fernandez's 32,380 to Herve Racivitch's 25,275 in the First Congressinal District, Archie Higgins' 64,487 to Walter Gleason's 49,661 for the Supreme Court seat, and James P. O'Connor's 67,146 to Francis Williams' 52,233 for the Public Service Commission ("Louisiana's Vote is Promulgated," *New Orleans States,* 18 September 1934, p. 7, col. 5).

39. "Senator Long and His Supporters Listen to Returns at Hotel Suite," *New Orleans Tribune,* 12 September 1934, p. 2, col. 2; "O'Connor, Higgins, Maloney, and Fernandez Victorious," p. 1, col. 8; "Louisiana Gives Long a Big Margin," p. 1, col. 3; "Kingfish to King," *Newsweek* 4, no. 12 (22 September 1934): 11; Hodding Carter, "The Kingfish on His Way," *New Republic* 81, no. 1042 (21 November 1934): 40-42. The same mid-term contests that revived Huey's fortunes, however, absolutely electrified President Roosevelt's prospects. In the November mid-term general election, New Deal Democrats saw their party pick up nine seats in the House, increasing their membership there from 313 to 322, as they also won an additional 10 new seats in the Senate, giving them an overwhelming 69 to 29 margin, in an unprecedented mid-term victory for the party holding the White House, tangible proof for Huey that Roosevelt was still enormously popular across the country (James MacGregor Burns, *Roosevelt: The Lion and the Fox* [New York: Harcourt, Brace & World, 1956], 197-203).

40. "O'Connor, Higgins, Maloney, and Fernandez Victorious," p. 1, col. 8; "Long Ticket Wins in City; Wilson Only Congressman to Face Second Primary," *Times-Picayune*, 13 September 1934, p. 1, col. 4; "Long's Candidates Win in Democratic Primary for Various Positions," p. 1, col. 7; "National Guardsmen Held in N.O. for Nearly Week Are Sent Back to Homes," p. 1, col. 3; Mel Washburn, "The Spotlight," *New Orleans Tribune*, 12 September 1934, p. 7, col. 1. Mel Washburn, the entertainment columnist for the *Tribune* who frequently encountered Huey on his dancing and drinking outings in the Blue Room, noted the effects of the balloting on the city's two most famous hotels: "Voters yesterday," Washburn said, "moved the blue room from the Roosevelt Hotel to the St. Charles!"

41. "Guard Moves Out of City," *New Orleans Tribune*, 13 September 1934, p. 1, col. 3.

CHAPTER 9

1. "National Guardsmen Held in N.O. for Nearly Week Are Sent Back to Homes," p. 1, col. 3; "Guards Pack, Ready to Quit Orleans Today," *New Orleans Item*, 12 September 1934, p. 1, col. 1; "Guard Moves Out of City," *New Orleans Tribune*, 13 September 1934, p. 1, col. 3; "Troops Demobilize, Pack Up Guns, and Set Out for Home," *Times-Picayune*, 13 September 1934, p. 1, col. 8; *Special Orders, A.G.O., L.A., 1934-1935*, 13 September 1934, Order Number 71, the Military Library at Jackson Barracks, New Orleans, La.

2. "Guards Pack, Ready to Quit Orleans Today," p. 1, col. 1; "Militia Departs from Office of Registrar Here," *Times-Picayune*, 14 September 1934, p. 1, col. 3; "Guard Moves Out of City," p. 1, col. 3. At least one bullet entered Long's mansion, lodging itself in a book on the life of Benvenuto Cellini, the Italian sculptor (Long, interview; Gouaze, interview).

3. "Guard Moves Out of City," p. 1, col. 3; "National Guardsmen Held in N.O. for Nearly Week Are Sent Back to Homes," p. 1, col. 3.

4. "Beauties to Parade," *New Orleans Item*, 13 September 1934, p. 4, col. 1; "Beauty Show Again Tonight," *New Orleans Item*, 14 September 1934, p. 4, col. 3.

5. "Blue Room Opens at the Roosevelt," Times-Picayune, 3 October

1934, p. 16, col. 3; Mel Washburn, "Blue Room Reopened," New Orleans Item, 2 October 1934, p. 22, col. 6; "Blue Room Opens in the Roosevelt," New Orleans States, 2 October 1934, p. 18, col. 2.

6. Tulane University, *Jambalaya Year Book 1935* (Nashville: Benson Printing Company, 1935), 134-35, 142-43; Carter, *The Past as Prelude,* 206-7.

7. "House Moves for Passage of 44 Bills," *Baton Rouge Morning Advocate,* 14 November 1934, p. 1, col. 1; "Bills Pass House with No Fight," *Baton Rouge Morning Advocate,* 15 November 1934, p. 1, col. 1; "Legislators to Adjourn Before Noon," *Baton Rouge Morning Advocate,* 16 November 1934, p. 1, col. 8; "Long Cracks Whip and Speeds Bills," *New York Times,* 14 November 1934, p. 5, col. 1; "Long on the Dais 'Passes' Bill," *New York Times,* 15 November 1934, p. 16, col. 1; "Long Bills Voted by Senate Group," *New York Times,* 16 November 1934; "Debt Moratorium Voted in Louisiana," 17 November 1934, p. 30, col. 2; "Huey Long's Forty-Four Laws," *New Republic* 81, no. 1043 (28 November 1934): 63; Williams, *Huey Long,* 726-28.

8. "The Time Machine—December," *American Heritage Magazine* 36 (December 1984): 22; Raymond Gramm Swing, "The Menace of Huey Long, Part I," *Nation* 140, no. 3627 (9 January 1935): 36-39; "Long Sets Session to Widen Power," *New York Times,* 16 December 1934, p. 37, col. 1; "Huey Long Files 35 'Mystery' Bills," *New York Times,* 17 December 1934, p. 3, col. 4; "Long Legislature Does His Bidding," *New York Times,* 18 December 1934, p. 12, col. 5; "Joker Makes Long School 'Dictator,'" *New York Times,* 19 December 1934, p. 2, col. 1; "Long Usurps Rule at State Capital," *New York Times,* 20 December 1934, p. 25, col. 6; "Session Gives Long Power Over Cities," *New York Times,* 21 December 1934, p. 18, col. 1; "350 Laws Enlarge Huey Long Realm," *New York Times,* 23 December 1934, sec. 2, p. 1, col. 6; *Official Journal of the Proceedings of the House of Representatives, Second Extra Session,* (Baton Rouge: Remieres-Jones Printing, 1934), 41-78; *Official Journal of the Proceedings of the House of Representatives, Third Extra Session* (Baton Rouge: Remieres-Jones Printing, 1934), 74-102. Both journals provide page after page of the consistent, lopsided majorities Huey was commanding by late 1934.

9. Russell Owen, "Huey Long Gives His View of Dictators," *New York Times,* 10 February 1935, sec. 6, p. 3, col. 1; "Long Maps Battle

for Vote on Farley," *New York Times,* 10 March 1935, p. 33, col. 3; "After the Storm," *New York Times,* 20 March 1935, p. 20, col. 4; "Share-the-Wealth Wave," *Time* 25, no. 13 (1 April 1935): 15-18; "Kingfish: 'Gamewarden' Long Takes University to Its Game," *Newsweek* 4, no. 18 (3 November 1934): 10; "Louisiana: The Kingfish Stops Presses with Big Round Oath," *Newsweek* 4, no. 22 (1 December 1934): 8; "L.S.U.: 26 Students Get Theirs in Huey Long vs. Press Row," *Newsweek* 4, no. 23 (8 December 1934): 14; "L.S.U.: Two Heavy Brickbats Hit Huey Long's University," *Newsweek* 5, no. 1 (5 January 1935): 34; "Kingfish: Square Dealers Attack Huey; Huey Attacks Millionaires, Colleague Asks to Be Butler," *Newsweek* 5, no. 4 (26 January 1935): 7; "Demagogues: Johnson Lambasts Senator and Priest; Long Counters with Utopia; Coughlin Parries with Spirit of '76," *Newsweek* 5, no. 11 (16 March 1935): 5; Swing, "The Menace of Huey Long, Part I," 36-39; Raymond Gramm Swing, "The Menace of Huey Long, Part II," *Nation* 140, no. 3628 (16 January 1935): 69-71; Raymond Gramm Swing, "The Menace of Huey Long, Part III," *Nation* 140, no. 3629 (23 January 1935): 98-100; "The Build-up of Long and Coughlin," *Nation* 140, no. 3637 (20 March 1935): 325-26; "Dictated, But Not Dead," *Business Week,* 9 February 1935, p. 12, col. 1; "Facts Are Stubborn," *Saturday Evening Post* 207, no. 35 (4 May 1935): 26; W. Davenport, "Too High and Too Mighty,"*Collier's* 95, no. 3 (19 January 1935): 7-8; "Rabble-rouser," *Collier's* 95, no. 7 (23 January 1935): 70; V. F. Calverton, "Our Future Dictator—Is It Huey Long?" *Scribner's Monthly* 97, no. 3 (March 1935): 174-75; "Churches and American Fascism," *Christian Century* 52, no. 11 (13 March 1935): 327-29; Fielding, *American Newsreel,* 285; Fielding, *March of Time,* 12, 46-53.

10. Fielding, *March of Time,* 12, 46-53; "Huey Long a Film Censor Now? Kidding Subject Deleted from 'Time' in N.O.," *Variety* 118, no. 6 (24 April 1935): p. 1, col. 4.

11. Brinkley, *Voices of Protest,* 169-71, 284-86; McElvaine, *The Great Depression,* 246-49; Schlesinger, *The Politics of Upheaval,* 63-67.

12. "Long's Acts Delay New Orleans Funds," *New York Times,* 18 November 1934, p. 1, col. 30.

13. Williams, *Huey Long,* 795-99; Hair, *Kingfish and His Realm,* 286-87; Stan Opotowsky, *The Longs of Louisiana* (New York: Dutton, 1960), 113-14; Martin, *Dynasty,* 112; Kane, *Louisiana Hayride,* 163-70.

14. Whitley to Hoover, 4 October 1934, serial number 62-32509-

58; Hoover to Attorney General Stephens, 12 October 1934, serial number 62-32509-58; G. N. Lowden to Hoover, 31 January 1935, serial number 62-32509-60; Hoover to Assistant Attorney General William Stanley, 8 May 1935, serial number 62-32509-69; C. I. Lord to Hoover, 27 July 1935, serial number 62-32509-73.

15. Harold Ickes, *The Secret Diary of Harold L. Ickes: The First Thousand Days, 1933-36* (New York: Simon & Schuster, 1953), 346-47; Smith, *New Deal in the Urban South,* 108-11, 114, 115, and 118; "Long's Acts Delay New Orleans Funds," p. 30, col. 1; "Ickes Warns Long; Halts PWA Funds," *New York Times,* 23 November 1934, p. 2, col. 2; "Long Acts to Rule Belief Bills Fund," *New York Times,* 15 April 1935, p. 7, col. 1; "Long Gets Control of Federal Grants," *New York Times,* 16 April 1935, p. 12, col. 2; "Ickes Scores Long; Threatens to Halt Works in Louisiana," *New York Times,* 17 April 1935, p. 1, col. 3; "Loans to Georgia Revoked by Ickes; Louisiana Also Hit," *New York Times,* 19 April 1935, p. 1, col. 1; "Long Defies Ickes: Forms Relief Rule," *New York Times,* 20 April 1935, p. 2, col. 3; "PWA May Cancel All Louisiana Jobs," *New York Times,* 21 April 1935, p. 22, col. 1; "Long Threatens 'Boston Tea Party,'" *New York Times,* 22 April 1935, p. 12, col. 4; "Long Excoriates President's Aids, Talks Succession," *New York Times,* 23 April 1935, p. 1, col. 6.

16. "New Orleans Pay Pledged by FERA," *New York Times,* 23 June 1935, p. 24, col. 1.

17. Weiss, interview; Gillis, interview. There is some question as to how serious Long was about removing Walmsley. "No, that would be bad psychology," he told an associate who suggested that he simply get rid of the mayor through the necessary two-thirds vote of the legislature. "You always leave a figurehead for your boys to fight against." Huey added that Walmsley had become a perfect target because "he's impotent and can't do us any harm" (Williams, "The Gentleman from Louisiana," *Huey P. Long—Southern Demagogue or American Democrat?* [Lafayette: The Center for Louisiana Studies, 1976], 74).

18. "Long Asks 'People' to Oust Walmsley, *New York Times,* 13 July 1935, p. 3, col. 6; "Long Victory Seen in Walmsley Fight," *New York Times,* 21 July 1935, sec. 4, p. 6, col. 8; "City Workers Still Ponder Over Wages," *New Orleans Tribune,* 17 July 1935, p. 1, col. 8; "PWA Projects in Louisiana Hinge on Long," *New Orleans Tribune,* 18 July 1935, p. 3, col. 1; "U.S. Withholds PWA Funds Until Long Repeals

Control; Mayor to Push Water Fight," *New Orleans Tribune*, 19 July 1935, p. 1, col. 6; "Further Loss of PWA Funds Is Revealed," *New Orleans Tribune*, 20 July 1935, p. 3, col. 1; "Mayor Flays Tax Collection as Thievery," *New Orleans Tribune*, 22 July 1935, p. 1, col. 6; "Will Not Resign, Plans Continued Fight, Declares Mayor to Public," *Times-Picayune*, 15 July 1935, p. 1, col. 1.

19. "Long's Hand Bared in Garbage Strike; Workers Apologize," *New Orleans Tribune*, 3 July 1935, p. 1, col. 8.

20. Ibid.

21. Fairclough, "The Public Utilities Industry in New Orleans," 49-63; Carpenter, "The New Orleans Street Railway Strike of 1929-30," 50, 109, 142, and 163; Cook and Watson, *Louisiana Labor*, 199. While Walmsley was willing to work with organized labor, the evidence suggests that Long was not: Cook and Watson say Huey's record was "poor inasmuch as he failed to enact any legislation of notable benefit to the labor movement," 210-11; Sindler calls Huey's labor record "sorry" (Sindler, *Huey Long's Louisiana*, 105); while another scholar, Arthur Pearce, accuses Long of "union-busting" in the 1929 streetcar strike by failing to support the striking drivers (Pearce, "The Rise and Decline of Labor in New Orleans," [master's thesis, Tulane University, 1938], 229). George Wallance, a top official with the American Federation of Labor also found Long's labor record wanting, charging that behind Huey's "sweet words about 'sharing our wealth,' is a ruthless anti-labor program" (Hodding Carter, "Walmsley Finds Strong Sentiments in Parishes," *New Orleans Item-Tribune*, 21 July 1935, p. 14, col. 1). Long, however, thought he had a good labor program and frequently advertised himself as the pro-labor candidate (see circular 47, "Huey P. Long's Work for Labor," in the William B. Wisdom Collection, Special Collections, Howard-Tilton Memorial Library, Tulane University).

22. Gouaze, interview.

23. Williams, *Huey Long*, 850-53; "Long's Bills Seize All City's Taxes, Empower Police, Fire Boards to Borrow, Fix Penalty for Misuse of Relief Funds," *New Orleans Tribune*, 5 July 1935, p. 1, col. 5; C. E. Frampton, "Last Minute Moves Awaited with Bills Up for Vote Today," *New Orleans Tribune*, 6 July 1935, p. 1, col. 8; "Legislature Ready for New Long Bills," *New York Times*, 5 July 1935, p. 14, col. 1; "Legislators Rush to Pass New Long Bills," *New York Times*, 6 July 1935, p. 2, col. 1.

24. "Long's Bills Seize All City's Taxes," p. 1, col. 5.

25. "Long Is Branded As Party Traitor," *New York Times*, 25 July 1935, p. 20, col. 1; "Walmsley and One Aide Alone Now Combat Long," *New York Times*, 30 July 1935, p. 14, col. 2.

26. Hair, *Kingfish and His Realm*, 256-66; *Bisso Towboat Company, Incorporated* (company pamphlet that gives a brief sketch of Captain Bisso's political career [New Orleans: Rosemary James and Associates, 1991]); for more on James E. Comiskey, see Leibling, *The Earl of Louisiana*, 57-64; Eric Wayne Doerries, "James E. Comiskey, the Irish Third Ward Boss: A Study of a Unique and Dying Brand of Politics," (master's thesis, Tulane University, 1973), 3-8; Hoke May, "Personality—Jim Comiskey," *New Orleans Magazine* 3, no. 6 (March 1969): 39-44.

27. "Long, Regulars Make Peace Providing for Ouster of Walmsley by His Own Forces," *New Orleans Tribune*, 13 July 1935, p. 1, col. 7. During the meeting, Long referred to his guests as "you birds," prompting Burke to complain, reminding Huey that he had earlier promised to refer to the Regulars only as gentlemen. The following day cartoonist John Chase in the *New Orleans Item* pictured a disconsolate Old Regular ward leader, hiding his tears behind his hands as he cries: "He called us 'boids'" (John Chase cartoon, *New Orleans Item*, 16 July 1935, p. 4, col. 3).

28. "Long, Regulars Make Peace Providing for Ouster of Walmsley by His Own Forces," p. 1, col. 7; "Old Regulars Plan Mass Meeting for Walmsley's Ouster," *Times-Picayune*, 13 July 1935, p. 1, col. 8; and "Walmsley Gets Pay for City Forces, Byrne Fires 3 Stanley Assistants," *New Orleans States*, 13 July 1995, p. 1, col. 8.

29. J. K. Riggs to Walmsley, 18 July 1935, T. Semmes Walmsley Papers, Louisiana Division, New Orleans Public Library; Father Rombouts to Walmsley, 13 August 1935, Walmsley Papers. See also Leroy Stafford Boyd to Walmsley, 20 July 1935; R. H. Bruce to Walmsley, 21 July 1935; W. G. Caldwell to Walmsley, 31 July 1935; Perry Young to Walmsley, 20 August 1935; and Milton Montifue to Walmsley, 21 August 1935, Walmsley Papers.

30. Louis B. Davis to Walmsley, 23 July 1935, Walmsley Papers.

31. "Mayor to Keep Job; Loses Council Rule; Long Goes After F. D.," *New Orleans Item-Tribune*, 14 July 1935, p. 1, col. 7; "Blocks Long's Move to Oust Walmsley," *New York Times*, 16 July 1935, p. 10, col. 5. For more information on the Square Deal Association

and a subsequent abortive coup they would launch against Huey, see Kane, *Louisiana Hayride,* 113-14. Williams, *Huey Long,* 783-90; Fleming, interview; Mrs. J. S. Roussell to Hoover, 3 March 1935, serial number 62-32509-65; Ernest K. Bourgeois to Hoover, 8 March 1935, serial number 62-32509-63; and Hoover to Bourgeois, 16 April 1935, serial number 62-32509-63.

32. "Roosevelt Picture Back in Long Club," *New York Times,* 29 July 1935, p. 17, col. 5; "Arrest of Mayor's Aide Due," *New Orleans Item,* 27 July 1935, p. 1, col. 7; "Reyer Orders Walmsley Aide Be Arrested," *New Orleans Item-Tribune,* 28 July 1935, p. 1, col. 5; "Choctaws Order Romaguera Arrest," *New Orleans States,* 27 July 1935, p. 1, col. 8.

33. "Reyer Orders Walmsley Aide Be Arrested," p. 1, col. 5.

34. "Mayor to Keep Job; Loses Council Rule; Long Goes After F. D.," p. 1, col. 7; "The Fighting Mayor of New Orleans," *New York Times,* 15 July 1935, p. 9, col. 3; "Block Long's Move to Oust Walmsley," *New York Times,* 16 July 1935, p. 10, col. 5.

35. "Long Leaves; 'Can't Help with Mayor,'" *New Orleans Tribune,* 18 July 1935, p. 1, col. 7; "Bolting Regular Chiefs Getting No Cash from Long," *Times-Picayune,* 17 July 1935, p. 1, col. 5; "Roosevelt Bars New PWA Grants Under Long Rule," *Times-Picayune,* 18 July 1935, p. 1, col. 6; see also circular number 73 on Long's demand for Walmsley's resignation in the William B. Wisdom Collection, Special Collections, Howard-Tilton Memorial Library, Tulane University.

36. Mrs. John Singer to Walmsley, 8 August 1935, Walmsley Papers.

CHAPTER 10

1. "'Square Dealers Halted Petition,' Asserts Whilden," *Times-Picayune,* 17 July 1935, p. 2, col. 5; "Whilden, Incensed at Cossack's Raid, Will Seek Legal Redress," *New Orleans States,* 18 July 1935, p. 1, col. 2; "Give Two Versions of the Raid," *New Orleans Item* 18 July 1935, p. 1, col. 7; Oscar Whilden to Walmsley, 11 July 1935, Walmsley Papers.

2. "Square Dealers Halted Petition, Asserts Whilden," p. 2, col. 5; "'No Home Safe,' Asserts Whilden," *Times-Picayune,* 18 August 1935, p. 16, col. 1.

HUEY LONG INVADES NEW ORLEANS

3. "Give Two Versions of Raid," p. 1, col. 7.

4. *The Congressional Record, Proceedings and Debates of the First Session of the Seventy-Fourth Congress* (Washington: Government Printing Office, 1935), 79, pt. 12:12786-12791; Williams, *Huey Long,* 839-40; David Zinman, *Day Huey Long Was Shot* (Jackson: The University Press of Mississippi, 1993), 231-39; Kane, *Louisiana Hayride,* 132-33; Hair, *Kingfish and His Realm,* 318; "Give Two Versions of Raid," p. 1, col. 7; "Long Predicted He Would Be Shot," *New York Times,* 9 September 1935, p. 1, col. 7.

5. "Long Predicted He Would Be Shot," p. 1, col. 7.

6. Gibbons, interview.

7. Morgan, interview.

8. Leroy Stafford Boyd to Walmsley, 20 July 1935, Walmsley Papers.

9. Perry Young to Walmsley, 20 August 1935, Walmsley Papers; James Gill, *Lords of Misrule—Mardi Gras and the Politics of Race in New Orleans* (Jackson: University Press of Mississippi, 1997), 14, 185, 190.

10. "Pay Promised City Employees," *New Orleans Tribune,* 8 August 1935, p. 1, col. 3; "Worker Held for Threat Against Pratt," *New Orleans Tribune,* 8 August 1935, p. 1, col. 3; "1 Dies of Heat; 15 Collapse," *New Orleans Tribune,* 9 August 1935, p. 1, col. 1; "City Workers to Get Half of August Pay," *New Orleans Tribune,* 15 August 1935, p. 1, col. 3.

11. "Widow's Plight Blamed on Long," *New Orleans Tribune,* 24 August 1935, p. 1, col. 3.

12. Ibid.

13. "FERA Pay Cut; Meet in Protest," *New Orleans Item,* 6 September 1935, p. 1, col. 3; Smith, *New Deal in the Urban South,* 110-11.

14. "The Longs Hear Huey," *New Orleans Item-Tribune,* 1 September 1935, p. 7, col. 3; Williams, *Huey Long,* 859.

15. "Extra Session Reported Set," *Tribune,* 7 September 1935, p. 1, col. 5; "Senate Receives 39 Bills Passed in Brief Session of Lower House," *Times-Picayune,* 10 September 1935, p. 1, col. 1; "Long's Condition Improved; Rallies from Rival's Shot," *Christian Science Monitor,* 9 September 1935, p. 1, col. 6; Williams, *Huey Long,* 859-63; Zinman, *Day Huey Long Was Shot,* 13-21; Thomas A. Becnel,

Senator Allen Ellender of Louisiana—A Biography (Baton Rouge: Louisiana State University Press, 1995), 63-64.

16. The lay of the land for Walmsley was clear as early as the first week of August when the city commission, now with a working Long majority—thanks to the defections of Old Regulars Skelly, Pratt, and Gomilia—began to regularly overrule Walmsley, even going so far to declare that they, not Walmsley, would now decide who to hire for new city jobs ("Long Cohorts in Council Vote Mayor Down," *New Orleans Tribune,* 7 August 1935, p. 2, col. 3).

17. Mel Washburn, "The Spotlight," *New Orleans Tribune,* 9 August 1935, p. 2, col. 4; Weiss, interview.

18. "Long to Slap Fine on U.S. Officials in State," *New Orleans Item-Tribune,* 8 September 1935, p. 1, col. 8; Becnel, *Senator Ellender of Louisiana,* 63; Robert Heilman, *The Southern Connection* (Baton Rouge: Louisiana State University Press, 1991), 5-6; Charles East, "The Death of Huey Long: A Photographic Essay," *Southern Review* 21, no. 2 (spring 1985): 247-56.

19. Williams, *Huey Long,* 863-64; Zinman, *Day Huey Long Was Shot,* 101-2; in a letter to his longtime editor, Maxwell Perkins, on September 7, 1935, Hemingway wrote "Harry Hopkins and Roosevelt, who sent those poor bonus marchers down to get rid of them, got rid of them all right" (Carlos Baker, ed., *Hemingway—Selected Letters, 1917-1961* [New York: Charles Scribner and Sons, 1981], 186). According to Anna E. Rowe and the New Yorker's gifted Richard Rovere, Hemingway nursed a grudge against FDR because New Deal programs, with their emphasis on public works and building, threatened to alter the sleepy ambiance of his beloved Key West. The classic northern transplant, Hemingway viewed all change on his island as bad and went so far as to mock government workers for the New Deal in his classic *To Have and Have Not* (Rowe, *The Idea of Florida in the Literary Imagination* [Baton Rouge: Louisiana State University Press, 1986], 92-95; Richard Rovere, "End of the Line," *The New Yorker,* 15 December 1951, 75-90); Hemingway, *To Have and Have Not* (New York: Charles Scribner Sons, 1937), 81, 137. The hurricane resulted in the deaths of more than 450 people, most of them working for the CCC building bridges that would connect the Florida Keys. Huey's initial comment to Frampton equaled Hemingway's for

tastelessness: "Mr. Roosevelt ought to be very happy tonight. Every soldier he gets killed is one less vote against him" (*Hemingway—Selected Letters, 1917-1961*, 186).

20. Zinman, *Day Huey Long Was Shot*, 114-26; Williams, *Huey Long*, 862-67.

21. Fleming, interview.

22. Benezach, interview.

23. Zinman, *Day Huey Long Was Shot*, 141-42; Robert Mann, *Legacy To Power—Senator Russell Long of Louisiana* (New York: Paragon House, 1992), ix-xv; Salvaggio, *New Orleans' Charity Hospital*, 127-28.

24. Salvaggio, *New Orleans' Charity Hospital*, 127-28.

25. Salvaggio, *New Orleans' Charity Hospital*, 127-28. Dr. Edgar Hull, longtime professor of medicine at LSU Medical School who arrived at Huey's bedside the day after his shooting, has never bought the theory that Huey died because of internal hemorrhaging. "He was not bleeding," Hull claimed nearly sixty years after Huey's death. Dr. Hull believes that Huey was dying from "fulminating peritonitis" because he had been shot through the colon and it was a couple of hours after the shooting before he was operated on ("Dr. Hull Remembers," *LSU Medical Center Alumni Quarterly* [fall 1983]: 27; "Ready to Teach," *LSU Medical Center Alumni Quarterly* [fall 1983]: 1-3).

26. Zinman, *Day Huey Long Was Shot*, 174; "Long Tells How 1,000 Poor Lads Will Receive L.S.U. Education," *New Orleans Item*, 6 September 1935, p. 1, col. 1.

27. The White House released an official message upon the news of Huey's death, quoting the president condemning the "spirit of violence" as un-American, with "no place in a consideration of public affairs." But when asked by reporters the following day if he wanted to expand upon the formal statement, FDR replied: "No. Naturally I sent a telegram to Mrs. Long and the family" (*The Complete Presidential Press Conferences of Franklin D. Roosevelt, Volume 5-6*, 6:157-158).That Long's death suddenly and dramtically changed Roosevelt's fortunes for 1936 is beyond dispute. "Honest horror must have mixed with jubilation that what had appeared to be the most serious threat to his Presidency was now removed," author T. H. Watkins later noted in his biography of longtime Huey Long foe Harold Ickes, Roosevelt's influential secretary of

the interior (T. H. Watkins, *Righteous Pilgrim—The Life and Times of Harold L. Ickes, 1874-1952* [New York: Henry Holt and Company, 1990], 416-17); Michael Beschloss, *Kennedy and Roosevelt—The Uneasy Alliance* (New York: W. W. Norton and Company, 1980), 119, 120.

28. Agent Magee to Hoover, 7 September 1935 and 8 September 1935, serial number 62-32509-74; Hoover's response, 11 September 1935, serial number 62-32509-75.

29. East, "Death of Huey Long," 247-56; Burns, *Huey Long.*

30. Mary Morrison, interview by author, tape recording, New Orleans, La., 10 December 1995.

31. F. Raymond Daniell, "Throngs Pass Long's Bier As Friends Discuss 'Plot,'" *New York Times,* 12 September 1935, p. 1, col. 3; Gibbons, interview.

32. "Senator Huey Long Dies of Wounds After 30-Hour Futile Fight for Life; Troopers Guard Louisiana Capitol," *New York Times,* 10 September 1935, p. 1, col. 4; "Long to Get State Funeral; Gov. Allen to Run 'Machine'; Foes See Chance to Beat It," *New York Times,* 11 September 1935, p. 1, col. 5; "High and Humble Send Messages to Senator Long," *Times-Picayune,* 10 September 1935, p. 1, col. 3; "Senator Long Will Rest Under Shadow of State's Capitol," *Times-Picayune,* 11 September 1935, p. 1, col. 8; "Body of Long Lies in State Capitol, Public Files Past," *Times-Picayune,* 12 September 1935, p. 1, col. 7; "Long's Funeral Will Be Held Thursday at 4 p.m.; Body to Rest in Capitol," *Baton Rouge Morning Advocate,* 11 September 1935, p. 1, col. 6; "Thousands View Remains of Long in State Capitol," *Baton Rouge Morning Advocate,* 12 September 1935, p. 1, col. 7; Zinman, *Day Huey Long Was Shot,* 186-88; Hair, *Kingfish and His Realm,* 325-26; Page Smith, *Redeeming the Time: A People's History of the 1920s and the New Deal* (New York: McGraw-Hill, 1987), 651-52. Long's funeral produced the most emotional outpouring of grief since the burial of Jefferson Davis in 1889, a funeral attended by more than 50,000 mourners. In Southern history, only the grand send-offs for Martin Luther King, Jr., in 1968 and Elvis Presley in 1977, both attracting up to 80,000 people, come close to Long's ("Thousands Mourn As Long Is Buried," *New York Times,* 13 September 1935, p. 1, col. 2); Peter Applebome, *Dixie Rising—How the South Is Shaping America's Values, Politics, and Culture* (New York: Times Books, 1996), 299 and 335.

33. Fleming, interview; "Honor Guard to Baton Rouge," *New Orleans Item,* 10 September 1935, p. 4, col. 1; Gouaze, interview.

34. Alexander, interview; although recent scholars have argued that Long was no friend of blacks because he did little to challenge the racist and segregationist ethos of his day, that same argument can easily be turned on its head: in the face of rampant racism, Long somehow managed to spread the benefits of his programs to both blacks and whites. See *Louisiana Weekly,* which ruefully noted that with Huey's death "died the hope of Louisiana Negroes for the early granting of of their right to vote" (Maybe Osby Brown, "Huey Long Killed; His Murderer Is Slain," *Louisiana Weekly,* 14 September 1935, p. 1, col. 1; "Huey Long Is Dead," *Louisiana Weekly,* 14 September 1935, p. 8, col. 1). The infamous Black Panther Huey P. Newton, raised in Louisiana, was named after Long, notes Newton's biographer Hugh Pearson, who adds that Newton's father, Walter Newton, "had been impressed by Long's populist efforts on behalf of the state's ordinary citizens, which brought free schools, paved roads and jobs to Negroes as well as to whites" (Pearson, *The Shadow of the Panther* [Reading, Massachusetts: Addison-Wesley Publishing Company, 1994], 46); similarly Andrew Young in his 1996 autobiography notes that his father, Andrew Young, Sr., a respected New Orleans dentist, was impressed with Long because he created a program that provided free dental care to the rural poor. "Huey Long showed great concern for the poor," Young writes, "and his programs helped black citizens as well as white" (Young, *An Easy Burden—the Civil Rights Movement and the Transformation of America* [New York: Harper-Collins Publishers, 1996], 12). For more critical views on Long's racial attitudes, see Glen Jeansonne's "Huey Long and Racism," *Louisiana History* 33, no. 3 (summer 1992), 265-82; Hair, *Kingfish and His Realm,* 99, 127, 151, 170-71, 202, 274-75, and 303-4; Adam Fairclough, *Race and Democracy—The Civil Rights Struggle in Louisiana, 1915-1972* (Athens: The University of Georgia Press, 1995), 21, 22-23, 35-36, and 44-45.

35. "Thousands Mourn As Long Is Buried," p. 1, col. 2; "Throngs to See Long's Burial on Lawn of Louisiana Capitol," *Times-Picayune,* 13 September 1935, p. 1, col. 7; Zinman, *Day Huey Long Was Shot,* 187-92; Harrison E. Salisbury, *A Journey For Our Times—A Memoir* (New York: Harper and Row, 1983), 130-31.

36. "Thousands Mourn As Long Is Buried," p. 1, col. 2; "Throngs to See Long's Burial on Lawn of Louisiana Capitol," p. 1, col. 7

37. "Thousands Mourn As Long Is Buried," p. 1, col. 2; "Throngs to See Long's Burial on Lawn of Louisiana Capitol," p. 1, col. 7; Glen Jeansonne, *Gerald L. K. Smith—Minister of Hate* (New Haven: Yale University Press, 1988), 41-42.

38. "In Token of Love and Friendship," *New Orleans Tribune,* 9 October 1935, p. 7, col. 3; "Mayor Seeks Carnival Joy," *New Orleans Tribune,* 25 February 1936, p. 7, col. 4.

39. "Regulars Sit with Leaders of State Camp," *New Orleans Tribune,* 27 September 1935, p. 1, col. 3; "Regulars Will Back State Ticket; Ask 'Repeal' Platform," *New Orleans Tribune,* 28 September 1935, p. 1, col. 1; *Official Proceedings of the Commission Council of the City of New Orleans,* July 13, July 27, August 2, August 6, and December 3, 1935, microfilm copies in the Louisiana Division, New Orleans Public Library; Kurtz and Peoples, *Earl K. Long,* 84-86; Kane, *Louisiana Hayride,* 203-4; Haas, *DeLesseps S. Morrison and the Image of Reform,* 13.

40. *WPA Guide to New Orleans,* xxii-xxiii, 55, 281, and 371; "Bridge to Be Dedicated in Ceremonies Today with Historical Pageant As Climax," *New Orleans Tribune,* 16 December 1935, p. 1, col. 3; Jesse H. Jones, *Fifty Billion Dollars—My Thirteen Years with the RFC (1932-1945)* (New York: Macmillian Company, 1951), 165-66; C. S. Garner (general manager of the American Bridge Company) to Walmsley, 31 July 1933, under the American Bridge Company file, Walmsley Papers; John Maxwell (chairman of the Commander's Council) to Walmsley, 21 August 1933, under the "A" miscellaneous file, Walmsley Papers; Gus Blanchard (manager of the city's employment office) to Walmsley, 20 March 1933, under the "A" miscellaneous file, Walmsley Papers; Walmsley to Jesse Jones, 13 July 1933, under the Reconstruction Finance Corporation files, Walmsley Papers; also Walmsley to Jones, 11 November 1933, Walmsley Papers; Walmsley to President Roosevelt, 6 October 1933, Franklin D. Roosevelt file, Walmsley Papers; FDR's response to Walmsley, 11 October 1933, Franklin D. Roosevelt file, Walmsley Papers.

41. Jones, *Fifty Billion Dollars,* 165-66; Walmsley to Blanchard, 25 February 1933, under the "A" miscellaneous file, Walmsley Papers.

42. "Throngs Attend Dedication of Bridge; Mayor Booed at Span, Cheered at Banquet," *New Orleans Morning Tribune*, 17 December 1935, p. 1, col. 1; "Walmsley Is Booed at Bridge Ceremony," *New York Times*, 17 December 1935, p. 13, col. 2.

43. "Throngs Attend Dedication of Bridge; Mayor Booed at Span, Cheered at Banquet," p. 1, col. 1.; Jones, *Fifty Billion Dollars*, 165-66.

44. "Mayor Hits Machine at War Rally," *New Orleans Morning Tribune*, 4 January 1936, p. 5, col. 6; "Machine Gets Six; Dear Ticket Four in Poll Allotment," *New Orleans Morning Tribune*, 7 January 1936, p. 1, col. 1; "Louisiana Voters Go to Polls Today; Fair Weather Forecast," *New Orleans Morning Tribune*, 21 January 1936, p. 1, col. 7.

45. "Leche and State Ticket Win," Dear Trailing by 77,713; Returns Slow," *Times-Picayune*, 22 January 1936, p. 1, col. 7; "Leche Majority Grows As Country Ballot Is Counted," *Times-Picayune*, 23 January 1936, p. 1, col. 8; Kurtz and Peoples, *Earl K. Long*, 79-80; Sindler, *Huey Long's Louisiana*, 123; Martin, *Dynasty*, 155-56; Becnel, *Senator Allen Ellender of Louisiana*, 69-70.

46. "Governor Allen's Body Lies in State Today in Memorial Hall of Louisiana Capitol," *Baton Rouge Morning Advocate*, 29 January 1936, p. 1, col. 6; "O. K. Allen's Body Is Sent to Winnfield," *Baton Rouge Morning Advocate*, 30 January 1936, p. 1, col. 8; "Governor's Last Rites to Be Held Today in Church of Home Parish," *Times-Picayune*, 30 January 1936, p. 1, col. 8; "Gov. O. K. Allen, Heir to Huey Long, Dies," *New York Times*, 29 January 1936, p. 5, col. 2; "NOE TO CARRY ON POLICIES OF PAST AS NEW GOVERNOR; ALLEN'S BODY LIES IN STATE," *New Orleans Morning Tribune*, 29 January 1936, p. 1, col. 5; "Allen's Body Borne on Special Train to Home Town Plot," *New Orleans Morning Tribune*, 30 January 1936, p. 1, col. 7.

47. "Earhart Goes Over; Self-Rule Off Until May, Thinks Pratt," *New Orleans Morning Tribune*, 7 February 1936, p. 1, col. 7; "Walmsley Offers to Resign If City Is Given Home Rule," *New Orleans Morning Tribune*, 10 March 1936, p. 1, col. 7; "New Orleans Mayor Sets Terms for Resigning," *New York Times*, 10 March 1936, p. 9, col. 2.

48. Haas, *DeLesseps S. Morrison and the Image of Reform*, 13-14; Kurtz and Peoples, *Earl K. Long*, 85-86; Don Eddy, "Kingfish the Second,"

American Magazine 127, no. 5 (November 1939): 16-17, 77-82; "Maestri Accepts Support of Old Regulars for Mayor if Walmsley Quits Office," *New Orleans Morning Tribune*, 11 March 1936, p. 1, col. 7; Edward Haas, "New Orleans on the Half Shell: The Maestri Era, 1936-1946," *Louisiana History* 13, no. 3 (summer 1972).

49. "Mayor to Resign Office Today; Maestri Will Run," *Times-Picayune*, 26 June 1936, p. 1, col. 2; "Epoch in Municipal History Passes As Walmsley Resigns," *Times-Picayune*, 1 July 1936, p. 1, col. 8; "Walmsley Out, Is Honored," *New Orleans Item*, 26 June 1936, p. 1, col. 1; "Walmsley Leaves Post As City's Mayor," *New Orleans Item*, 30 June 1936, p. 1, col. 8; "Shakeup at City Hall," *New Orleans Morning Tribune*, 26 June 1936, p. 1, col. 4; "Pratt Is Now Mayor," *New Orleans Morning Tribune*, 1 July 1936, p. 3, col. 4; *Official Proceedings of the Commission Council of the City of New Orleans, Special Session, June 30, 1936*, 1-5 (on microfilm in the Louisiana Division, New Orleans Public Library); Gibbons, interview.

50. "Walmsley Leaves Post As City's Mayor," p. 1, col. 8.

51. Weiss, interview.

52. Weiss, interview; Kane, *Louisiana Hayride*, 185-86; "The 1928-1936 Scrapbook," Allen J. Ellender Papers, Nicholls State University, Thibodaux, La.; Kurtz and Peoples, *Earl K. Long*, 81-82.

53. Gillis, interview; John Wilds, Charles L. Dufour, and Walter G. Cowan, *Louisiana Yesterday and Today—A Historical Guide to the State* (Baton Rouge: Louisiana State University Press, 1996), 124-26; "Seymour Weiss Taken to Begin Four-Year Term," *Times-Picayune*, 20 November 1940, p. 1, col. 5; Zinman, "Seymour Weiss Is Man Who Climbed Back from Disaster," p. 3A, col. 1; Joe Scaffidi, interview.

54. "Seymour Weiss, A Key Advisor in Huey Long's Regime, Is Dead," p. 47, col. 3; "Business, Civic Leader Is Dead," *Times-Picayune*, 18 September 1969, p. 1, col. 5; Zinman, "Seymour Weiss Is Man Who Climbed Back from Disaster," p. 3A, col. 1; "Hotel Is a Community Industry," *New Orleans Item*, 20 May 1951, p. 9, col. 4; Weiss Succession, Number 498-163, Civil District Court of New Orleans, Clerk's Office; in the mid-1960s, Weiss married the former Elva Kimball, leaving her upon his death one half of his enormous estate, eventually valued at more than $15 million. For his critical remarks concerning Louisiana's segregation laws, see "Business Loss Blamed on Law" (*Times-Picayune*, 15

August 1962, p. 25, col. 2), "Business Loss Involves Laws" (*Times-Picayune*, 8 September 1962, p. 11, col. 4), and James, "The Majority Leader—A Short Biography of a Controversial Man," 42.

55. Lester D. Langley and Thomas Schoonover, The Banana Men—American Mercenaries and Entrepreneurs in Central America, 1880-1930 (Lexington: The University Press of Kentucky, 1996), 161-63; "Molony Final Rites Arranged," p. 8, col. 2; "Guy Ross Molony, Police Chief, Soldier," p. D3, col. 2; "General Data" and "Names and People I Remember," Guy R. Molony Papers, Special Collections, Howard-Tilton Memorial Library, Tulane University, New Orleans, La.; Molony, interview; Deutsch, "Guy Molony's Off Again; But This Time on Peaceful Pursuits," p. 3, col. 5.

56. "More Pickets Arrested at 'Red Salute,'" *New Orleans Morning Tribune*, 11 December 1935, p. 3, col. 1; "Mayor Urged to Intervene for Pickets," *New Orleans Morning Tribune*, 12 December 1935, p. 9, col. 4; "Score Arrest of Pickets at 'Red Salute,'" *New Orleans Morning Tribune*, 13 December 1935, p. 3, col. 5; "Plan Protests of Arrests of Film Pickets," *New Orleans Morning Tribune*, 14 December 1935, p. 11, col. 5; *Red Salute* featured actress Barbara Stanwyck as an impressionable college peace activist exploited by Soviet agents, implying that all student activists of the day were in similar danger. Hale Boggs, editor of Tulane University's student newspaper, the *Hulaballoo*, was among those who lauded the protestors and slammed the film as reactionary (T. Hale Boggs, "The Front Row," *Hulaballoo*, 11 October 1935, p. 1, col. 1; *New York Times Film Reviews, 1913-1968* (New York: The New York Times and Arno Press, 1970), 1209; *Variety Film Reviews, 1934-1937* (New York: Garland Publishing, 1983), no page number given, but review is dated October 2, 1935. For information on Jessen's later years see "Funeral Tomorrow for Louise Jessen, Veteran UH Aide," *Honolulu Star-Bulletin*, 15 May 1952; "Jessen Rites Today; Sleeping Tablets Held Cause of Death," *Honolulu Star-Bulletin*, 16 May 1952. I am indebted to Susan F. Tucker of the Center for Research on Women at Tulane University's Newcomb College for her help piecing together the final years of Jessen's life.

57. Kelso, "When the Caucus Ruled the World," 20; David Lloyd Singer, "Downfall of a Political Machine: The New Orleans Mayoralty Election of 1946," (master's thesis, Tulane University,

1968); Robert Maloney, interview; Cangiamilla, interview; Gillis, interview; Fitzmorris, interview.

58. "'Bigot' in Office Peril to State, Says Walmsley," *Times-Picayune,* 1 October 1939, p. 24, col. 3; "Walmsley Backs All Save Three of Amendments," *Times-Picayune,* 5 November 1940, p. 3, col. 2; Gibbons, interview.

59. "Walmsley Is Exonerated in Highway Car Death," *New Orleans States,* 13 December 1937, p. 1, col. 1; "Walmsley's Auto Kills," *New Orleans Item,* 14 December 1937, p. 2, col. 1.

60. "Walmsley's Auto Kills," p. 2, col. 1.

61. Edwin Watson (secretary to President Roosevelt) to Walmsley, 30 January 1942, Mayor T. Semmes Walmsley file, Franklin D. Roosevelt Presidential Library, Hyde Park, New York; Watson to Walmsley, 30 January 1942, Mayor T. Semmes Walmsley file, Franklin D. Roosevelt Presidential Library, Hyde Park, New York.

62. Fred King, interview by author, tape recording, New Orleans, La., 3 May 1996; "Walmsley Dies," *Times-Picayune,* 18 June 1942, p. 1, col. 4; "Major Walmsley, Foe of Huey Long," p. 12, col. 3; Gibbons, interview; Walmsley Succession, Number 24556, Civil District Court of New Orleans, Clerk's Office.

63. Williams, *Huey Long,* 427; Hair, *Kingfish and His Realm,* 198, 206, 264-66; Haas, *DeLesseps S. Morrison and the Image of Reform,* 9-20; Opotowsky, *The Longs of Louisiana,* 220-25; Sindler, *Huey Long's Louisiana,* 113—all give varying accounts of Walmsley and his status as Huey's favorite Turkey Head. Walmsley was also called, according to author Mel Leavitt, "Turkey Neck" and "Old Buzzard Beak" by brother Earl (Leavitt, *A Short History of New Orleans* [San Francisco: Lexicos, 1982], 143); Kurtz and Peoples, *Earl K. Long,* 80.

64. The elections seeing a Long at the head of the ticket—Earl's gubernatorial bids in 1940, 1948, and 1956 in particular—inevitably incorporated Long and anti-Long themes usually centering more around issues of public corruption associated with the Longs, not with what Earl later called the "do-everythingism" of Long rule—more roads, pensions, and welfare benefits. So successful and popular had these Long programs, by the 1950s, become that even anti-Long candidates ran on programs of expanded government benefits. The emergence of Edwin Edwards, the gifted and controversial Cajun Populist who won the

statehouse in 1971, 1975, 1983, and 1991, only extended the Long program into a newer generation, more than fifty years after Huey's first election as governor (Errol Laborde, " Louisiana Politics," *PS* 17, no. 3 [summer 1985]: 593-600; Wilds, Dufour, and Cowan, *Louisiana Yesterday and Today*, 133-34; John C. Chase et al., *Citoyens, Progress et Politique de la Nouvelle Orleans, 1889-1964* [New Orleans: E. S. Upton Printing, 1964], 86-103; William L. Havard, *The Changing Politics of the South* [Baton Rouge: Louisiana State University, 1972], 544-59; Peirce and Hagstrom, *Book of America— Inside Fifty States Today,* 494-96, 498-500).

65. Sindler, *Huey Long's Louisiana*, 108-16; see also Paul Grosser, "Political Parties," *Louisiana Politics—Festival in a Labyrinth* (Baton Rouge: Louisiana State University Press, 1982), 264-71.

66. William J. Dodd, *Peapatch Politics—The Earl Long Era in Louisiana Politics* (Baton Rouge: Claitor's Publishing, 1991), 10-28; "Long's Goodbye Had Some Nostalgia, But No Regrets," *Baton Rouge Morning Advocate,* 28 December 1986, p. 1, col. 1; "Long's Career a Lesson in History," *Baton Rouge Morning Advocate,* 29 December 1986, p. 1, col. 1. For an inclusive view of the remarkable success of the Long family up to 1960 in politics see Martin's *Dynasty—The Longs of Louisiana* and Opotowsky's, *The Longs of Louisiana.*

67. Long's legacy is a richly literary one: besides the epic Pulitzer Prize-winning book by T. Harry Williams, *Huey Long,* published in 1969, Long is the subject of more than twenty-five books, most notably Willian Ivy Hair's *The Kingfish and His Realm* and Glen Jeansonne's *Messiah of the Masses,* both of which were published in the early 1990s and are far more critical of Long than Williams' book. Five other books stand out: Harnett T. Kane's *Louisiana Hayride,* originally published in 1941 by a decidedly anti-Long author, is nevertheless a detailed chronicle of the downfall of Huey's machine after his death; Sindler's *Huey Long's Louisiana,* published in 1956, broke new ground examining Longism demographically and electorally. The two previously mentioned books on Long's family—Martin's *Dynasty,* and Opotowsky's *The Longs of Louisiana,*—are both engagingly written, detailed accounts of Huey and his heirs; while Alan Brinkley's 1983 *Voices of Protest— Huey Long, Father Coughlin and the Great Depression* is one of the few books to present Long in his role as a national arbiter of dissent.

Three other books, all on Huey's death, are even-handed, detailed accounts of the events surrounding his assassination: Hermann B. Deutsch's *The Huey Long Murder Case* (Garden City: Doubleday, 1963); Zinman's *Day Huey Long Was Shot*, and Ed Reed's *Requiem for a Kingfish*.

As previously mentioned, Huey Long as a figure of fiction has also inspired literature, most notably Robert Penn Warren's *All the Kings Men*, published in 1946; John Dos Possos's trilogy *USA*, and Upton Sinclair's *It Can't Happen Here*.

Huey Long's posthumous career as a film star is also lengthy, including the 1949 movie version of *All the King's Men*, which won two Academy Awards; a documentary by historian Ken Burns in 1985 called *Huey Long*; and at least three feature films that easily mix fiction with fact: *The Life and Assassination of the Kingfish* (1976), *Blaze*, the 1989 film starring Paul Newman as Earl Long, which repeatedly refers to Huey and his times; and *The Kingfish: A Story of Huey Long* a 1995 television movie putting Huey in a sympathetic light (directed by Thomas Schlamme, 100 minutes, TNT Productions).

Huey is also the inspiration for a play published in 1992 by Larry L. King and Ben Z. Grant called *The Kingfish: A One-Man Play Loosely Depicting the Life and Times of the Late Huey P. Long of Louisiana* (Dallas: Southern Methodist University, 1992).

Historians and reporters also regularly return to Huey Long whenever they seek to explain some new disturbance on the political scene, almost as though the very words "Huey Long" have come to represent chaos in the same way that McCarthyism represents demagoguery. Curiously, the parallels are usually made with candidates from the right, ignoring Huey's historical anti-corporate, anti-establishment appeal. For comparisions between Huey and George Wallace, see R. W. Apple, Jr., "Humphrey Says He's Even with Muskie, and Has '3 Chances in 7' of Being Nominated," *New York Times*, 12 March 1972, p. 43, col. 1; and T. Harry Williams, "He's No Huey Long," *New York Times*, 6 April 1972, p. 43, col. 3. For the parallels with David Duke, the former Ku Klux Klan Grand Wizard who very nearly became a U.S. Senator from Louisiana in 1990 and its governor the following year, see Douglas Rose, ed., *The Emergence of David Duke and the Politics of Race* (Chapel Hill: University of North Carolina Press, 1992), 21, 31,

43, 244, and 252. Those same parallels were restated with the emergence of Patrick J. Buchanan in the 1992 and 1996 presidential elections, Alan Brinkley, "A Swaggering Tradition," *Newsweek* 128, no. 10 (4 March 1996): 28-29; and Michael Barone, "Once Again, the Pitch of the Populist," *U.S. News & World Report* 120, no. 9 (4 March 1996): 8-9.

Index

Agnelly, Edward, 154
Alexander, Avery, 54, 198
Alferez, Enrique, 99-100
All the King's Men, 113
Allen, Oscar K., 28, 62, 100,
  120, 121, 124, 130, 132, 168,
  173, 194, 195, 198, 200; in
  1936 election, 200-202
Amant, Alfred D., 149
Anderson, Sherwood, 54, 114
Arcade Theatre, 82
Arkansas Southern Railroad, 46
Armstrong, Louis, 15, 55, 80
Avedano, Numa, 141

Ballard, Marshall, 90
Barker, Danny, 53
Barnes, C. S., 88-89, 91, 93, 104
Behrman, Martin, 35, 37, 40, 42
Behrman, Stanley, 183, 184
Bel, George, 57
Benezach, Edward P., Jr., 135,
  136, 141, 195
Benezach, Edward P., Sr., 135,
  138
Benny, Jack, 156
Beverly Gardens nightclub, 80
Bisso, William, 183, 186

Boggs, Hale, 15
Boggs, Lindy, 92
Boston Club, 34, 37, 39, 41, 55,
  107, 209
Boyd, William Stafford, 191
Bryan, William Jennings, 48, 116
Burke, Ulic, 183, 184, 191
Burns, Ken, 113
Business Week, 177
Butera, Angelo, 25, 128

Campbell, Rachel Violette, 55
Cangiamilla, Joe, 89
Capone, Al, 153
Capote, Truman, 55
Carazo, Castro, 20-21, 131
Carter, Betty Brunhilde, 100
Carter, Hodding, 98-99, 100
Casey, Clarence, 181
Caso, Evans, 117
Charity Hospital, 26-27, 57, 211
Chase, John, 156
Choctaw Club, 37-39, 42, 55,
  117, 183, 186, 201
Christian Century, 177
Christian Science Monitor, 129, 152
Christmas, Lee, 164
Civil Works Administration, 90

Civilian Conservation Corps, 194
Claverie, Dominick, 138
Coad, George, 106
Collier's, 114, 177
Comiskey, James, 183
Cooke, Alistair, 76
Coughlin, Charles, 196
Crosby, Bing, 156-57

Daily Courier, 98
Daniell, Raymond F., 33, 147-49, 150, 160-61, 170-72, 198
Darrow, Clarence, 67
Davis, Jefferson, 117
Davis, Louis B., 185
DeMille, Cecil B., 153
Democratic National Committee, 62, 178
Democratic National Convention (1932), 64-67
Democratic National Convention (1936), 203
Dent, Fred, 195
DePriest, Oscar, 43
DeSoto Hotel, 190
Deutsch, Hermann, 79, 84, 86, 108, 110-11
Dies, Martin, 160
Dixon, Mason, 77
Dock and Cotton Council, 56
Dore, Hugo, 110
Dos Passos, John, 115

Earhart, Fred, 183, 202
Ellender, Allen, 100, 116, 194, 202
Escarra, Walter, 191
Escorial Theatre, 81
Eskimo (movie), 82
Estopinal, J. A., 140-41

Every Man a King, 60, 116, 131
Ewing, Robert, 62

Farley, James, 67
Faulkner, William F., 54
Federal Emergency Relief Administration, 90, 181, 191, 192
Ferguson, Harry, 96
Fernandez, Joachim, 154
Fiebleman, James, 54
Fisher, Joseph, 178
Fisher, Jules, 178
Fitzmorris, James, 39, 157
Fleming, Raymond, 30, 31, 117-19, 121, 124, 133-34, 135-36, 140-41, 151, 152, 162, 194-95, 197
Fournet, John, 100
Frampton, Chick, 194

Gallier Hall, 32, 26, 42, 55, 61, 88, 90, 117, 120-21, 124, 145, 167, 203, 209
Gamble, Harry P., 84
Garden, 191
Garner, James Nance, 179
Gaurino, Sam, 21-22
Gendusa, John, 56
George's Tavern, 82
German consul, 23, 29-30
Gervais, Pershing, 39-40, 52
Gibbons, Kathleen, 34-35, 190, 197, 207
Gillis, James, 18, 23, 59, 88-89, 99, 150, 162
Gouaze, Edward, 135, 136-38, 182, 197
Grenada Theatre, 82
Grosjean, Alice Lee, 131, 132-33
Grunewald, Louis, 18-20

Grunewald, Theodore, 20

Haas, Edward, 42
Haas, W. Davis, 189
Haesler, Jack, 177
Hagstrom, Jerry, 47
Hammond, Hilda Phelps, 68,
    97-98, 106, 147
Hardy, George, 105, 108
Harris, Phil, 20
Harrison, Pat, 69
Heilman, Robert, 194
Heineman, Alexander J., 56-57
Hemingway, Ernest, 194
Henry, Burt, 97
Hibernia National Bank, 34
Higgins, Archie, 154
Hitler, Adolf, 149
Hoffpauir, Smith, 111
Hoover, Herbert, 25
Hoover, J. Edgar, 146, 167, 196
Hopkins, Harry, 96
Howell, Roland B., 96
Huey P. Long Bridge, 199-202
Hullabaloo, The, 92
Humphrey, Joseph, 170

Ickes, Harold, 179
International Longshoreman's
    Association, 143
Isis Theatre, 81
It Can't Happen Here, 115-16
Item, 76, 90, 108, 123, 138, 154,
    207-9
Item-Tribune, 76, 79, 106

Jackson, Andrew, 48, 126
Jackson, Joy, 56
Jackson, Rachel, 126
Jackson Barracks, 124, 135,
    140, 149, 151, 194
Jeansonne, Glen, 68, 111
Jessen, Louise, 58, 141-46; final
    years, 206-7
Jessen, Otto, 145, 206
Jews in New Orleans, 81, 87, 168
Johnson, Lyndon B., 69
Jones, James T., 115
Jones, Jesse, 200-201
Jung Hotel, 100

Kane, Harnett, 160
Kennedy, Robert, 55
Klorer, John, 74, 82, 85-86, 88,
    90-91
Knoblock, K. T., 108, 109
Ku Klux Klan, 99, 164, 185

La Guardia, Fiorella, 199, 203,
    209
Lang, Fritz, 211
League for Industrial Democ-
    racy, 143
Leche, Richard, 201, 202, 205
Lewis, Sinclair, 115-16
Liebling, A. J., 17
Liberty Theatre, 81
Lindsey, Coleman, 108
Literary Digest, 99
London *Times*, 77
Long, Earl, 51, 121, 128, 203, 211
Long, Huey, 15-18, 20, 21, 23,
    24, 33; and the Old Regulars,
    44-46, 49-52, 60-74; back-
    ground of, 46-49, 53, 54, 55,
    76, 77, 82; in 1934 mayor's
    race, 83-93; in Washington,
    95-97; hatred of, 98-103, 106-
    10, 111, 112; as literary inspi-
    ration, 113-16, 117, 119, 120,

121, 123, 124, 125, 126, 127, 128, 129; and Daniell, 130-32, 133; and National Guard, 133-38, 141, 142; and Jessen, 145-46, 147, 149, 151, 152; and vice commission, 153-61, 166-67; and 1934 congressional election, 168-73, 175; and late 1934 legislative sessions, 176-78; and New Orleans, 179-83; and Old Regulars' abdication, 183-88, 189, 190, 191, 192, 193; assassination and funeral of, 194-99, 201, 202, 203, 205, 206, 209; and his legacy, 211
Long, Rose McConnell, 49, 60, 63-64, 198, 200
Long, Russell, 18, 21, 92-93, 102-3, 151, 163, 195, 211
Louisiana Democratic Association, 51, 87
Louisiana Highway Commission, 104
Louisiana National Guard, 117-19, 120, 121, 122, 124, 134, 135-38, 146; at the Port of New Orleans, 149-51, 173, 175
Louisiana State University, 194, 195-96
Louisiana State University marching band, 23
Louisiana Women's Committee, 89
Loyola University, 35, 87

McCain, Thomas P., 164
McCormack, Thomas, 181
McShane, Andrew, 164, 165

Maestri, Robert, 23-24, 28, 30, 51, 121, 195, 198, 202-3
Maloney, Paul, 39, 40, 154, 203
Maloney, Robert, 39, 40
Manetta, Manuel, 15
March of Time, 177
Mardi Gras, 43, 100, 199
Martin, Bernie, 56
Martin, Clovis, 56
Martinez, Elsie, 127
Mayflower Hotel, 95-97
Mitchell, Niclaise, 21
Molony, Guy, 91-92, 163-67, 206
Molony, Isabel, 165
Monteleone Hotel, 82
Morgan, Cecil, 18, 97, 103, 190
Morrison, Mary, 196-97
Mosely, V. H., 117
Mostly Mississippi, 127
Mouledoux, Gabe, 97
Moviegoer, The, 33-34
My First Days in the White House, 130

Nation, 177
National Industrial Conference Board, 59
Neu, Kenneth, 88
New Orleans: in the 1930s, 53-60; gambling and vice in, 126-28; hunger in, 142, 191-93; economic crisis in, 179-82
New Orleans Athletic Club, 85
New Orleans Cotton Exchange, 104
New Orleans Public Service, 56, 182, 191
New Regulars, 62
New Republic, 98, 172
New York Times, 33, 63, 64, 77,

99, 106, 130, 147-49, 160, 170, 198
New York World, 17
New Yorker, The, 114
Newlin, Floyd, 58
Newsweek, 129, 172, 177
Noe, Jimmy, 150-51

O'Connor, James P., 154
O'Hara, Joseph, 181, 200
O'Keefe, Arthur, 35-36, 37
Old Regulars, 31, 37-46; and Huey Long, 49, 60-74, 77, 83, 84, 86, 87, 88, 91, 100, 102, 104, 105, 109, 111, 112, 132, 134, 154, 159, 161-62, 168-73; and effort to dump Walmsley, 183-88, 193, 201-3, 207
Orpheum Theatre, 18
Overton, Jon, 67-68, 103

Palmisano, Charles, 133
Parker, John, 98
Patio Cafe, 140
Pegler, Westbrook, 129
Peirce, Neal, 47
Percy, Walker, 33
Perez, Leander, 110
Perrault, George K., 100
Pickwick Club, 17, 34, 107
Pleasant, Ruffin G., 98
Populists, 47
Porter, Cole, 72
Porter, Katherine Anne, 115
Pratt, R. Miles, 183
Prima, Leon, 53-54
Prima, Louis, 53-54
Prohibition, 79-80, 81

Ransdell, Joseph E., 51-52

Raven-Hart, R., 126
Reconstruction Finance Corporation, 199-201
Red Salute, 206
Reyer, George, 84, 119-20, 151-52, 159, 160, 162
Reynolds, George M., 40
Riggs, R. K., 185
Rogers, Will, 67
Romaguera, Arthur J., 186
Rombouts, Edwin, 185
Roosevelt, Eleanor, 129
Roosevelt, Franklin D., 17-18, 25, 30, 31, 64-67; and Huey Long, 70-71; and Walmsley, 74-76, 82, 90, 91, 96, 129, 138, 146-47, 178-79, 180, 186, 192, 194, 196, 200, 205
Roosevelt, Theodore, 18
Roosevelt Hotel, 18-20, 21-25, 26, 54, 55, 60, 62, 72, 80, 83, 114, 115, 120, 121, 128, 130-31, 145, 153, 154, 157, 168, 183-85, 193, 205-6
Rose, Al, 53

Saenger Theatre, 17
St. Charles Hotel, 24-25, 92, 165, 166, 167, 172
Sanders, Jared Y., Jr., 190
Sandlin, John, 190
Saturday Evening Post, 116, 177
Saunders, Dufour and Dufour (law firm), 35
Saxon, Lyle, 54, 127
Scafidi, Joseph, 20, 25, 205
Scribner's Monthly, 177
Semmes, Raphael, 34
Semmes, Thomas, 34
Shaffer, W. D., 140

Share Our Wealth program, 30, 69-70, 178, 187, 192
Shushan, Abe, 178
Sindler, Allen P., 47, 211
Singer, Mrs. John, 188
Skelly, Joseph, 183
Smith, Gerald L. K., 198
Smith, Howard K., 37, 57
Smith, James Monroe, 196, 205
Smith, Webster, 62
Socialists, 47, 58, 141-46
Souchon, Edmond, 53
Soule Building, 119, 121, 124, 130, 138-40, 151
Southern Railway Station, 15, 17
Southern Review, 113, 115
Speakman, Harold, 127
Square Dealers, 98, 186, 189-90, 201
Standard Oil, 49
State Railroad Commission, 49
States (New Orleans), 60, 62, 74, 84, 102, 129, 138
Stein, Gertrude, 114
Stitch, Frank, 105
Stratford Club, 34

Tharpe, William, 133
Thomas, Norman, 145-46
Thurber, James, 114
Time, 129, 177
Times-Picayune, 43, 62, 102, 121, 123, 124, 126, 149
Truman, Harry S., 69
Tucker, Sophie, 20
Tugwell, A. P., 103-4
Tulane University, 33, 34, 37, 58, 80, 85, 92, 143, 186, 191, 206

Tyler, Pamela, 41

Valeton, Oscar, 149-50
Van Vechten, Cal, 114
Vandervoort, George, 102
Variety, 81, 177
Vidrine, Carl, 195
Voitier, Paul, 121
Von Hoven, Herman, 181

Walmsley, Augustus, 80
Walmsley, Julia Havard, 35, 96, 200
Walmsley, Myra, 83
Walmsley, Robert, 34
Walmsley, T. Semmes, 31; background of, 33-36, 37; and the Old Regulars, 41-43, 51, 52, 56, 58-59, 60, 61, 63, 64, 65, 66, 67, 71, 74, 76, 77, 82; in 1934 mayor's race, 83-87, 88, 90-93; in Washington, 95-97; anti-Long coup, 100-10, 111, 112, 117; response to militia, 119-24, 126, 130, 132, 138, 141, 142; and Jessen, 143-45, 151, 152, 154, 159, 165, 172-73, 176, 180, 181; move to oust him, 182-88, 189-91, 192-93, 197; as a figurehead, 199-202; resignation, 202-4; final years, 207-9
Warren, Robert Penn, 113, 196
Washburn, Mel, 80
Washington Post, 64, 99
Washington Star, 64
Watson, Tom, 48
Weber, Joseph, 105
Wegmann, John, 106
Weiss, Carl, 194

Weiss, Seymour: background
of, 24-25; and Huey Long,
25-30, 46, 51, 61, 63, 65, 67,
74, 80, 83-84, 92, 121, 128,
131, 168, 178, 180, 193, 195,
197, 198, 202, 203; final
years, 205-6
Wells, H. G., 114
Whilden, Oscar, 189-90
White League, 106-7, 109
Whitley, R., 167
Whitney National Bank, 34

Williams, Francis, 76, 84, 90
Williams, Gus, 62-63, 68, 74
Williams, Lavinius, 97
Williams, T. Harry, 39, 115
Winn Parish, 46-47

Young Businessmen's Association, 83, 84, 85
Young, Perry, 191

Zemurray, Samuel, 164
Zero Hour, 116